Divots,
Shanks,
Gimmes,
Mulligans,
and
Chili Dips

Divots, Shanks, Gimmes, Mulligans, and Chili Dips

A LIFE IN 18 HOLES

Glen Waggoner

VILLARD BOOKS

NEW YORK

1993

Library of Congress Cataloging-in-Publication Data

Waggoner, Glen.
    Divots, shanks, gimmes, mulligans, and chili dips : a life in
    18 holes / Glen Waggoner.
        p. cm.
    ISBN 0-394-58005-2
    1. Golf—Miscellanea. 2. Golfers. I. Title.
GV967.W28 1993
796.352′02—dc20   92-50492

9 8 7 6 5 4 3 2
First Edition
Book design by JoAnne Metsch

For Henry, Jayne, and Frances.
We were a great foursome.

CONTENTS

A Life in 18 Holes

Golf is the cruelest of sports. Like life, it's unfair. It's a harlot. A trollop. It leads you on. It never lives up to its promises. It's not a sport, it's bondage. An obsession. A boulevard of broken dreams. It plays with men. And runs off with the butcher.

—Jim Murray, in the
Los Angeles Times

I gave up golf once and for all in June 1962.

Gave it up cold turkey, once and for all, irrevocably and without possibility of parole, for what seemed at the time like two excellent, well-considered, grown-up reasons.

The first was that I would be leaving my home in Dallas at the end of the summer to go to graduate school in New York City, where I would be way too busy going to Broadway shows and the opera, visiting museums and galleries, attending poetry readings, chewing the fat with intellectuals in Greenwich Village bars, taking walks in Central Park, finding out about French food, and hanging out in Times Square to have time for childish pursuits. (I wasn't taking my baseball glove, either.)

The second reason was that my clubs got lost.

Not lost, actually. Nor even misplaced. I knew exactly where they were because I had put them there. Threw them, if you must know. And unless some kid had come along with a fishing pole and gotten lucky, they were still where I put—threw—them: next to the thirteenth green of the Stevens Park Municipal Golf Course at the bottom of a small but deep pond.[1]

Let me explain.

Golf played an important supporting role in my life when I was a teenager. During the school year, we would sometimes play in the afternoons between the end of football season and the beginning of baseball season, plus weekends and most holidays. (I say "we" because I usually played in a fivesome or sixsome. It might have begun as a twosome or threesome, but by the fourth hole, when everybody had sneaked on, we were a virtual golf posse.)

In the summers, though, we played a lot.

Sometimes we would head for Stevens Park right after throwing our paper routes, play a quick seven (skipping two long holes at the far end of the course) before the clubhouse opened, liberate a box of donuts stacked in the doorway of a nearby grocery market before it opened, and be home in time for breakfast.

Other times, depending on baseball practice, job schedules, and available funds, we would stay at the course in the morning, pay our greens fees when the clubhouse opened, and play all day. The only problem was that Dallas can get pretty hot in July and August, and walking forty-five holes in the broiling sun when the temperature hits 102 degrees can be tough, even when you're young. Our solution, when we got a little older and more resourceful, was to buy a large, plain snow cone from a little stand over on Hampton Road and fill it with Mogen David wine. It was the perfect pick-me-up on a hot summer day.

(Boone's Farm and Ripple hadn't been invented back then. If they had, I might never have given up golf.)

---

[1] They flip-flopped the nines about ten years ago, so it's the fourth green now. I mention this just in case anybody might be interested in a set of used clubs, including bag.

A strapping youth, I could hit the ball a country mile, and usually did, *well* into the country. There are a lot of trees at Stevens Park, and at one time I was personally acquainted with most of them—although, by the end of my adolescence, some of them were no longer speaking to me.

I was wild. Long, but wild. Wild left, wild right, I never knew which it would be. I never had a golf lesson—can you tell?—and I had no clue what I was doing. None of us did. We were gripping and ripping when John Daly was still a chromosome.

Some days, ah, some days it would be great. A stretch of play that made me think, Yes! I've got it! Big drives that found the fairway. Punch-and-run shots that bounced straight and true across the dried-out Bermuda grass and rolled to a stop eight feet from the pin. Eight-foot putts that went in. Hey, if I can play this way once, I can play this way every time!

Like the time I caught fire on the back nine and made eight straight pars. *Eight straight pars!* Normally I shot in the mid- to high eighties, very high if you insist on counting every single mulligan, gilligan, and foot mashie. But this day I was shooting legit, on-the-level, as-Ben-Hogan-is-my-witness *even par.* If I could make a four on the final hole, then my thirty-six on the back nine plus my forty-three on the front nine would mean that I had broken eighty *for the first time in my life.*

I made an eight.

That was in April. Two months later, I quit the game.

I don't remember the shot that did it. Golfers are like that: we never remember the bad shots, only the good ones. That's why we come back.

It may have been a chili dip from the fringe, or possibly a third putt, because the burial at sea took place near a green. But I would suspect the underlying causes of the final declubbing of my golf bag would be found many holes, many rounds, many angry years of hacker golf earlier.

In any case, I vaguely remember flinging a club in the general direction of New Mexico, only to have it land in the pond. A moment of silence for it to sink in—and with it, full realization of what I had done—and another club followed. Then another.

At this point it must have dawned on me that this method of club reassignment was slow and inefficient. Or perhaps I became aware that the group behind us on the tee was waiting to hit. Or maybe I realized that if I was going to make a complete ass of myself in front of friends and strangers alike, I might as well go whole hog, do it big time, grab the brass ring.

So I picked up my blue Sears Roebuck golf bag, held it high above my head like Hercules offering a sacrifice up to Zeus, walked slowly and (I hoped) dramatically over to the water's edge, and threw the thing—well weighted by my remaining clubs, six or seven X-outs, a handful of tees in assorted colors, a badly torn golf glove, and my wristwatch—smack into the middle of the pond.

And that was that.

For the next twenty-two years, my word was as good as my bond.

I got married, moved to New York, earned two graduate degrees, sired three children, lived two years abroad, grew a beard, taught at a Midwestern university for five years, moved back to New York, got divorced, quit teaching, got married again, put three children through college, and started writing magazine articles and books.

But I didn't even so much as touch a golf club for twenty-two years. During that time, I kept up with the pro game: mourning when Palmer gave way to Nicklaus, exulting when Lee Trevino (like me, a muni golfer from Dallas) came on the scene, applauding when Stanford graduate Tom Watson kicked Nicklaus off the throne, and crying with joy and excitement when Nicklaus won the 1986 Masters.

As a recovering golfer, I could follow the game and watch the majors on TV, but I never played myself, never was even tempted.

And then Sharon came along and offered me a bite of apple.

.   .   .

We were on our way back to New York from a quiet weekend in the country when we passed a golf course up in the Catskills. It wasn't much: a flat track laid out in a narrow valley, straight holes mostly running parallel to one another, obviously short, not much bunkering, flat greens, no character. (I might not play anymore, but I could still look.)

"Did you ever play golf?" Sharon asked innocently enough. We had only been married a year, and she didn't know all the skeletons in my closet.

"Yeah, a long time ago," I said. I believe that good relationships are built on honesty.

"Why don't we stop and you play here?"

"What?" (The car swerved onto the shoulder, but I got it back under control.)

"Good, it's a nice day"—she thought I was pulling over— "and you'll have fun."

"But I don't have any clubs." (I had to think of some way to nip this in the bud.)

"I bet they rent them."

Oh, God. I bet they do.

"Come on," she said. "Turn around and let's do it. It's pretty here. You play and I'll just walk."

I thought of quoting Mark Twain ("Golf is a good walk spoiled"), but then I thought, What the hell, why not? It can't hurt anything, not after all these years. Anyway, it's just this once.

Famous last words.

Flash-forward four years. The scene is the west coast of Florida, near Clearwater. Four grown men are sloshing around a golf course in a torrential downpour. They are the only people on the course. They are just about the only people in this part of Florida not in boats. It has been raining hard for an hour, but they are only on the fourteenth hole and show no signs of quitting. Neither does the rain, but they are determined to finish the round, come hell or . . . more hell, high water having long since arrived.

I am one of those four men.

It hadn't happened overnight, my getting hooked on golf again. After that time in the Catskills, I had tried to put the game out of my mind because I knew in my gut that that was where it belonged. And I had mostly succeeded, when one day my pal Lee asked me to come with him and Michael to play golf.

You guys play golf? Since when? They were two of my best friends, and I never knew this dark secret about them. Since one round a couple of months before, it turned out. Both had played when they were teenagers, both had stopped when they went off to college, both had decided to take it up again. They were baby boomers, just turning forty. It figured.

And so we played. And played some more. And soon we were playing everywhere and anywhere we could. At a couple of scruffy public courses in the Bronx that we referred to collectively as "the shithole." At a big, sprawling mountain course that ice-cream peddler Tom Carvel had built about a two-hour drive north of the city. (By going up there, we avoided the two-hour wait for a tee time at all local public courses.) And in Florida, where we let golf ruin a wonderful, special thing that had recently come into our lives—Spring Training.

The guys playing golf in that Florida downpour happened to be four of the founders of a phenomenon called Rotisserie League Baseball. If you know what it is, you either love us or hate us for it: no more needs to be said. If you don't know by now what Rotisserie League Baseball is, you don't want to know: even the twenty-five-words-or-less explanation has been known to cause acute dyspepsia or premature ejaculation. (Different people react differently. Do not take without consulting your physician.)

One of the Rotisserie League rituals, dating back to 1982, was an annual trip to Florida for Spring Training. Eleven of us would go down to Clearwater in late March, check into the

Belleview Biltmore Hotel (a grand old palace from the early part of the century), and head straight for the ball park. We went to games in Clearwater (Phillies), St. Petersburg (Cardinals), and Bradenton (Pirates). Once we drove to Winter Haven (then the Red Sox) for a day game and then to Lakeland (Tigers) for a night game. We went to rookie camps and intrasquad games. We went early for batting practice and stayed until the last out. We spent most of our waking hours away from ball parks at a batting cage in a strip mall. And we spent the rest of our waking hours on the back veranda of the Belleview Biltmore, drinking funny rum drinks with little parasols and talking baseball.

Nobody paid much attention those first few blissful years to the two Donald Ross golf courses that wrapped around the hotel. Nice places for a walk, sure. Pretty. Say, what time do we leave for the game?

Golf ruined all that.

The first spring after that fateful day when Lee, Michael, and I played golf, we tried to combine golf with baseball: the agreement was that we play golf early enough in the morning to finish in time to get to the ball park for batting practice, even if it meant stopping before we'd finished the round. The second day we broke that rule. The third day we played in the torrential downpour. (Why not? The baseball game had been postponed.)

The second year the golfers among us decided that we would meet the others at the game as soon as we could. Sometimes that was even after the game started. The nongolfers shot us dirty looks, but we ignored them.

The third year I skipped the game Saturday afternoon to get in another round of golf. The fourth year I saw a grand total of seven innings of baseball spread over three days. The fifth year I didn't see a single inning.

Last year the Rotisserie League Baseball founders didn't even go to Florida for Spring Training.

We stayed home and played golf.

· · ·

It was about this time that golf for me became vocational as well as avocational. I began to write about it for magazines. I traveled around the country playing all the best golf resorts and wrote a book about them. I went to Scotland and played the Old Course at St. Andrews.

As part of my new job, I began to follow the PGA Tour, and not just on TV: I started going to tournaments. To the Tournament of Champions in January and the Tour Championship (it was Nabisco in those days) in October. To the Hope and the Crosby. (Sorry: the Bob Hope Chrysler Classic and the AT&T Pebble Beach National Pro-Am.) I picked up the Florida swing in March (Doral, Honda, Bay Hill, the Players). Out to the Memorial, down to the Colonial. I saw a U.S. Open and a PGA Championship. I paid my respects at the Masters. I traveled to England for the Ryder Cup Matches.

But learning a lot about the pro game didn't have any effect on my game, the Hacker's Game. The more I played, the more things stayed the same. I got down to the low nineties and stayed there. Once in twenty rounds I would shoot 89; once in twenty rounds I would shoot 101. As I said, the more things stayed the same.

My golfing pal Ziggy says that our problem—mine, his, every hacker's problem—is not that we are inherently bad golfers; it's that we are inherently bad *people,* and therefore unable to play good golf. It's an interesting twist on Original Sin, and I think Zig may be on to something. If you think of the Garden of Eden as a golf course, then the snake becomes a two iron and the apple a golf ball.

It would explain a lot.

But how is it, the hacker in me asks, that two or three times a round I hit shots that are absolutely perfect, hit them as well as Couples or Kite or Strange or any of those guys hit them? And if I can do it two or three times, why can't I do it every time? *Because we are bad people, not bad golfers,* Ziggy says. But the hacker in me insists, No, there *is* a way to get better at this game, I just haven't found it.

And so, taking up the Hacker's Holy Mission, I went to golf school, and doubled my practice time. I changed balls monthly in hope of finding a brand that flies straight, bought new clubs, subscribed to all the golf magazines. I listen to advice from strangers, watch Ken Venturi and David Leadbetter explain shots on TV, and sacrifice a chicken every full moon. And I study Fred Couples's every move because he has the most beautiful golf swing I have ever seen.

In the pages that follow, I offer a progress report on my quest. In "Front Nine," I talk about the Pro Game. In "Back Nine," I talk about *our* game, the Hacker's Game.

Ours may not be as pretty as theirs. In fact, it's not even the same game. But I do think we have more fun. Even if we are bad people.

The
Pro
Game

Thank You, Mr. Palmer

The other day a guy said to me, "If you didn't know how old you were, how old would you think you were?" About twenty-nine, I told him.

—Arnold Palmer, at age fifty-nine

No book about golf in the modern era should begin with anyone other than Arnold Palmer.

No book about golf by me could possibly begin with anyone else because the first time I ever saw Arnold Palmer in person he did something I had never, ever seen before.

It was on a hot, windy afternoon in May at the Colonial Country Club in Fort Worth, Texas, during the second round of the Colonial National Invitational Tournament.

The year was 1962.

"Cut class and go to the Colonial with me tomorrow," Kenny Scott said, taking a small bite of pizza and chewing it carefully. It was Thursday, the first day of the tournament, and we were thirty miles away in Dallas, sitting in the back room at Gordo's, the official beer joint of the Southern Methodist University student body. Located just off campus and about a hundred yards outside the jurisdiction of University Park's no-beer, no-liquor, no-damned-fun-of-any-kind laws, Gordo's was a required course for any SMU undergrad who was halfway serious about higher education.

The owner was a muscular ex-marine named Gordo Gordon. He probably had another name, but you never could be sure in Texas. Once I had an assignment from a magazine to do a story on Angelo's, a barbecue temple in Fort Worth. Proceeding in the hallowed Woodward-Bernstein tradition of investigative journalism, I polished off a double order of ribs with a side order of smoked sausage as background research prior to interviewing owner Angelo George's son, Skeeter, who managed the place. "Skeeter," I said, flipping to a sauce-free page of my reporter's notebook, "tell me your real first name." He looked at me sort of funny and said, "Skeeter."

The back room at Gordo's was normally reserved for SMU's scholar-athletes who wished to get shit-faced in semiprivate. But during the off season and on those occasions when our heroes were off preparing to beat the snot out of TCU, Gordo permitted a few privileged nonathletic regulars to enter. I was there because of Kenny, who dutifully took Gordo's money on the golf course every Monday afternoon, which made them best buddies.

"Drive all the way to Fort Worth?" I snorted at Kenny. "To *watch* golf? Why not stay here and *play*?"

Cutting Friday classes late in the second half of my senior year didn't exactly confront me with an existential dilemma. Nor was it altogether unprecedented. But only one thing usually drew SMU boys to Fort Worth, and the Jackson Hotel wasn't the kind of establishment one visited in broad daylight. Besides, a free Friday meant a chance to play a round with Kenny instead of caddying for him, which is what I did almost every Saturday morning at Tenison Park.

Students of Lee Trevino's career may have heard of Tenison Park, a huge expanse of rolling prairie land in northeast Dallas that contains a dozen or so baseball and softball diamonds, a swimming pool, acres of woods and picnic areas, and two fine public golf courses, Tenison West and Tenison East. Both were—and still are—tough, well-designed courses: plenty long, lots of live oak and pecan trees, not much sand or water, fairways tighter than my first father-in-law.

In those days, Tenison Park was the site of some mighty serious golf and some even more serious betting. Anytime you spotted a gallery of fifteen to twenty spectators following a foursome around, you had to figure they were interested in something besides picking up a few swing tips. For the big-money matches played at Tenison Park every weekend from dawn to dusk, Kenny was always in great demand. So was Trevino, who, along about the same time, was teaching himself to play at other people's expense.

Kenny was a terrific golfer with a sweet swing who might have taken a shot at the pro tour after leaving college a few years earlier if there had been any money in it at the time—and if he'd had the mental discipline to spend enough hours on the practice range working on his short game. A long hitter who loved to hit his driver off the hardpan Texas fairways on par-five holes, Kenny was a scratch shooter whose pride and lust for challenge caused him to give away so many strokes when making bets, that he lost more matches than he won. But he was always great on the presses, which is when I'd try to get my five bucks down.

If God is in the details, then golf betting is in the presses. A lot of golfers play a standard Nassau—match-play bets on the front nine, the back nine, and the match—with one optional press per nine, i.e., a new bet for the remaining holes when a side is closed out. This means that if your opponent wins the first five holes on the front nine, you can make a new bet for the remaining four holes. Sometimes people make the presses automatic, leaving you no choice but to throw good money after bad. In Kenny's game, you could press anytime you were down so much as a single hole, which meant you had virtually unlimited opportunities to lose money if your game went south—or to win back a bundle if your putter got hot.

Nor were the initial wagers and presses limited to the golfers:

Kenny's foursome was always accompanied by ten or fifteen speculators who bet on everything from the hang time of a full wedge to the number of times Fat Travis would fart during an opponent's backswing. A beer-bellied former fireman with a half-chewed El Producto permanently implanted in the corner of an unshaven cheek, Fat Travis was usually the big winner, despite the fact that he broke wind more often than he broke 85. Fat Travis made it a policy never to shoot better than was needed to finish one-up.

"Hey, we can play anytime," Kenny insisted, polishing off the last slice of Gordo's pizza before I could get to it. "This is the *Colonial*."

And then the clincher: "We'll get to see Palmer."

And so it came to pass: the following day, after spending the morning at my first-ever professional golf tournament following one golfer after another, some of whom are still hacking away on the Senior Tour, I found myself behind the green at the seventeenth hole at Colonial waiting for Arnold Palmer to play his second shot.

The Colonial, now unfortunately the Southwestern Bell Colonial, has always been one of the pros' favorite stops on the tour. For decades it's been firmly ensconced in the second tier of tournaments, just below the majors, and for good reasons. It's contested on a great, classic course, one the pros love to play. It has world-class fringe benefits in ample supply, from knowledgeable galleries to frozen margaritas to a hot band that pounds out solid rock from the clubhouse veranda after the close of play on Saturday. And it traditionally attracts the largest legally permissible assembly of halter tops and tight shorts this side of Paradise.

The Colonial always attracts a terrific field, as good as any to be found outside the majors. Take 1962, the year I saw Arnold Palmer for the first time, if you want a list of blue-chip players. The top twenty finishers included, in ascending order, Julius

Boros, Al Geiberger, Phil Rogers, Byron Nelson, Kel Nagle, Ben Hogan, Billy Maxwell, Don January, Jack Burke, Jr., Billy Casper, Gary Player, Doug Sanders, Doug Ford, Bob Wininger, Gay Brewer, Jim Ferree, Jack Nicklaus, and Bruce Crampton.

Crampton, who finished third, would have won if he hadn't hit so many balls in the water hazard at the eighteenth hole. To this day the hazard is known as "Crampton's Lake." Old-timers say that Crampton used to have a sunny, warm disposition before that fateful year at Colonial.

Kenny and I had been zigzagging across the course all day, following Hogan for a while, then Doug Sanders for a close-up look at the funniest swing we'd ever seen, and then Gary Player, who we figured must have been sweltering in his all-black outfit. We'd seen Palmer play some shots, but for some reason we hadn't stuck with him, despite our original intentions. We did see him make par on fourteen and hit his drive on fifteen, but we decided to let him play the par-three sixteenth on his own and pick him up when he came back up to the seventeenth green.

The seventeenth at Colonial is a 387-yard par four that dog-legs right through a canyon of live oak and pecan trees to a small green cut into a slight rise. Spray it a little either way off the tee and you have to trim treetops to hit the green. But even from the right-center of the fairway, where Palmer was, the second shot is no bargain, because you're usually hitting into the teeth of a southwest wind that bats down lofted shots like so many Ping-Pong balls.

At that moment Palmer was at the apex of his career. Earlier in the spring he had won his third green jacket at Augusta. Later in the summer he would win his second straight British Open. By the end of the year he would have won eight tournaments and the huge sum of $81,448, making him the tour's top money winner for the third time in five years. By a wide margin, he was the most popular golfer in the world. Millions of fans were on a first-name basis with Arnie.

To counter the wind in his face this day at Colonial, Palmer—Arnie—hit something relatively low and plenty hard, directly on line to the pin and my nose. Too long! My brain was on the verge of issuing a red alert to my feet when the ball slammed into the green just short of the back fringe, hopped in place, and then spun miraculously back toward the flag as if pulled by an invisible string, stopping about eight feet from the cup.

I was stunned. Not once in my twenty-one years had I ever seen a golf ball do that. Okay, so maybe mine was a pretty sheltered life to that point, but all my golf had been played on hardscrabble public courses baked by the Texas summer sun. Remember the hard, dry fairways at Royal Troon in the 1989 British Open? Your average Dallas public course thirty years ago would make Royal Troon look like a subtropical marsh. The greens we hit to were a little softer than concrete, but not much, so the bump-and-run-run-run was the only shot we ever learned. Kenny was good enough to stop a lofted shot on one of those hard greens, but I'd never before seen any golfer hit a ball that low and make the damned thing actually *back up*.

We followed Arnie on to the eighteenth, where he carded a textbook par to finish at 72 for the day, one stroke off the lead after 36. The next day my pal Kenny carried his own bag at Tenison: I returned to Fort Worth to see my new hero shoot 66. And again on Sunday to see him shoot 76 and blow a chance to win outright. And then again on Monday for the eighteen-hole play-off to see him shoot 69 to beat Johnny Pott by four strokes for the championship.

These numbers come from checking the Colonial record book, of course, not from memory. I don't even remember how I came up with the money for tickets. Whatever they cost, it was way more than I could afford, that much is certain. After nearly three decades, pretty much everything about those four days in Fort Worth is a blur. Everything, that is, except Arnie's shot to the green on seventeen.

I can still see him marching up the hill toward us, shoulders

O

slightly hunched, head thrust forward, shirttail hanging out. That walk, that look, have been so much a part of golf for so long that it's easy to forget that they were once new. Back then, pro golfers looked like our fathers. Not Palmer. Palmer looked like your best friend's older brother, the one who had the '55 stickshift Olds and who would sometimes let you hang out with him on Friday night.

And I can still remember exactly what I said to my buddy three decades ago when that ball smacked onto the green, slammed into reverse, spit cider in my ear, and rolled back toward the hole: "Holy shit, Kenny! *Did you see that?*"

The second time I saw Arnold Palmer in person he was monumentally pissed off.

Flash-forward nearly three decades to the La Costa Country Club in Carlsbad, California. Arnie had just finished the second round of the 1989 Tournament of Champions (Senior Division). He was explaining to the press his reactions when he and Harold Henning were penalized two strokes on the second hole for hitting from the back tees instead of the senior tees. And he was not happy.

After attaining sufficient years to buy a six-pack of beer legally, no one gets all tingly with joy about the prospect of another birthday. Getting older is better than the only known alternative, but not many of us are secretly looking forward to our first liver spots, even if they do give a boost to our Señor Wences impersonation. Most of us, however, are at least permitted to age in private. And in most lines of work, getting older usually means getting better, at least up to a point.

But for athletes not named Nolan Ryan, getting older means not winning as much as you once did, and then not winning at all, and then not even being competitive—all out there in the open, for everyone to see. As fans, we conspire with athletes to deny this process. We keep alive the memory of peak performances of our sports heroes well past the time when they can realistically be expected to reach such heights again. By keeping them young in our minds, we keep ourselves young. And when the marvelous skills that once so excited our imaginations finally fade away, when we finally recognize that our sports heroes can no longer perform heroically, we freeze them in our memories, and we go out and find new, younger heroes.

Arnie transcended this process. He made no pretense of going gently into that good night. But he didn't sulk in public, or retreat into a shell, or turn bitter. He stayed out there on center stage and got old, right before our eyes, and he did it with courage and without a trace of self-pity. He showed us how it should be done.

Sure, along the way he took on part-time jobs as a motor-oil salesman, a holding company, a land developer, even a designer of golf courses. (Although he's picked up many millions in pocket change for adding his name and reputation to golf course developments, course design is not exactly Arnie's raison d'être. One year at the Bob Hope Chrysler Classic, where one of the four courses used bears his name as designer, Lanny Wadkins said, "Have you ever noticed that when Arnold plays a course he designed that [design partner] Ed Seay has to show him where the first tee is?")

Arnie became a major business enterprise, a conglomerate in spikes, but he continued to be what he'd always been: a golfer.

That's why, with nothing whatsoever to gain and plenty to lose, Arnie breathed life into the Senior Tour in the early eighties, thereby giving a hundred or so former fraternity brothers a chance to be reborn. Care to imagine where the Senior Tour would be today if Arnie hadn't hitched up his pants and played it? About the same place the regular tour would be if Palmer hadn't come along in the late fifties and early sixties, won the hearts of an army of followers, played the TV cameras as brilliantly as he played Augusta National, and almost single-handedly transformed professional golf into a spectator sport. Nowhere, that's where. Instead, it's a $24 million oldies-but-goodies show—all because Arnie loves to play golf.

And what did he get out of it? A break from corporate outings and business meetings. A little less time explaining to TV audiences how Pennzoil keeps the old machinery working. A few more nineteenth holes with guys he'd bent elbows with for three decades. And a chance to play in a final twosome on a Sunday afternoon with a championship on the line, a chance to win again. For Arnie, that added up to a good deal.

But damnit, don't insult his pride by setting up the Tournament of Champions track 207 yards shorter for him and his generation than for the young bucks! If he can't cut it, he can't; just don't rub his nose in it. No wonder he hit from the back tees on the 526-yard par-five second hole instead of twenty yards forward: that's where he'd been hitting from since 1969, when the Tournament of Champions (an event he'd won three times before) was moved to La Costa.

When informed of the infraction and penalized the two strokes, Arnie nearly exploded: "It's the closest I've ever come to just walking off a course." Not because of the penalty strokes, but because of the tour's gratuitous concession to the fact that the seniors were, well, seniors, and couldn't hit the ball as far as the juniors: "They might as well give us all golf carts and petticoats."

Now, if that's not a straight line, then Chi Chi Rodriguez never heard one. The next day, when he spotted Arnie approaching the practice tee, Chi Chi whipped out a petticoat and slipped it on over his pants. Minutes earlier, Arnie had found three copies of *The Rules of Golf* left in his locker by less courageous perpetrators of lèse-majesté. Said Chi Chi to the King: "You can use my cart today, Arnold. I'm going to follow your orders and walk."

Arnie laughed, but he'd made his point.[1]

The third time I saw Arnold Palmer in person it was at the 1989 PGA Championship at Kemper Lakes Golf Club, an upscale

---

[1]And the point was taken by the PGA Tour's politburo. The following year at La Costa, seniors and regular PGA Tour winners played from the same tees. Only one senior—fifty-year-old rookie George Archer—managed to break par.

public course set amidst soybean fields masquerading as Chicago suburbs, about thirty miles west of Wrigley Field. And he turned back the clock.

There are a lot of ways to make birdie. You can spray the ball around, slap it to the wrong side of the green, and roll in a forty-foot no-brainer. You can misclub into a greenside bunker and skull a sand wedge that hits the stick halfway up and drops straight down. You can even do it my way, which is very, very rarely.

Or you can do it the way Arnold Palmer did in the first round of the 1989 PGA Championship at Kemper Lakes. You can drive it long and straight, hit medium and short irons to just the right spot on the green, and putt with a steady hand. Textbook birdies. Five straight times on the front nine. Just enough to bring 25,000 or so solid citizens to the brink of mass hysteria.

No. 4: Par 5, 508 Yards. Arnie grabs attention of a platoon of onlookers with a twenty-foot putt.

No. 5: Par 4, 442 Yards. Arnie hits a four-iron stiff and rolls a three-footer into the back of the hole.

No. 6: Par 3, 180 Yards. By the time he's ready to hit his tee shot, Arnie's following has swelled to battalion size. He puts starch in their uniforms with another four iron to eight feet and a dead-center putt.

No. 7: Par 5, 557 Yards. Fifteen feet away from the cup after three solid shots, Arnie elicits a triumphant roar from the regiment around the green with his fourth straight yipless birdie putt.

No. 8: Par 4, 421 Yards. His army is now at full divisional strength and growing as Arnie lines up a tough, downhill twenty-six-footer for a three. The reaction when the putt drops is heard as far away as the Loop: something very big is happening out there in the soybean fields.

"Palmer's five under! Palmer's five under!"

Not since "To arms! To arms! The British are coming!" had a public service announcement caused such a hullabaloo. People all over Kemper Lakes' 250 acres checked their course maps and began to chart vectors to the nearest intercept point. Golfers with names like Norman and Ballesteros saw their entourages melt away. Fans sitting quietly in the stands behind the eighteenth green squinted at the scoreboard, wiped their sunglasses, looked again, and promptly deserted their precious vantage points in order to reenlist as foot soldiers in the most popular army ever assembled—Arnie's.

To get from the ninth green to the tenth tee at Kemper Lakes, you walk past the practice green and across a parking lot large enough to accommodate commoners who line up to pay the $90 greens fee (cart included) on other summer Fridays. On the practice green this day was a cadre of pros, most of whom had still been looking ahead to the first grade when Arnie had won his last major championship, the 1964 Masters.

Professional athletes aren't generally known for their sense of history, and pro golfers aren't exceptions to the rule. To the youngest of them, Palmer is the old guy who used to hang out with O. J. Simpson at airports, a legend worthy of homage, but certainly not someone to be reckoned with. Just as most baseball players don't have a clue about the role Curt Flood played in making them millionaires, most of the younger PGA Tour golfers don't really grasp the significance of Arnold Palmer. Haven't golf tournaments *always* offered million-dollar purses and free courtesy cars?

But today at Kemper, as Arnie strode by, to a man they stopped putting to look at the legend who had just shot 31 on the front side. All of them looked, but only one of them, another graybeard, said anything. Dave Stockton, the man who had beaten back a Palmer charge to win the PGA Championship in 1970, the last time Palmer had been in contention for the only major title he never won, stepped forward to shake an old friend's hand.

"Hey, Arnold," Stockton asked, "what course you playing today?"

From the size of the grin on Arnold's face, one he used to play regularly.

By now Arnie's newly reassembled army lined the tenth fairway five deep, as more fresh recruits pushed ahead along the cart paths, extending the beachhead and fighting for a vantage point. The press tent emptied so fast you'd have thought they had run out of lunch. Inside the ropes a phalanx of armbanded photographers hunkered down to record every grimace, every slashing stroke. If history was in the making, and Palmer was about to shoot 59 or something, they damned sure better have a picture of it or *they* would soon be history.

No. 10: Par 4, 453 Yards. After hooking his tee shot dangerously close to the bullrushes that line the left side, the most popular golfer who ever lived hits his approach on the green— but forty-five sloping, dipping feet away from the hole. Then, as the huge gallery holds its collective breath, Arnie freezes over the long putt. He's motionless for what seems an eternity, as everyone present intones the same silent prayer: "Please, God— let him pull the putter back!"

Finally, he does—and leaves his putt five feet short. More agony, another wait, and his second putt stops one inch from the lip.

Bogey, four under.

No. 11: Par 5, 534 Yards. Under his floppy straw hat, he looks more like Uncle Fudd than Arnie. But even at a distance, you recognize the familiar gait: chin out, shoulders rounded, purposeful stride. Waiting for him to approach, you hear the clapping give way to cheers, then to a full-throated ovation as he moves past.

Par, four under.

No. 12: Par 4, 393 Yards. Tightest driving hole on the course, and Arnie draws it too close to rough on left-hand side. Not a good place to be because of the big trees protecting green. He needs a delicate draw to have a chance for three, but too much hook spin and the ball will skip through the green to the trap at back left.

He steps up and takes a swipe. His body twisting and bending as he follows flight of ball, Arnie virtually wills the damned thing to curve left around a tree branch, hit fifteen feet from the pin, and roll down the slope to nine feet.

"AR-NEEE! AR-NEEE! AR-NEEE!"

The old chant echoes down from another era. Before square grooves. Before Nabisco. Before stadium courses and all-exempt fields and million-dollar purses. Even before Jack Nicklaus. The closer he gets to the green, the louder the chant. He looks up, greeting old friends with a familiar grin. He has, always will have, one of the great faces. A face that's seen a lot of sun and wind and its fair share of scotch. A face that's known plenty of good living. A face that's done a heap of grimacing and grunting and growling to make sure the ball got the message. A face that is the face of golf.

He makes the eight-footer.

Birdie, five under.

"AR-NEEE!"

No. 13: Par 3, 219 Yards. Not enough club leaves him thirty-five feet away on immense green. (The greens at Kemper Lakes are huge. Collectively, they are the size of Rhode Island.) Playing partners Jeff Sluman and Larry Nelson putt first whenever possible, even when Palmer's away, to avoid getting sucked up by the back draft when the gallery moves on to the next hole.

Par, still five under.

No. 14: Par 4, 420 Yards. Routine four, except that nothing is routine this afternoon. Gallery goes apeshit every time Arnie swings a club. Drive to left trap—"Uuuwwooo!" Second shot to twenty feet—"Yes!" Putt—"Get in the hole!" It doesn't, but the tap-in does—"AR-NEEE!"

Par, five under.

No. 15: Par 5, 578 Yards. Following through on his drive, Arnie's left elbow flies up like it's going into orbit, his body twists to maintain balance, his head tilts to the side as he follows the flight of the ball. He looks like Peter Jacobsen mimicking Chi Chi Rodriguez mimicking the famous Palmer swing. The ball lands in the fairway bunker, but his recovery is in the middle. Seven iron to eight feet. The putt splits the center of the hole.

Birdie, six under to tie Mike Reid for lead.

"AR-NEEE! AR-NEEE! AR-NEEE!"

No. 16: Par 4, 469 Yards. Toughest hole on the course, with water down the entire right side. All Arnie does is boom one down the middle and knock approach to twelve feet. Play stops on the seventeenth until the roar on sixteen finally subsides. His birdie attempt burns the right side of the hole but doesn't drop.

Par, still six under and tied for the lead.

And then the string that has tied so many people together, tied yesterday to today, finally breaks. A six iron finds the back bunker on the tough seventeenth, a nine iron runs through the green to the back rough on the eighteenth, and Arnie finishes bogey-bogey for a 68. He's still four under, still only two strokes off the lead, but it's over, this last hurrah. We all know it, we who have mustered for this final brave charge, and we don't care.

"This morning I just thought, Why can't I play as well as I used to?" Palmer was in the press tent now, savoring what had just happened. "Well, today I did."

Earlier, Jeff Sluman had explained that Arnie could easily have birdied the first and third holes and been seven under at the turn, he was playing so well. This was the same Arnold Palmer who shot 80–81 to miss the cut in the Masters four months previously, who didn't even try to qualify for the U.S. Open, who posted 82–82 in the British Open before catching his return flight in July, and who was only playing here in the PGA because of a special exemption.

What were you thinking about out there, Arnold?

The question came from someone in the front row, a reporter

who knew Palmer well enough to call him Arnold.[2] It was a lazy question, but it didn't really matter. The idea was just to keep Arnie talking about the day for as long as he would. Mike Reid and Leonard Thompson might be tied for the lead, but nobody cared: the only way either would make it into a headline the next day would be if he shot somebody. There was only one story today.

"After the birdie at fifteen," Arnie answered, taking level aim at the slow pitch, "I just thought to myself, 'Hey, this is great—don't screw it up!' "

Do you think you can still win?

The easy grin on Arnie's face gave way to a cold, hard stare, and it became instantly clear that this question was not only lazy, it was just plain dangerous. Paul Newman's eyes may be a tad bluer, but for flashing anger I'll take Arnold Palmer's any day.

"If I didn't think so," he said slowly, his words biting the air, "I wouldn't be out here. The day I think I don't have a chance to win is the day I stop playing."

(Memo to File: Never, ever ask Arnie if he thinks he can still win. *Never.*)

Taking pity on the poor soul he had just walloped, Arnie went on to talk about what good shape he was in physically. It was sort of like having Patrick Ewing explain that he's tall, because Palmer looked really terrific—gray, wrinkled, tired from the day's exertions, but terrific. "I've been doing exercises every day for five years," he said, and everybody in the room knew he was not exaggerating by so much as a day. "But psychologically, I can't concentrate for as long I used to be able to do, for as long as I need to."

But Arnie wasn't about to end the day on a negative note, so he recalled the wisdom of Norman Vincent Peale and *The Power*

---

[2]Winnie Palmer once said that there were two sets of people who called her husband Arnie: "There are the fans and the people who don't know him at all. Then there are a few people very close to him. I call him Arnie. His friends call him Arnold."

of Positive Thinking, "one of the few books I ever read." (Nobody in the room held this fact against him. We don't require our heroes to be well read. We just require them to be heroes.)

"I want to play if I can be of value to the tournament, to myself, and to the game," Arnie said. "I considered not playing because of the way my game has been lately, but I decided to give it a try. I'm glad I did."

He wasn't the only one.

The last time I saw Arnold Palmer in person I broke an ancient taboo.

It was the week after the PGA Championship at the 1989 Fred Meyer Challenge in Portland, Oregon, or "Peter's Party," as the event is more colloquially known. Spearheaded by Portland native Peter Jacobsen, the Fred Meyer Challenge is the biggest golf event of the year in the Pacific Northwest, a region without a regular tour stop for a quarter of a century. Besides raising a big chunk of money for Portland charities, the two-day tournament also gives a couple of dozen of the top pros who need it the least a chance to pick up some spare change. The $100,000 first prize for the winning two-man team is unofficial (i.e., it doesn't count in calculating the tour's money list), but it spends pretty well, and everyone has a good time.

Sitting at a picnic table near the pool at the Portland Country Club after his round on Tuesday, Arnie was feeling flush. He and Jacobsen, his playing partner, had just finished third in the tournament. But what mattered more to Palmer was the side bet on the round he had made with Greg Norman. In the featured foursome of the day, Palmer and Jacobsen defeated Norman and Curtis Strange, and Palmer was now $100 richer.

"Believe me," said Jacobsen, "I had no trouble getting my partner pumped up for today's round. That hundred bucks with Greg did the trick."

Not surprisingly, talk turned to Palmer's performance in the PGA. After the stunning 68 in the opening round, he came back with a 74 on Friday to leave him nine strokes off the lead going into the weekend. A quarter of a century before he would still have been in the hunt, but an 81 in the third round quashed any hopes of a Sunday miracle. He did finish strong with a final-round 70, including a birdie on the final hole, and a week later in Portland he was still basking in the afterglow.

"I was tingling all the way to my toes," Arnie said. "The crowd gave me a huge ovation as I walked up toward the green after my second shot. I turned to my caddie and asked him, 'Do you think they'll go a little crazy if I make this one?' He said, 'Why don't you do it and let's see.' "

He did, and they did.

"Mr. Palmer, will you sign my program, please?"

A ten-year-old boy who'd been hovering in the background for ten minutes had finally worked up the courage to make his move. Palmer shot him a collegial smile and took the program and pen. Before he signed, he extracted from the young fan confirmation that Yes, he played golf, and Yes, he practiced a lot.

"Well, you keep it up," Arnie said with a parting smile. From the look in the kid's eyes, you figured him to head straight to the practice tee.

As Palmer signed and talked, my mind wandered back to the only autograph I can ever recall getting. It was in the late 1940s at a grocery store in the Oak Cliff section of Dallas, four blocks up from the Texas Theater, where I always spent Saturday mornings and where, a couple of lifetimes later, Lee Harvey Oswald would seek final refuge. The grocery store was sponsoring some sort of promotion with the Dallas Eagles of the Texas League ("Eagles Ticket Free with Bag of Groceries" rings a bell).

My all-time favorite ballplayer at the time, Eagles first base-man Jerry Witte, was going to be there. No way was I going to miss meeting him, so there I was, first baseman's mitt and pen in hand, every bit as nervous and excited as the junior golfer from Portland. I got my autograph, too.

"Thank you, Mr. Palmer," the boy called back over his shoulder as he walked away, his awe intact but his nervousness gone.

"Just to have the old adrenaline flowing again," said Mr. Palmer, turning back to the PGA, "that, by itself, was good news."

And then he put it all in perspective.

"You know," he said, "I can keep in shape, and do my best, but everything would have to be just right, and I'd have to make sacrifices to be ready to win that I'm just not prepared to make."

It's barely a week since he snapped at a reporter for asking him if he thought he could still win. But that had been in the heat of battle, in the middle of a tournament, in the middle of the only major championship he'd never won, when a voice in the back of his head was still whispering, "Maybe, just maybe." Now, on an overcast, misty afternoon in Portland, Arnold Palmer was going head-to-head in match play with reality.

"I've had my time," he said quietly, without a trace of regret or self-pity. "If I can't win, I'm ready to accept it."

"No cheering in the press box" is maxim number one of the Sports Reporters Creed. Traditionally attributed to veteran Chicago sportswriter Jerome Holtzman, it is honored by most sportswriters most of the time. This taboo against displays of childlike enthusiasm while observing and chronicling the games played by overgrown children extends, most definitely, to autographs. Never once have I seen a sportswriter in a clubhouse or a locker room—or anywhere else, for that matter—ask a player for an autograph. It just isn't done.

But as Arnie stood up to leave to go to the Portland airport, something came over me. It wasn't anything he had done this week at an exhibition that was more of a party than a tournament. It wasn't the 68 the week before at the PGA, or all those triumphant charges so many years back. It wasn't the sixty-one victories or the six majors or even the enduring, abiding, passionate love he has for the game. No, it was something else. It was the memory, still fresh as tomorrow's sunrise, of a seven iron

backing up on the seventeenth green at Colonial a preposter-
ously long time ago, back when we were young.

And so I handed him my pen: "Will you sign my program,
please?"

Thank you, Mr. Palmer.

Who *Are* Those
Guys, Anyway?

The traditions of the game are rich with memories of dramatic triumphs as well as heartbreaking failures. The best players fail the most because they are in the hunt all the time. You learn to handle it—accept it or you don't survive. To be out there is like no other experience. I've been out there and I know.

—Deane Beman

The most often heard question in the gallery at a professional golf tournament is "Who is that guy?"

Now, it's quite true that all but a handful of professional athletes—Michael Jordan, Magic Johnson, Muhammad Ali, Arnold Palmer, O. J. Simpson, not as many others as you might think—could walk through a crowded airport without being recognized. So it's not so strange that fans in a golf gallery would not recognize most of the players in the field on sight.

The problem is that the question—"Who *is* that guy, anyway?"—frequently gets asked *after* the fans have seen the signboard with the guy's name on it. Except for a handful of marquee stars who hog the headlines even if they don't dominate the game, most members of the PGA Tour labor in relative anonymity. A full field consists of 156 players, a tournament comes to town once a year, and media coverage of golf is scant, certainly when compared with that accorded to the Big Three team sports plus hockey—so how can a golf fan be expected to tell Brad Fabel, Brad Faxon, and Brad Bryant apart?

At the Fred Meyer Challenge the highlight of the tournament is a big Monday night party where a lot of people get together in a big tent to eat, drink, and be merry—and raise a lot of money for local charities. One year, for example, Arnold Palmer's blazer was auctioned off for $6,000, and somebody paid $4,000 for Curtis Strange's pants. (I *said* it was a party.)

After the affair I shared a ride back to the hotel with tour veteran Mark Lye, who had performed with a rock group called Jake Trout and the Flounders (featuring Peter Jacobsen on vocals, Payne Stewart on harmonica, and Lye laying down strong bass lines). "So," said Lye, "I guess after tonight you guys can't say we're a bunch of faceless clones anymore."

Oh, sure—it's the *media's* fault.

Okay, no problem: we'll just fix it, here and now. Applying highly scientific investigative methodologies, we—I mean "I," but Mark said "you guys" when the person he was talking to was "me," so we/I guess it's okay to speak for us/me—will now examine the full membership of the PGA Tour and provide an up-close and personal look at just who those guys are, anyway.

MR. EVEN PAR

The "typical" golfer on the PGA Tour is thirty-five years old, stands 5'11" in height, weighs 176 pounds, was born in California, North Carolina, or Texas but lives in Florida, went to college but did not graduate, has been on the tour for 10.3 years, has won 3.5 tournaments, is married, has 1.5 children, plays in twenty-six official tour events a year, makes seventeen cuts, uses Titleist balls (100 Compression), makes five charity appearances a year, pays his caddy $28,500 a year, carries three wedges, prefers fishing to hunting but likes all sports, incurs $56,000 a year in tax-deductible job-related expenses, owns a boat, votes Republican if he votes at all, and earns $303,000 per year in prize money.

But that's merely scratching the surface.

THE LONG AND THE SHORT OF IT

The first time I saw Jack Nicklaus in person, he reminded me of the Alamo—neither is anywhere near as big as I had expected. In fact, just about the only thing average about Jack Nicklaus is his height. At one inch under six feet, he hits the PGA Tour mean height right on the screws.

The tallest golfer on the tour is Phil Blackmar. At 6'7", Blackmar looks a lot like the guy on your college basketball team who sat at the end of the bench and never got into games until the last few minutes. The starting five: Tom Sieckmann and Howard Twitty at 6'5", Steve Jones, Bob Tway, and Andy Bean at 6'4".

The shortest golfers on the tour are Bill Britton, Ed Fiori, and Jeff Sluman at 5'7", although Gene Sauers may be fudging a big when he says he's 5'8". Craig Parry from Australia, who made a good run at a green jacket (38 short) at Augusta in 1992, is 5'6", but he's not a member of the PGA Tour, so Commissioner Deane Beman (5'8") insists that he doesn't count. All of them tower over 1991 Masters winner Ian Woosnam, who, at 5'4½", is only slightly taller than Bruce Lietzke's putter.

Most of the great golfers of history have been under six feet in height. Examples: Nicklaus, Trevino, Watson, Palmer, Player, Hogan, Snead, Hagen, Jones. The principal exceptions: Byron Nelson, Henry Cotton, Johnny Miller.

Conventional wisdom has it that too much can go wrong in taller guys' swings—at least that's what taller guys like Bob Tway and Steve Jones say. Teaching guru David Leadbetter is 6'3", which may have something to do with his success in working with prize pupil Nick Faldo (also 6'3").

Shorter guys have lower centers of gravity, which Newton or somebody figured out is better for swinging a golf club. This principle of swing dynamics has its limits, as anyone who has ever watched Mickey Rooney play in the Hope Chrysler Classic will readily attest.

AGE BEFORE BEAUTY

The mean age for PGA Tour golfers is thirty-five, at least five years older than for any other major sport. Golfers start their professional careers a little later and last a lot longer than athletes in other sports. Most are twenty-five or twenty-six when they get on the tour to stay (i.e., make the top 125 on the money list and don't fall off), a few years older before they win their first tournament. At that age swimmers are washed up and tennis players are at their peak.

Prime time for golfers in the modern era is exactly 32.8 years of age. That's the average age of the winner of the twenty majors in the last five years. Throw out John Daly (twenty-five when he won the PGA in 1991) and the average age of recent major winners is 33.8.

At that age the average football player has been out of the NFL three years and has just begun to walk without a limp, a basketball player is weighing an offer to play in Italy, and a baseball player prays three times a day for expansion.

MARRIED, WITH CHILDREN

Ninety-three percent of pro golfers are married. Nationwide, the number for all men in their age group (twenty-five to forty-five) is only 70 percent, so there must be something to the wholesome family picture the PGA Tour's Image Management Department paints.

The 127 married golfers on the tour have 198 kids. This works out to 1.56 per married pro, quite close to the national average for American couples in the same age group. One statistically interesting fact that bodes well for the *L*PGA in the twenty-first century: 109 of the PGA Tour kids (55 percent) are girls.

The PGA Tour is silent on the subjects of D-I-V-O-R-C-E, single parenthood, nontraditional relationships, and other departures from its official Family Values Creed.

BORN IN THE USA

The prime breeding ground for professional golfers in America—and this should come as no surprise—is California, birthplace of eighteen of the 136 pros (12.7 percent) in the survey sample. Tied for second are North Carolina and Texas with twelve each, also no surprise. Next are Georgia and Missouri, each with seven native sons who make their living by chasing birdies.

You might figure that Florida, with more golf courses per capita than any state in the union, would be a prime producer of touring pros. Not so. Only three native-born Floridians are on the pro circuit, a number topped by a bunch of states and tied by Canada, which is covered with ice and snow half the year.

HOME IS WHERE YOU HANG YOUR HAT

While only three members of the PGA Tour were born in Florida, nearly a third—forty-three of the sample group of 136—make their home there.

Some of the obvious reasons: good weather for golf during the "off season" (October-December) . . . a lot of first-rate courses with good practice facilities . . . four Florida tournaments on the Florida circuit in March-April (Doral, Honda

Classic, Nestlé Invitational, Players) and another in October (Walt Disney World/Oldsmobile Classic) . . . excellent airline service to Europe as well as the rest of the U.S. from Orlando, Miami, West Palm, and Jacksonville . . . business opportunities (e.g., a huge number of lucrative corporate outings take place at Florida golf resorts).

But the main reason that so many pros live in Florida is that the Sunshine State has no state income tax. The second most popular residential choice—Texas, with sixteen tour members—likewise has no state income tax.

BEYOND FAIRWAYS AND GREENS

If pro golfers shoot and cast as well as they hit seven irons, American wildlife is in deep trouble: one half of them list hunting, fishing, or hunting *and* fishing as their primary "special interest." In distant second place: "all other sports" (40 of 136). Also in double figures: skiing (18), music (13), basketball (10), water sports (10), and reading (10).

I wonder if golfer Dan Quayle would be happy to learn that ten pros list "family" as their number one special interest? (I wonder if anyone still cares what Dan Quayle thinks? I wonder if anyone still remembers who he is?)

God makes a surprisingly poor showing—only nine pros list church and/or bible study as a special interest. This is surprising, given the notices of "Bible Group" meetings posted in clubhouses at every tour stop, not to mention the frequent "witnessing" by born-againers who've just fired 66 to take the third-round lead. ("First, I want to thank our Lord for giving me the strength to make all those great shots, and I want to say that if He shows up and helps me read my putts tomorrow, I'll *really* show Him something.")

Could it be that some of them are lying? After all, Fuzzy Zoeller says the reason you never run into any of the younger players at nineteenth holes on the tour is that "they're all back in their rooms, reading the Bible and putting on the carpet."

Golfers on the PGA Tour are emphatically mainstream when it comes to hobbies, but there are three scuba divers, two martial artists, four cooks, two wine enthusiasts, and one bird-watcher—Ben Crenshaw, not Robert Wrenn. Speaking of Wrenn, he lists "thrill seeking" as his special interest—which, coming from a guy who wears an Eskimo Pie logo on his visor, could mean just about anything.

Anyone who pays attention to these matters has to lament the passing from the active scene of Mac O'Grady. He listed his special interests as "modern times, science, history"—and meant it.

LONE RANGER

There are a lot of former NCAA champions on the tour. There are several former U.S. Amateur winners. But there is only one former U.S. Public Links champion—Jodie Mudd. A native of Louisville, Kentucky, Mudd learned the game at local public courses and won the national Public Links title twice, in 1980 and 1981. His familiarity with municipal golf courses sets him apart from pros his age on the tour, most of whom learned the game on country club courses. Mudd won the two richest tournaments on the tour in 1990, the Players Championship and the Nabisco Championship, and earned over $900,000 to finish fifth on the money list. The following year he dropped to 102nd, then to 141st in 1992, when he entered only twenty events. Exempt from qualifying until the year 2000 because of his victory in the Players Championship, Mudd said he might even take off a couple of years to raise horses on a farm he bought recently near Louisville—which proves that you can take the boy out of Kentucky, but you can't take Kentucky out on tour with you.

THE SPEEDY GONZALEZ FASTEST PLAYER ON TOUR AWARD

Lanny Wadkins. Nobody else is even close. Lanny is halfway down the fairway before his tee hits the ground after his drive. If everybody played as fast as Wadkins, an average round at a PGA Tour event would take three hours, tops. You like to watch a man being tortured? Watch Lanny Wadkins waiting to hit (and waiting after he hits) during the five-hour rounds with three amateur partners at the Hope.

FAST IS GOOD. VERY FAST IS BAD.

At the end of the third round in the Nabisco Championships at Pebble Beach in 1988, Greg Norman and Mark O'Meara were so far off the lead that they were the first pair to tee off on Sunday morning. Neither was inclined to grind for four hours just to finish in twentieth place, especially since dead last paid $30,000 in this season-ending bonanza for the tour's top 30 finishers on the year's money list. So they decided to have some fun.

With about a thousand fans chugging along with them, they ran—sometimes literally—through eighteen holes in one hour and twenty-four minutes, an unofficial tour record.

Both shot 79.

Flash-forward to the 1992 Players Championship, where Mark Calcavecchia and John Daly found themselves in the same boat—and tried to break the Norman-O'Meara streaking record. They didn't come close, taking two hours and three minutes to play the round. Daly had an 80, Calcavecchia an 81.

This time, though, hall monitor Deane Beman was not amused. After all, one does not make sport of the Players Championship, the fifth major in Beman's dreams, any more than one would take a whiz against a tree at Augusta.

The players were admonished by the tour's deputy commissioner for "failure to exert their best effort" and warned that a fine might be forthcoming, at which news Calcavecchia went ballistic: "This is going to be appealed, big time."

The tempest returned to the teapot. It is tour policy not to reveal the terms—or even the fact—of disciplinary proceedings against players, but you can assume that the worst the two golfers got was the public scolding. If either had been fined so much as a dollar, we would have heard more on the subject. Big time.

THE JACK W. NICKLAUS SLOWEST PLAYER ON TOUR TROPHY

The winner and all-time champion is the Golden Bear himself. In the under-forty set, there is a three-way tie among Ian Baker-Finch, Chip Beck, and Larry Mize.

LIKE A PAGE OUT OF *ESQUIRE*

The two snappiest dressers on tour—Keith Clearwater and Tommy Armour III—have not yet come up with the game to match their wardrobes.

WORST-DRESSED PLAYER ON TOUR

Brad Bryant. His nickname is "Dirt," and he comes by it honestly. A hundred others are tied for second.

DUMBEST-DRESSED PLAYER ON TOUR

Payne Stewart and his NFL-logo knickers. Can't really blame him, though. For $350,000 a year, I'd wear my underwear outside my clothes.

KEEP ON TRUCKIN' MEDAL IN BRONZE

John Adams, Buddy Gardner, Brad Bryant, and Bobby Wadkins have been on the tour a collective fifty-nine years, during which time they have played in nearly two thousand tournaments, and among them they have exactly *no* victories.

HALF-TIME JOB

Pro golfers are on the road more than Willy Loman. In most sports, the better you are, the more you play. The reverse is true in golf: the better you are, the fewer tournaments you play. A journeyman trying to grind out a living and keep his tour play- ing card will enter thirty or more events a year. The leader of the pack the last two years was Ed Dougherty, a forty-five-year-old veteran of thirteen undistinguished seasons on the tour. In 1991 Dougherty entered thirty-six events and made twenty cuts to earn $202,000. Last year he logged another thirty-six tourna- ments in his travel diary while earning $237,525 to finish sixty- sixth on the money list, his best ranking ever.

IT'S A LIVING

Just to give you some perspective about how much money pro- fessional athletes make, the *average* salary of a major-league baseball player in 1992 was $969,000. The average salary of a basketball player in the NBA was $1.78 *million.* In the NFL the average starting offensive *guard* made $364,000. That gives you some idea of where the average touring pro and his $303,000 in winnings last year rank in the financial pecking order of profes- sional sports.

99⁴⁴/₁₀₀ PERCENT PURE

Professional golf is white. Lily white. White as freshly driven snow. White as Wonder bread. White as Cypress Point and Augusta National and Pine Valley and 99⁴⁴/₁₀₀ percent of the other private golf clubs in America. White as a gallon of vanilla ice cream topped with a pinch of chocolate sprinkles.

Race is not one of the information categories in the PGA Tour's media guide. It doesn't have to be. You get the picture just by looking at the faces of the 239 professional golfers whose photos appear there: only 2 are black.

One of the black faces belongs to Calvin Peete. He has played sparingly in recent years because of injuries, but in the mid-1980s Peete was one of the tour's legitimate stars. He won a dozen tournaments, including the 1985 Tournament Players Championship, which gave him a ten-year exemption from qualifying for tour events. (That's why he's still listed as an active member of the PGA Tour.) He won a Vardon Trophy for low-stroke average. He played on two Ryder Cup teams. He won ten straight driving accuracy titles: he still misses fairways about as often as Gerry Ford pays greens fees. And he accomplished it all without benefit of country club training or even a straight left arm. (When he was a kid, growing up with eighteen brothers and sisters on a hardscrabble Florida farm, Peete broke an elbow that never mended properly.)

You might say that Calvin Peete is something of an exception.

When Peete turns fifty in the summer of 1993 and joins the Senior Tour, the only black face on the PGA Tour will belong to Jim Thorpe—and it won't be seen very often along the circuit. A solid journeyman whose career got derailed in 1987 and 1988 by severe injuries, Thorpe has three victories carved onto his belt, which is three more than a lot of guys who make good livings on the tour. But he's not had much success the last couple of years, finishing 133rd (1991) and 200th (1992) on the money list. At forty-three, Thorpe is too old to be a factor on the regular tour and too young to start counting the days until he can go play on the Senior Tour.

Among the old geezers playing from the forward tees on the PGA Senior Tour, big Jim Dent has made a big splash, but he's the *only* African American on the circuit—and will continue to be so until Calvin Peete arrives.

It's not that PGA Tour players are especially prejudiced against people of color—some are, some aren't, some are indifferent. But they are definitely not accustomed to playing with blacks, so they may well be less tuned in to racial issues than other athletes. When the host golf club's racially discriminatory admissions policy became a public issue at the 1990 PGA Championship held at Shoal Creek in Birmingham, defending PGA champion Payne Stewart probably expressed the majority view: What's the big deal?

The fact is that PGA Tour golfers as a group are about as sensitive to racial issues as your average country club golfers: not much.

Commissioner Beman and his PGA Tour staff worked mightily after the Shoal Creek incident to secure at least token changes by golf clubs hosting tour-sponsored events so that the public relations issue would go away. The tour now requires that host clubs have an "open" admissions policy and actual, real, live minority members. If certain private clubs (e.g., Cypress Point in Monterey, Butler National in Chicago) tell the PGA Tour to get stuffed, that's okay so long as enough others (e.g., Colonial in Fort Worth) remove any nominal barriers to minority membership and scrounge the neighborhood for upper-middle-class blacks who can pony up cash to join. It is immaterial that this policy change will have no substantive effect on the racial composition of the clubs affected; it is material to the PGA Tour that it will take some of the heat off professional golf.

The pro tour is 99⁴⁴/₁₀₀ percent white because golf is a country club game, and the country clubs of America are $99^{44}/_{100}$ percent white. Nothing will change until there is a more equitable distribution of wealth in America and blacks and other minorities can afford to join golf clubs—and are invited to do so—in the same proportions as whites.

We should all live so long.

Nice Guys Finish First

Every kid learning how to play golf dreams about winning the Masters, about winning the Open, not about being the leading money winner. I've never shortchanged myself on dreams.

—Tom Kite

If Thomas O. Kite, Jr., had been called to the first tee of the Elysian Fields Country Club in the sky prior to June 21, 1992, he would already have earned the right to have any number of admirable achievements carved on his tombstone back here on earth: Good Husband and Loving Father . . . Stand-Up Guy . . . Straight and True . . . Fairways and Greens . . . Loyal Texas Longhorn . . . Money Machine on the PGA Tour.

But because the Gods of Golf revel in being capricious, heartless, vindictive, and spiteful, Kite's epitaph would inevitably have been the tag that was hung around his neck back in the mideighties, a description that should have been rendered as his own personal logo and stitched on the front of his golf shirt—a little circle composed of the letters B-G-H-N-W-M, with his name in the middle, for "Tom Kite: The Best Golfer in History Never to Win a Major."

"Tom Kite?"

Somebody would have brought up the name at a nineteenth hole in the middle of the twenty-first century. Oh, yeah, good golfer, some graybeard would have recalled. Nice guy, too. Terrific short game. All those freckles. Thick glasses, like the bottoms of Coke bottles. (What are Coke bottles? a youngster would have asked.) Didn't hit it very far, but won a lot of money for those days. Went on to win another fortune on the Senior Tour.

Never won a major, though, did he?

Fortunately, for those who believe that hard work and dedication and courage should be rewarded, that last question will never be asked, and in its place will appear this substitute: He finally got the monkey off his back with that great chip at the Open at Pebble Beach, didn't he?

Yes, Tom Kite did finally get the monkey off his back. But it took a whole lot more than a great chip to win the 1992 U.S. Open. First he had to recover from what happened at the U.S. Open in 1989, when the earth opened up and swallowed him whole.

The United States Golf Association says that its goal in staging the U.S. Open is to identify the best player in the world. In fact, says former USGA executive director Frank Hannigan, "The USGA generally sets up [an Open] course to identify Ben Hogan."

Hogan, wrote Jerry Tarde a few years back in *Golf Digest*, "played a golf course the way a locomotive runs down a railroad track, making only scheduled stops." In other words: fairways and greens, fairways and greens, with nary a detour.

There are other ways to play golf. Seve Ballesteros's way is to hit a bank shot against a brick wall, blade a putt with a sand wedge, and make a pitch shot stop in midair and sing a chorus of "Malagueña" before dropping next to the flagstick for a tap-in birdie. Tom Watson's way is to hit a three iron from somewhere in the next zip code to thirty feet, then one-putt to save par. Ben Crenshaw's way is like Tom Watson's, only not as good. And John Daly's way is to grip it and rip it to set up an eagle or a triple bogey, depending on the phase of the moon.

But for the past four decades the USGA has chosen to create its flagship tournament in the image of Ben Hogan, which translates as the narrowest fairways, the fastest greens, and the tallest, thickest, deepest, nastiest rough in the universe.

The site of the 1989 U.S. Open was the East Course at the Oak Hill Country Club in Rochester, New York. Designed by Donald Ross and opened for play in 1926, the course endured many alterations over the years, including major overhauls by Robert Trent Jones and George and Tom Fazio that removed most traces of Ross. Any traces of forgiveness in the long, narrow, tree-lined track were removed by the USGA.

By Monday of tournament week the course was in quintessential U.S. Open shape: fairways trimmed closer than Michael Jordan's head, Formica-hard greens coated with Teflon, and rough up to Ian Woosnam's chin. But then, between Tuesday morning and Saturday night of Open week, it rained for forty days and forty nights, turning Oak Hill into a northeastern facsimile of the Okefenokee Swamp.

Lee Trevino, who had won his first U.S. Open at Oak Hill in 1968, had warned before the tournament that rain would make hash of short hitters. "At old courses like this," he said, "there's an opening in front of most greens. That helps a short hitter, at least when it's dry, because he can run it up."

Not only would a wet track make the course play longer, but it would also levy an extreme penalty for hitting into the thick rough. "At Augusta I just take three deep breaths and hit it as hard as I can," said Trevino. "You don't have to worry about rough because there isn't any. Do that here and you might never be heard from again."

Trevino also spoke of how shaky a golfer's grip on the lead could get at the Open: "In 1968, if I'd had a one-stroke lead with four holes to go instead of four strokes, I wouldn't have won. I was too damned nervous."

・ ・ ・

On Sunday morning, Tom Kite had a one-stroke lead with eighteen holes to go and he looked anything but nervous. If there is any justice, I concluded while watching the first twosomes of the day tee off, if the gods in charge of the game of life pay off for hard work, dedication, and professionalism, then Tom Kite will win the U.S. Open today.

The guy is the soul of self-discipline, the heart of devotion to his craft. He has done more with his natural abilities than anyone else on the tour. He never cops an excuse, never ducks a question, never dodges responsibility for his own game and his own performance. For a bunch of years he has hit the ball straight and dealt with people the same way.

Temper tantrums? Prima donnaism? Childish petulance? Not exactly unknown on the tour, but never associated with Tom Kite. Not ever.

The worst thing Tom Kite can be accused of is being colorless because he doesn't do those things that supposedly add "color" to sports. Guilty as charged. He's no Andre Agassi, no Charles Barkley, no José Canseco. Thank goodness. He's just plain old Tom Kite from Austin, Texas. What you see is what you get.

What you see is not exactly your archetypal athletic hero. He's a haircut over 5'8" and weighs 155 pounds after a big lunch. His uncorrected vision is legally blind (20/480). Except for golf, he has no evident athletic skills. Yet sports shrink Bob Rotella believes that Kite "gets more out of himself physically than anybody who's ever played the game." And just about everybody on the PGA Tour would agree with the assessment of fellow pro Tim Simpson: "There are a hundred guys out here on tour with more talent, but very few with as much of what it takes to win."

There was every good reason on this soggy Sunday in 1989 to believe that this nice guy with the suspect body was finally going to win his first major. Coming into Oak Hill, Kite was number one on the money list, he was riding a string of twenty-four tournaments without missing a cut, and he had two wins already that season, at Bay Hill and the Players Championship.

Ordinarily, what a player did that long ago—Bay Hill and the Players Championship took place in March—wouldn't amount to a bag of broken tees. "You stay out here all year," Ken Green once said, "just to catch that four or five weeks when everything comes together."

But in the first three rounds of the Open Kite had posted a 67 and two 69s, and he would enter the final round one stroke ahead of Scott Simpson, three over Curtis Strange, and four in front of Larry Nelson, Jumbo Ozaki, and Jay Don Blake. Of Kite's pursuers, Blake clearly had no business being there, Ozaki was a wild card, and Simpson, Strange, and Nelson all played the same game. Fairways and greens. Tom Kite's game.

Maybe somebody would make a run from the pack and throw up a lot of red on the scoreboard, but it wasn't likely. The course was a great green sponge and would play much longer than its 6,900 yards. And, as usually happens at U.S. Opens, it was getting harder to score as the tournament progressed. On Thursday, even par was only worth a tie for twenty-second place; at the end of play on Saturday, even par was good for a tie for seventh. It stood to reason that there wouldn't be many birdies made this Sunday, so the winner would be the guy best able to hang in there, keep his nervous system from short-circuiting, and play steady golf.

After what Tom Kite did at the third hole, I was certain he was that guy.

What he did was run a twenty-two-footer into the back of the cup for a birdie. That gave him a three-shot lead over Simpson, who bogied the same hole, and a four-shot advantage over Strange, who was doing nothing up ahead but making pars.

That did it. All he had to do now was play his own game the rest of the way in. Fairways and greens. Tom Kite, U.S. Open champion.

The gallery walkways along the fourth and fifth holes were virtual swamps, and, anyway, I wanted to get over to the hill above the thirteenth to watch play on the course's longest hole.

So I left Kite, convinced that he had a hammerlock on his first major, and cut catty-corner across the hog wallow separating the fairways on the front nine. Only once did I lose a shoe to the muck, not bad considering that some people lost whole children.

On the way I ran into Tom McCollister, golf writer for the *Atlanta Constitution,* who was wading his way in the other direction to see how Atlanta-area veteran Larry Nelson was faring. Thinking to spare McCollister the trouble and a stiff dry-cleaning bill (so far he hadn't fallen in the mud once), I explained to him that Kite had birdied the third and pretty much wrapped things up.

"You're out of your mind," McCollister said, looking at me as if I'd just been beamed down by Scotty. "*Nothing* at a U.S. Open is settled this early on a Sunday."

"Oh, yeah?" was the best retort I could think of on the spur of the moment, but it dawned on me as he scurried away that I should have added, "Oh, *yeah?*"

Hadn't I predicted back in January after the third round of the Tournament of Champions that Steve Jones was going to win? And hadn't I been correct to tab Jones to cop the Bob Hope Chrysler Classic the next week after watching him come back from a skulled 100-yard tee shot to nail a birdie on a par-five hole? And hadn't I predicted even before the Players Championship began that Andy Bean—whom I'd seen spend four hours on the practice range—would finish in the top 10?

Hey, this golf handicapping wasn't so tough after all, and I was on a roll. Cut me some slack, McCollister. I think I know a U.S. Open winner when I see one.

Oh, yeah? Barely twenty-five minutes later, the three-stroke lead was history. On the fifth hole, Tom Kite—Mr. Dependable, the steadiest guy on the tour, the quintessential technician who never beat himself—had made a *triple bogey.* The steadiest golfer in the game had just gone up like the *Hindenburg.*

· · ·

Ray Floyd believed that Oak Hill had gotten tougher since the PGA championship was played there in 1980: "The trees have grown out a *lot*. Now it's like shooting down a tunnel. There is no play from rough to green. If you hit it in the rough, you're playing bogey. If you hit it straight, you're okay."

And what about the "improvements" made to the course since 1980? "If I owned a Rembrandt," said Floyd, "I don't think I'd want to go slapping on some reds and yellows just because it was kind of dull."

But as much as the pros disliked the new sixth hole and the new fifteenth hole ("It's totally out of character with the rest of the course," said Lanny Wadkins), the hole that they were most *worried* about was the fifth. Here's the official description from the USGA's media guide for the Open:

No. 5—(Double Trouble)—406 yards, par 4—This is one of the East Course's three most demanding holes. One mistake from tee to green can easily produce a double bogey. To reach the fairway, the drive must carry more than 200 yards through a corridor of trees. Allen's Creek at the right menaces tee shots and also fronts a small green.

Compounding the problem was the location of the tee box, tucked tightly against a stand of tall oaks that leaned far out into the fairway. Said Floyd: "On the fifth hole the tee placement selects the shot for you." Added Nicklaus: "I haven't figured out how to play it. Trees have grown out so much that faders can't start the ball left and bring it to the middle. They have to start the ball in the middle and hope it doesn't go too far right."

And so it came to pass, in the fourth round of the 1989 U.S. Open, that Tom Kite—in confident possession of a three-stroke lead on the field—tried to start the ball in the middle from the fifth tee. But instead of starting it straight and bending it, Kite blocked his tee shot straight right and into Allen's Creek. After a drop and a penalty stroke, he didn't have a shot to the green, so he laid up in front. A sand wedge got him to twelve feet. His first putt slid two feet past the hole. His second putt rolled four inches past. He made the tap-in for a triple-bogey seven.

Easy, huh?

What happened, of course, is that the Gods of Golf—perhaps out of boredom, perhaps out of sheer meanness—decided at that moment to turn Tom Kite into one of *us* for the rest of the afternoon. Bogey on eight. Bogey on ten. Double bogey on thirteen when he tried to force a four wood through wet, ankle-deep rough. (Hey, I did that last weekend!) Double bogey on fifteen when he pushed his tee shot into the water.

If only he had been playing baseball, Tom Kite would have had a great day: two doubles and a triple.

Golf fans like to see eagles. They like to see sand saves. They like to see big drives. ("You the Man, Shark!") They really like to see pros pull out their drivers on the fairway. ("Give it a ride, Big John!") But most of all, they like to see the pros get in trouble, the way they themselves always do, and then get out of it, in ways they never dreamed were even possible.

What they don't like to see is a good man destroy himself, which is what Tom Kite did at the fifth hole.

Making triple bogey when in position to win a tournament had never been part of Tom Kite's game. He missed, forcing Jack Nicklaus into a play-off at the 1986 Masters when a twelve-foot birdie putt wouldn't fall. But there's a big difference between not making a birdie and making a triple bogey, and it's a lot more than three strokes. What Kite's catastrophe at the fifth hole in the 1989 Open did was let Curtis Strange, two holes ahead, back into the hunt.

"Tom's triple bogey played into my hands," Strange said later. "It let me stay with my plan to just put it in the fairway and put it in the hole."

After hearing the news of Tom Kite's fifth-hole disaster, Strange continued to do what he'd been doing all day: grind out pars, one after another, like a metronome setting a beat. Fairway-green-putt-putt; fairway-green-putt-putt. "Like watching paint dry," Strange has often described his game, but when you're one stroke off the lead in the final round of the U.S. Open and people ahead of you and behind you are finding it harder and harder to swallow, it's the only game in town.

And on that damp, partly sunny Sunday in Rochester in 1989, it was enough game to earn Curtis Strange his second straight U.S. Open title. He made only one birdie all day, at the sixteenth hole, but that was enough cushion to absorb his only bogey, a "safe" five at eighteen when all he needed to do was protect against catastrophe.

As Strange's victory celebration began, Tom Kite closed out with a par on eighteen. Three hours before, he had enjoyed a three-stroke lead with fifteen holes to play; he ended the day five strokes back, tied for ninth. In the most important round of golf in his entire career, he had just shot 78, eight strokes over par, his worst score in competition in living memory.

As he walked from the scorer's table to the golf cart that would take him to the press tent, Kite stared blankly ahead of him. People lining his path were still, as if observing a funeral procession. Finally someone said, "Tough luck, Tom."

Baseball philosopher Branch Rickey was fond of saying that luck is the residue of design. "And also of execution," a professional golfer, if he were being honest with himself, would add.

"When you're swinging well and you push the ball, the hook spin will cause the ball to kick back toward the fairway," Kite mused one afternoon at a practice range. "But if you're not swinging well and push it, the slice spin will cause the ball to kick away from the fairway deeper into the rough. So sometimes 'luck' has more to do with execution than chance."

So on this gray day when the sky had fallen on him, Tom Kite turned his head and nodded in acknowledgment, a half smile fixed on his face. But he knew better. Luck had nothing to do with it.

• • •

After every round in a golf tournament, the tournament leaders come to the press room to answer questions and to participate in a ritual called "birdies and bogies," in which they go over the highlights (and lowlights) of the day's round, hole by hole. Given the nature of a golf tournament, with the action spread out over 150 acres and forty or so pairings, it's the only way reporters can determine how the winner and the runners-up arrived at their scores.

Under normal circumstances, a player who finished tied for ninth wouldn't be asked to come to the interview room. But the circumstances were hardly normal, so here was Tom Kite, sitting behind a table on a riser at one end of a large tent, 500 reporters in front of him on folding chairs, a dozen video cameras aimed at him, trying his best to explain what had happened.

"What can I say? I stunk. Every shot I missed cost me dearly. I played thirteen holes one under par. The other five holes killed me."

The familiar Hogan visor was pushed back on his forehead. His face was flushed. He gazed blankly out toward the back of the tent. His shoulders slumped as he leaned forward on thick forearms. His voice was the dazed, flat monotone of a boxer who isn't sure where or who he is.

Excuse me, Tom—the USGA media coordinator seated next to Kite said, breaking a painful silence—but could you give us birdies and bogies?

"Birdies and bogies?" Kite asked. "You don't really want me to go through . . ." His voice trailed off without finishing the thought because he knew the answer, knew the press-tent ritual, knew what was expected of him, knew he would have to relive the day, hole by hole. No one would have blamed him had he not come to the interview room at all: he was still recovering from open-heart surgery that he had performed on himself. But he was here, and he wasn't going to duck anything.

"Okay, I birdied number three. Triple-bogied number five.

Bogied number ten. Double-bogied number thirteen—three wood to left rough, left a four wood in the grass. Blocked it into the water on fifteen. Bogied eighteen. Any questions? Make 'em easy."

They were easy. No one had to ask Tom Kite how he felt. No one had to ask what the day meant to him. No one wanted to prolong his suffering.

"I'll survive it. No question. You don't like to have a chance to win a tournament, much less a major, and perform this way . . ." His voice trailed off, while suddenly everybody in the tent decided it was time to look down and scrutinize their notes.

Among those watching and listening and taking notes was Iva Green, a press-room veteran and the wife of Bob Green, chief Associated Press golf correspondent since before typewriters. The Greens and the Kites go way back, all the way to Tom's first year on the tour (1972). Like the Kites, the Greens are from Texas. Their home in Weatherford is about four hours from the Kites' home in Austin.

When the questions mercifully ended, Kite got up and made his way to the back of the tent toward the exit, beyond which more TV and radio crews were waiting for a sound bite. Iva Green was seated near the exit, and when Tom got almost to the door, she stood and walked up to him. Wordless, struggling to hold back the tears, she gave him a silent hug. "It's okay," he said, trying to comfort her. "It's okay."

Outside, after another fifteen minutes of the same questions, he finally broke away and started walking back across the parking lot toward the clubhouse. Just then a young boy with a program ran up to him. Please, Mr. Kite, can I have your autograph? Sure you can. A smile, a signature, a handshake.

And as the young boy ran off to brag to his friends, Tom Kite walked away to meet his wife, Christy, and to start the recovery process. "The best things you have going for you at a time like this," he had said a few minutes earlier in the press tent, "are your friends and your family."

. . .

Put away your hanky. As we all know, this story has a happy ending. Tom Kite is *not* the Best Golfer in History Never to Win a Major. Not anymore.

The USGA did its usual number in preparing Pebble Beach for the 1992 Open. The rough was as high as an elephant's eye, and on several holes it pinched the fairway tighter than a Victorian corset. The greens were jacked up to eleven and change on the Stimpmeter, which was maybe a couple of Stimps too severe even before weekend winds blew in and turned the putting surfaces into hardpan. It's not as if Pebble Beach was exactly toothless to begin with; the USGA seemed hell-bent on turning it into an unplayable lie.

"The U.S. Open is a joke," groused Raymond Floyd, who birdied the first two holes on Sunday on his way to an 83. He was talking about the way the course was set up, not the championship itself. And it was no laughing matter.

How tough did Pebble Beach play? Of sixty-six golfers who teed it up for the final round, only five shot par or better. None broke 70. Defending U.S. Open champion Payne Stewart shot 83, as did Davis Love III. Ian Woosnam shot 79. (Even par would have tied him with Kite and forced a play-off.) Seve Ballesteros, Mark Calcavecchia, and Paul Azinger shot 80. After a brilliant 68 on Saturday, Scott Simpson shot *88* on Sunday.

Tough.

Memorable images from the 1992 Open include Curtis Strange looking like he was *back,* at least for one round . . . Dr. (of Optometry[1]) Gil Morgan making history by being the first golfer in Open history to reach ten under par . . . Andy Dillard assuming the traditional mantle of Designated Nobody and shooting his way into second place after two rounds . . . Nick Faldo up a tree . . . Ian Woosnam seeing his five iron blown far

[1]The TV commentators almost always refer to Morgan as "Dr. Gil Morgan," but they practically never explain what he is a doctor of. That oversight is hereby corrected to 20/20.

left on the seventh and making bogey after dismissing the 107-yard jewel as a "practice hole" . . . Dr. (of Optometry) Gil Morgan getting to twelve under and then losing nine strokes to par in the next eight holes . . . the sun coming out after three days of fog, mist, clouds, and no blimp shots . . . Dr. (of Optometry) Gil Morgan picking up on Sunday where he left off on Saturday to finish with an 81, when even par would have won the tournament.

But the most indelible image—other than Tom Kite raising both fists in exultation on the eighteenth green on Sunday after finally, *finally*, getting that damned monkey off his back—was that of Jack Nicklaus and Tom Watson, paired together, competing against younger, stronger versions of themselves via the miracle of television.

Indeed, if you happened to doze off during TV coverage of last year's Open only to be awakened by a roaring gallery, you might have thought you had been caught in a time warp. There was Jack Nicklaus in long sideburns hitting the flagstick at seventeen with a three iron en route to his third U.S. Open title in 1972. God, he looks *young*. And hey, isn't that Tom Watson standing in ankle-deep rough at the same hole ten years later with a wedge in his hands? No way he's going to . . . he did it! He knocked it in!

Over and over the same exhilarating images flickered across the screen. Those images from a grander day provided a bittersweet antipode to their live performances. Watson shot 75–73 to miss the cut by one stroke; Nicklaus shot 77–74.

The hell with that: kill the live cameras and roll the promo again.

You figure that if Tom Kite was ever going to get his major, Mr. Consistent would do it by playing steady, conservative, fairways-and-greens, *bor*-ing, Tom Kiteish golf. And if you look only at his scores at Pebble Beach last summer—71, 72, 70, 72—it might seem that that was just what happened.

Not so. On Sunday Kite hit only seven fairways and six greens in regulation. True, everything is relative, and compared to what everybody else was doing, that was pretty steady and consistent. But what won the 1992 U.S. Open for Tom Kite was something beyond consistency. What earned him his first major championship was an aggressive play worthy of Lanny Wadkins, a display of true grit reminiscent of Ben Hogan, and a single, stunning, miraculous, once-in-a-lifetime chip shot.

If you were on vacation in Tierra del Fuego and missed the chip shot, don't worry: it will be shown again, and again, and *again,* in every TV preview and promo spot for the U.S. Open forevermore. And rightly so. The next time the Open returns to Pebble Beach, probably in 2002, look for Kite's chip-in for birdie at the 107-yard seventh hole to form a triptych with Nicklaus's flagstick-rattler of 1972 and Watson's fabulous flop from 1982. How do you win a U.S. Open at Pebble Beach? future generations will ask. Easy. You just make a single miraculous birdie at one of the par threes abutting the ocean.

The big difference in the three shots is that Nicklaus and Watson made theirs at the seventy-first hole of the golf tournament. When Kite made his, after punching a six iron under the wind and into deep rough well left of the postage-stamp green at the seventh, there were still eleven holes left to play, and it was a little premature to be running around the green yelping with joy. The chip-in gave him a commanding three-stroke lead, but the roughest part of the course lay ahead. Anyway, he had held a commanding three-stroke lead in the final round of a U.S. Open once before.

In 1989.

But this was 1992, and the true-grit factor came into play.

The eighth, ninth, and tenth at Pebble Beach form the toughest three-hole stretch of par fours in golf. "Cliffs of Doom" seems an ill-suited term for such a scenic swatch of oceanfront property, but this trio certainly spelled doom for most golfers in last year's Open. That day the eighth and ninth alone yielded just five birdies, forty-eight pars, and seventy-nine bogies or worse.

All Tom Kite did, with the memory of 1989 surely knocking around somewhere inside his head, was square his jaw, hitch up his britches, and shoot par-bogey-par to make the turn back home with his lead intact.

Intact, maybe, but by no means safe, not even after a thirty-five-foot no-brainer for birdie on twelve gave him some breathing space. The only safe lead in a U.S. Open is the one you still have when everyone is in the clubhouse. Kite figured it was no time to play safe. It was time to be aggressive.

The fourteenth hole at Pebble Beach is one of the trickiest par fives in golf. Not because of its length: at 565 yards, it's reachable by most of the big hitters, at least when the wind is from the west, as it was during the final round of last year's Open. Nor because of its tightness: too far right from the tee is OB, but there's plenty of bail-out room on the left and a nice wide fairway to receive your second shot.

What makes the fourteenth so doggone tough is the target presented for the approach shot. Guarding the front of the green is a deep, steeply walled bunker, from the bottom of which you can barely see the flag. Throw a lofted shot to the right-hand third of the green and the ball will back off the putting surface faster than a sand crab scuttling for cover. Hit on the back side and the ball will slide down a steep hill that the USGA mowed short to make sure overshooters would be sorely punished. What's left is a safe haven the size of a king-size bedspread, only it must look like a pocket handkerchief when the U.S. Open title is at stake.

The day before, Kite had hit a three wood off the tee, laid up with a two iron, chunked his wedge into the trap, blasted out and off the back side of the green, putted back up the hill to two feet, and knocked it in for a bogey six. That was not the model he wanted to follow on Sunday.

"Saturday night a friend told me that he had watched at fourteen all afternoon," Kite would later explain, "and he said that no one who laid up had been able to hold the green. The only guys able to hold the greens were the ones who went for it in two. Even if they weren't able to run it in on the right side, all they had was a little pitch."

That bit of intelligence helped forge Kite's decision on what to do when he got to fourteen on Sunday. And what he did was pull out his driver, a move that stunned caddie Mike Carrick. Then, after rocketing his tee shot far down the right side dangerously near but well beyond a fairway bunker, Kite shocked Carrick even more by grabbing his three wood. Even with a big west wind blowing at his back, Kite didn't reach the green. But his ball landed close enough in the left rough for him to employ his trusty sixty-degree wedge, the magic wand he had wielded to such startling effect on the seventh hole. He hit it to two feet and tapped in his birdie to go four strokes up with four holes left to play.

There was still some work to do. After a cautious par on fifteen, Kite seemed to slip into a four-corners defense and went bogey-bogey on the next two holes. (The second, on the par-three seventeenth, was a smart bogey: rather than try to drill through the headwind and risk being pushed left into the ocean, Kite underclubbed into the sand in front of the green to set up a worst-case four.) But he still had a two-stroke cushion when he stepped up to the eighteenth tee.

The eighteenth hole at Pebble Beach tops just about everybody's list as the most beautiful finishing hole in golf. But on the fourth day of the 1992 U.S. Open, with the wind ripping in from the ocean on the left and the fairway cut in half by ankle-high USGA alfalfa on the right, this beauty was a beast. To keep a drive out of the rough meant starting it so far over the ocean that all day long the best golfers in the world had arrived at the eighteenth tee, sized up the situation, and pulled out an iron.

Tom Kite arrived at the eighteenth tee, a lifetime of dreams

O

hanging on his next swing, and pulled out his driver. Then, in yet another example of gutsy, flawless execution under pressure, he drove the ball smack into the middle of the fairway. From there, the rest was a mere formality: five-iron lay-up, lob wedge to fifteen feet, and two putts for a par—and the U.S. Open championship.

Tom Kite finally had won his first major. And he had won it by being aggressive.

How much did winning a major *really* mean to Tom Kite? It depends on when you asked him.

Back in early 1989, a month after his thirty-ninth birthday, he had spoken almost wistfully, like a man who knows that time is running out: "You have to think about what might have been. When I came out, I had goals like everybody else. I was going to improve . . . and keep shoving at those at the top. Sometimes I think I don't know anything about winning. Some say, 'Be patient.' Then I hear, 'Just let it happen.' Then I hear these stories of guys who could 'make it happen.' And I just wonder what it all means."

A few months later, after he won the Players Championship, he spoke (unconvincingly) about how, as far as he was concerned, the Players felt like a "fifth major." Nobody agreed with him.

Then, in the three years after the heartbreak at Oak Hill, he had to deal with the hurt in a way that would let him keep on plugging. "Do you still think about it?" he was asked six months later. "Only about fifty or sixty times a day," he answered. But it was okay, *he* was okay, he would contend in majors again, that he was sure of. Nobody else was so sure.

Even after the third round of the Open last year, he was preparing himself mentally for another flaming crash: "No matter what happens tomorrow, Tom Kite has had a great career, has a great family. I have nothing to prove to anyone."

Except, deep down, to himself.

And after he won?

"I'm still scared that I'm going to wake up," he said on the Tuesday following his victory. He was in Rye, New York, for the Buick Westchester Classic after doing a post-Open corporate outing on Monday. After an hour on the range and nine holes on the course, he was going over to the Sleepy Hollow Country Club to work on his swing with an old friend, Jim McClean. Business as usual.

"I did the best job of concentrating in my life last week," he said. "Not just the last round, but from Monday on. I didn't play my best golf, but I kept focused better than I ever have. I stayed in the present tense all week."

To fight the inevitable letdown, Kite said, he planned to "get back into my routine" as soon as possible. That meant practice, play, more practice. (It worked: he finished tied for eleventh at Westchester.)

A couple of years before, he had bristled at a reporter's suggestion that if he had won a major title five years earlier he might not still be the last player to leave the practice range every day. How would winning the Open affect him now, at the age of forty-two?

"I don't know," he said. "I've never been here before. I know I won't cut short my practice time or my family time."

At the corporate outing on the previous day, Kite added, "they introduced me for the first time as the U.S. Open champion." He liked it a lot: "It dawned on me then that the rest of the year that's the way I'll be introduced on the first tee at tournaments; and after the Open next year, I'll be introduced as *former* U.S. Open champion. That's pretty neat stuff."

He was sure of one other thing: "I guarantee I'll enjoy it."

Tom Kite is 5'8". That's what the PGA Tour's media guide says. That's what every profile ever written of him says. That's what *he* says. But in a sidebar to the story of his victory the day after the 1992 Open, *USA Today* listed Kite's height as 5'9"—and I don't think it was a typo.

"I always thought Tom was a good player and a good man," Tom Kite, Sr., said after the 1992 Open. "I didn't think it took a major to make him one."

No, but it did make him taller.

Will There Ever Be Another Nicklaus?

It will happen. It's important for the game that someone does emerge, someone to shoot at. There's always been one to come along. History shows it, so I think it will happen again. But don't ask me who it will be.

—Jack Nicklaus

Once upon a time, the poets tell us, giants strode the fairways and stalked the greens and swept all before them, and it was good.

Epic figures dominated the game of golf, each putting his stamp on an era. Robert Tyre Jones, Jr., and Walter Hagen. Sam Snead, Lord Byron Nelson, and the incomparable Ben Hogan. The old king, Arnold Palmer. The new king—and the greatest of them all—Jack Nicklaus. And Tom Watson, whose reign ended so prematurely in 1984.

They were adventurers who explored the game's possibilities. Swashbuckling artists and precise scientists, imaginative innovators and orderly classicists, golfers utterly different in temperament and style and technique who nevertheless shared the ability and the will to transcend mere competence and fly on wings of greatness.

They spoiled us. For a quarter of a century following King Arnold's victory in the 1960 U.S. Open, golf was never without a Dominant Player (DP), someone who was a consensus favorite to win every time he stepped up to the first tee. And what the DP of the moment didn't manage to win, Gary Player, Johnny Miller, or Lee Trevino did.

So how did it come to pass that we find ourselves in the middle of the Corey Pavin Era? And how do we get out?

Nothing against Corey Pavin, the 1991 PGA Player of the Year, a nice guy and a swell golfer. And nothing against Wayne Levi, the 1990 PGA Tour Player of the Year, yet another nice guy and swell golfer. Nor against Tom Kite, Curtis Strange, Paul Azinger, Bob Tway, or Lanny Wadkins, all nice guys and swell golfers, who have been PGA of America and PGA Tour Players of the Year[1] since 1984. But none has been what you would call a DP.

You remember 1984. That was the fateful year when the last player to well and truly dominate golf, Tom Watson, lost his way on the Road Hole at St. Andrews. He was only thirty-four at the time, and we had no reason to expect he wouldn't be king of the hill for another five or six years. But Watson's bogey at the most famous par four in golf cost him more than his sixth British Open: it cost him his place on the hill. He lost the extra molecule of confidence or magic dust or mojo or whatever it was that had made him the game's best player the preceding seven years.

Since 1984, Watson has won only once on the tour, and that win—the 1987 Nabisco Championships—didn't really amount to anything more than cigarette money. Nowadays, Watson told Dave Anderson of *The New York Times* recently, the question his kids ask him most is "Daddy, did you make the cut?"

[1]The PGA Tour (i.e., touring pros) selects its Player of the Year by secret ballot. The PGA of America (i.e., club pros) employs a point system: thirty points for winning a major, twenty points for winning the Players Championship or the NEC World Series of Golf, ten points for other official tournament victories, plus points for the top 10 finishers on the year's money list and the scoring average list.

The fact is, it's just a lot more fun when there's a big dog out there on the course, kicking ass and taking names. Isn't it in the Constitution somewhere—I think maybe it's the Babe Ruth Amendment—that every American sports fan has the inalienable right to a hero, a star, a bigger-than-life persona in his sport of choice, someone who can float like a butterfly and sting like a bee?

There has been no bona fide, media-certified DP in professional golf for the better part of a decade. Without a DP to capture the imagination of fans just by showing up, your average golf tournament suffers a severe shortage in the pizzazz department. Without a DP, there is only competence on tour—and mere competence is about as exciting as watching your fingernails grow. Without a DP, the pro tour boils down to how many tax-deductible corporate dollars 150 blow-dried fraternity brothers in funny clothes can stuff into their Sansabelts.

Maybe it is too much to expect another Nicklaus per se—that is, someone to come along and win fifty-five tournaments on the PGA Tour and put together such a mind-boggling résumé in the major championships: six Masters titles, five PGA Championships, four U.S. Opens, and three British Opens. Oh, yes, and a couple of U.S. Amateurs for warm-up.

But is it too much to expect some golfer to take charge of the game and put his stamp on an era, if not for two decades, at least for a few years? Aren't we entitled?

Golf is the toughest of all sports to handicap. In tennis, the winners at Wimbledon and the U.S. Open always come from the three or four top seeds. In the NBA play-offs, it's the Bulls (and will be at least until Michael Jordan turns thirty). In the World Series, it's whichever team has the best starting pitching. And in the Super Bowl, it's practically a sure thing that half the country will be sound asleep by the middle of the third quarter.

But when *Golf Digest* picked Fred Couples to win the 1992 Masters, it was the first time in twenty years that the magazine's editors had correctly predicted the winner of a major golf title. That's four majors times twenty, or eighty events, with only one right call. Good thing those guys spend all their time at golf courses instead of racetracks.

Given the difficulty of predicting winners in golf, it figures that trying to pick the next Dominant Player in the game will always be tougher than Ray Floyd with a two-stroke lead. A quick trip down memory lane for a look at a few highly touted DP candidates from the recent past will underscore just how tough.

Remember Bobby Clampett? Just over a decade ago he rocketed out of the Monterey peninsula like a Jack Nicklaus one iron. In his first two years on the tour (1981 and 1982), Clampett finished fourteenth and seventeenth on the money list, and at the tender age of twenty-two he won his first tournament, the 1982 Southern Open. That was also his last, as a fiery temper contributed to his game's steady meltdown. A made-for-TV movie about him in the last decade would be called *Whatever Happened to Bobby Clampett?* He lost his tour card in 1990, won it back at the PGA Tour's Qualifying School that year, but found alternative employment as a part-time TV commentator. Fortunately for Clampett, he's a lot better with a mike in his hands than a putter, because in 1992 he finished 199th on the money list and lost his card again. He's certainly not the next Jack Nicklaus, but he could be the next Gary McCord.

Remember Scott Verplank? He won the U.S. Amateur in 1984, the NCAA Championship in 1986, and the first PGA Tour event he ever entered—the 1985 Western Open—when he was only twenty-one. He won again—the 1988 Buick Open—when he was only twenty-four. He was on his way to becoming the next Tom Watson when suddenly he started playing like Dr. Watson, primarily because of elbow injuries that required two operations. In 1991 Verplank entered twenty-six tournaments, made one cut, and finished 266th on the money list. In 1992 he entered thirteen tournaments, made one cut, and finished 309th on the money list. Verplank? Verplunk.

O

Remember the *S.I.* Four? Not to pick on *Sports Illustrated* or anything, but there is no better illustration of how frustrating this DP-predicting business is than a 1988 *S.I.* article, "APB for a Champion." In the article Jaime Díaz, now senior golf writer for *The New York Times,* took a look at the current crop of young talent on the tour and picked the most likely candidates to emerge as the game's next Dominant Player.

The four nominees were Keith Clearwater, Steve Pate, Chip Beck, and Paul Azinger, four young studs who had created a groundswell of excitement with their games, their attitudes, and their flair. One of them *had* to make it big, right?

Wrong. Fast-forward five years and take another look. Since the article appeared, the *S.I.* Four have won a grand total of six tournaments, none of them a major.

About the only way Clearwater has distinguished himself is as a trendsetter in fashion: until Ian Baker-Finch joined the PGA Tour two years ago, Clearwater headed a minority of tour players who wore pleated slacks and natural fibers, and he was the only one to turn up his collar, yuppie-style. More recently, he was the first pro on the tour to button the top button of his golf shirt, something at least a smattering of his colleagues will undoubtedly emulate. (Pro golfers are not exactly slaves to fashion, but even they recognize that Clearwater looks exceedingly cool.) That's something, but not enough to make him a DP.

As intensely competitive as any player on the tour, Pate more than earned his nickname—"Volcano"—with a temper that always seemed to erupt at the most inopportune times. He now claims to have outgrown that temper. If so, Pate may still fulfill the potential that earned him a star with a bullet five years ago.

Chip Beck is a money machine: six straight top-20 finishes on the money list, three times in the top 10. But he's won only four tournaments in fourteen years on the tour, and he turns thirty-seven in 1993, so he's no longer a serious contender for DP honors. He could, however, become the Four's first official ambassador of goodwill: pro-am partners love him, and he would win any Mr. Nice Guy tournament that Tom Kite wasn't in by ten strokes.

(When I started following the tour a few years ago, the first golfer I met was Chip Beck, and almost the first words out of his mouth were "You know, out here the big winner is charity." Nice turn of phrase, I thought. Not until later that same day did I learn that it was the official mantra of the PGA Tour's public relations program.)

Of the *S.I.* Four, Paul Azinger is the only one people are still talking about as a possible DP. Few golfers are more popular with galleries than the Zinger, and none is a more ferocious competitor. He was a hero of the 1991 Ryder Cup Matches, beating José-María Olazábal on the final day in a match charged with electricity.

Azinger is a cross between Dennis the Menace and Opie. He's direct, open, funny, self-confident, engaging, and he doesn't take himself too seriously. He has charisma and a great short game. And, like Chip Beck, he knows how to bang the cash register: five of the last six years, the Zinger has been among the top 10 money winners on the tour (and in his "off" year he finished eleventh).

Winning the Tour Championship in 1992 did more than pad Azinger's bank account. It showed him that he could still win a big tournament—not quite a major, but plenty big. That win could be just the push he needs to have a break-out year. At thirty-three, the Zinger should be hitting his prime.

But there is this one problem: since blowing the 1987 British Open at Muirfield with bogies on the last two holes and losing the 1988 PGA Championship by a heartbeat to Jeff Sluman, Azinger hasn't been a factor in the majors—and that's not the mark of a DP.

The point here is that back in 1988 each of the *S.I.* Four was a perfectly plausible candidate to be the game's next Dominant Player. Now it looks like we might as well be waiting for Godot to win his first major.

. . .

If Mother Nature abhors a vacuum so doggone much, how come She doesn't forget about the Greenhouse Effect for a few minutes and go out and find us a new Dominant Player? When is someone going to come along and pick up where Tom Watson left off? Why does it feel like we've been waiting for a DP longer than it takes Bernhard Langer to putt?

Everybody's got a pet theory. Here are five:

1. Too many good players.

This theory holds that the overall quality of play has improved so much that it's nearly impossible for any one player to step forward and dominate the pro tour.

Once upon a time, the corollary to this theory goes, Ben Hogan used to go out and win a half-dozen tournaments as a tune-up for the U.S. Open, and the only ones Hogan didn't win Sam Snead did. Jack Nicklaus told *Golf Digest* that in his heyday there were about "seven or eight" players he had to worry about at a Masters or British Open, i.e., seven or eight with a legitimate shot at winning. Now, he figures, there are "thirty or forty" in that category.

It's unquestionably true that a lot more guys are capable of winning on the PGA Tour today. How else do you explain Jay Don Blake, Rocco Mediate, Fulton Allem, Billy Andrade, Ken Perry, Russ Cochran, Dillard Pruitt, Bruce Fleischer, Billy Ray Brown, David Peoples, Lee Janzen, Mark Carnevale, Fred Funk, and Richard Zokol—all of whom won for the first time in 1991 or 1992?

"Share the wealth" has become the name of the game. Between 1960 and 1980, there were twenty-five instances of a golfer winning at least four tournaments in a year and seventeen cases of five or more wins. But in the dozen years since 1980, only five golfers have won as many as four times in a year. In 1991, nobody won more than *two* times. Last year, Fred Couples, Davis Love III, and John Cook each won three tournaments, but no one interpreted this as the Second Coming of the Palmer-Player-Nicklaus Golden Age.

Parity precludes dominance.

2. American golfers don't know how to win.

Two DP emeriti, Tom Watson and Jack Nicklaus, believe that the better European players—namely Seve Ballesteros, Nick Faldo, Ian Woosnam, José-María Olazábal—have risen to international prominence because they play against generally weaker competition on the European tour and find themselves in a position to win more often. This presumably hones the skills needed to finish off an opponent. (See corollary to Theory #1.)

On the tougher, richer American tour, the better young players don't get enough shots at winning, so they never quite acquire the knack. And they don't have to win at all to make a very decent living, thank you very much.

Nicklaus believes the core problem goes much deeper and that the American system producing today's pros breeds mediocrity: "There's no head-to-head competition in high school and college golf anymore. No match play, no head-to-head medal play. You'll have five players on a team, and they'll take the best four scores, and all the emphasis is on how the team does. Now, high school and college programs do a lot better job of golf instruction than they used to, but they're not teaching kids how to win. When I was in school, every weekend I had a match. It was win or lose, not a matter of finishing eighth or whatever as a team. Everything was determined by individual competition."

Call this the Grumpy Old Fart explanation of why no American has stepped forward to take over the game.

3. All-exempt tour breeds complacency.

Every year since 1983, when the "All-Exempt Tour" came into being, the top 125 finishers on the preceding year's official money list have been automatically exempt from qualifying for a PGA Tour event.

In golf as in war, there is no substitute for victory—mainly because winning a pro golf tournament carries with it a *two*-year exemption along with a check for $180,000 (and up). But winning is by no means necessary for a player to keep his union card. Enter a lot of tournaments, make two out of three cuts, manage a couple of top-20 finishes, play it safe, and you lock up a place on the tour next year. A whole lot tougher than it sounds, to be sure, but it's outside work and there's no heavy lifting. Just keep on chooglin' and don't take chances.

For a golfer who's long on talent but short in the ambition and work-ethic departments, the all-exempt tour is a perfect security blanket. Get off to a good start, cash some big checks, and then put it on cruise control. Who needs the anxiety of sweating a lot of four-footers to save par to win the tournament? If they fall, great. If they don't, tied for thirteenth is good enough. And why spend a lot of extra hours working on your middle irons when you've already banked 300K official bucks and could spend the time at a corporate outing? Blow off the range; let's go smell the roses.

Consider this: Ray Floyd, as fierce a competitor as ever put on spikes, loathes the all-exempt tour; Gary McCord, a genuinely gifted TV announcer, invented it. 'Nuf said.

Complacency is an inevitable by-product of the all-exempt tour, critics say, and it's always going to be one of the primary barriers to the emergence of the next Nicklaus.

Says the last Nicklaus: "You're never going to change a guy who's content to be twentieth on the money list. A lot of players on the tour are like that: they have the talent but not the drive to win. And there are also a lot of guys who want to be the best and who really work at it, but who don't have the talent."

So far, this sounds depressingly like life.

4. Too much money.

"More and more," says Frank Hannigan, heir apparent to Jack Whitaker as golf's philosopher-poet, "the PGA Tour is becoming the qualifying school for the really big money."

As evidence in support of that proposition, consider two extreme examples, Greg Norman and Curtis Strange:

○Greg Norman's first year of total income "in eight figures"—that translates from the Australian as "in excess of $10,000,000"—was as long ago as 1988, and it's safe to say that his annual haul hasn't dipped since then. From the beginning of 1989 through 1992, Norman won six tournaments on the PGA Tour (but no majors) for a grand total of "only" $3,512,000 (or about $700,000 per year) in *official* winnings. That's a lot of moolah, but the multimillion-dollar gap between Norman's "official" and "total" money in the last five years proves Frank Hannigan's point.

○Since winning his second straight U.S. Open in 1989, Curtis Strange hasn't won anything else on the PGA Tour through 1992. Last year he finished ninety-ninth on the money list, the lowest he's ranked in sixteen seasons on the tour. Not to worry. His nonofficial earnings during the three-year period were "in the neighborhood" of $25 million. Not a bad neighborhood, and over four times more than he has earned in official money in sixteen years on the tour.

The extra bucks come from endorsements, corporate outings, appearance fees for playing in overseas tournaments, personal appearances, and guaranteed money for playing in unofficial one- and two-day charity tournaments. (The charities make out, but so do the players.) And while Norman and Strange are certainly extreme cases, even farther down on the food chain an established middle-level pro can usually double his official earnings with off-tour activities—and that's without winning. Cop a tournament victory every other year or so and the multiplier goes up. Win a major somewhere along the line and it goes way, *way* up.

There's nothing wrong with trying to put a little something away for a rainy day, but when it comes to a point that a pro golfer can make more money off the course than on, then you have to figure that sooner or later it's going to affect his game. A player picking up five (or fifty) grand giving a clinic to XYZ

○

Corporation execs on Monday or Tuesday is neither recharging his batteries nor working on his short game. If he books a tournament in Europe the week before the PGA Championship (as Paul Azinger and Mark O'Meara did in 1992), he may make $75,000 (or more) just for showing up, but he's also cutting into preparation time and catching a dose of jet lag—just before a major.

Then there's the Second Season, consisting of made-for-TV junk matches and international tournaments featuring the game's best-known names. Last year's top Second Season events, with total purses: Johnnie Walker World Championship, an IMG product manufactured in Jamaica ($2.7 million); the Million Dollar Challenge in South Africa ($2.5 million); the PGA Grand Slam, starring the winners of the four majors ($1.1 million); the Shark Shootout, catered by McDonald's ($1 million); the Three-Tour Challenge, with guys, old guys, and dolls going head to head to head ($650,000); and, of course, the mother of junk golf, the Skins Game ($540,000).

Last year, Fred Couples made $981,858 in such events, just a few bucks less than he earned on the regular tour. No wonder he played in only twenty-two official tournaments: he had to save himself for the Second Season.

Says Nicklaus, now golf's elder statesman and the reigning expert on dominance of the sport: "There's so much money to be made today in Monday events and at foreign tournaments that it's hard for anyone to dominate. It's a lot harder to concentrate on big events when you have so many lucrative distractions."

5. The international factor.

Golf may have been invented by Scottish shepherds with too much time on their hands about a thousand years ago, but it's been an American game ever since Bobby Jones crossed the big water in the 1920s and showed everybody over there how to play.

Every now and then we'd let somebody named Henry Cotton or Peter Thomson win what they insist on calling "The Open," usually when Walter or Sam or Ben was too busy to make the trip. And once a young royalist named Tony Jacklin slipped over here and won *our* Open. But Masters and PGA champions were strictly "Made in the USA." (Gary Player doesn't count: he was an Honorary American.)

Then, in 1980, things changed. That was the year an ex-caddie from Spain named Severiano Ballesteros, who the year before had won a British Open, came over here and won a Masters. People in Europe started saying that this young kid was going to be the best player in the world, which was patent nonsense, of course, since Tom Watson was also young and *he* was the best player in the world and would be until the next Nicklaus came along. But then doggone if Ballesteros didn't win *another* Masters in 1983, and when he stole the British Open from Watson the following year, it began to look as if maybe he *was* the best player in the world.

After that, all hell broke loose in Augusta, Georgia. A German named Bernhard Langer won the 1985 Masters. (Who knew Germany even had a golf course?) A Scot named Sandy Lyle won the 1988 Masters. An Englishman named Nick Faldo won the 1989 Masters . . . and the 1990 Masters. A Welshman named Ian Woosnam won the 1991 Masters.

Things were just as strange over in Great Britain. From 1984 through 1992, eight of nine British Open champions did not carry American passports, and three of them were named Faldo, the guy with two Masters jackets. People began to whisper: Maybe this Faldo fellow is the best player in the world.

What had happened, of course, is that the quality of golf played in Europe and Australia improved dramatically during the eighties. Suddenly the best European golfers were as good— or better—than the best American golfers. The Europeans won the Ryder Cup in 1985, then won it again in 1987, then retained it with a tie in 1989. The world of competitive golf at its highest levels had, in the space of a decade, become exponentially more interesting.

But while the pool of potential Dominant Players grew larger and deeper, the likelihood of one emerging to take control of the game became less likely, in great measure because a potent mix of greed, jealousy, conflicting egos, and self-interest split the world community of golf. Or put it this way: Don't ever invite Deane Beman and Seve Ballesteros to the same dinner party.

The PGA Tour has a rule that a player must enter fifteen PGA Tour events a year to maintain full playing privileges. No problem for European players so long as the European PGA Tour was in its infancy and most of the action was over here. But as the European tour expanded in the 1980s, with appearance fees for stars and purses growing into serious money, Ballesteros and some of the other European stars began to balk at the fifteen-event PGA Tour requirement.

Too much, Ballesteros and friends said. Reduce it so we can play in America *and* support our own tour. No way, said Beman and the PGA Tour's board of directors. Play fifteen tournaments or be limited to the three majors played here (not under PGA Tour jurisdiction in any event), the Players Championship (if you're invited), the NEC World Series of Golf (if you qualify), and five others by sponsor invitation, as permitted by the All-Exempt Tour Priority Rankings (Category 1, Paragraphs 10b and 11). Nine, maybe ten events. Period.

"*¡Coraje!*" said Seve, or words to that effect.

"Take it or leave it," said Beman, speaking for the journeyman majority of his constituency, who weren't thrilled at the thought of Europe's best golfers coming over to win money that might otherwise end up in their pockets.

"There's got to be a way for the best to play against the best," said elder statesmen like Nicklaus and Watson, who urged doubling the exemptions for non–PGA Tour members, or giving an extra exemption for each major won, or permitting free access to anyone whose name ended in a vowel—anything to open up spots for Seve, Woosie, Nickie, and José-María.

"We want Seve," said sponsors of star-starved tournaments, but never publicly for fear of rocking the boat with Beman and his board.

Compromises were proposed and rejected, the matter degenerated into an ego thing between Ballesteros and Beman, both sides tried to claim the high ground in a public relations fight that everyone soon grew weary of, Beman dug in his heels—and Sandy Lyle, Nick Faldo, and Bernhard Langer gave up their PGA Tour cards. End of story.

Tempest in a teapot? Well, it's no Square-Grooves Controversy, that's for sure. But it does explain why American golf fans see so little of the top foreign stars, not to mention the younger generation of European golfers. It also helps explain why it's harder than ever to identify the next Dominant Player in golf: the haystack is now so much bigger.

What are the criteria for identifying and anointing an era's Dominant Player? I mean, if one actually comes along, how will we *know*? For starters, we can eliminate what are *not* particularly useful DP criteria.

Forget the Official PGA Tour Money List. The only people who really care about the money list are the players, their wives, their accountants, and the IRS.

Forget the Sony Rankings, a system that awards points to players for their performances in tournaments that are weighted according to strength of the field. It's better than nothing for taking the temperature of world golf, but it's still an apples-and-oranges deal.

Forget total number of victories. Not entirely, of course, because winning is always better than not winning. But not all tournaments are created equal: winning the Colonial and the Memorial is a lot sexier than winning Hardee's Golf Classic and the Las Vegas Invitational. (A moot point, in any case: these days nobody wins more than two or three times a year on the PGA Tour anyway.)

No, when it comes to naming an era after a Dominant Player, you can forget everything except the five major championships. Yes, *five*. The Masters, the U.S. Open, the British Open, the PGA Championship—and the Ryder Cup Matches.

Even with the majors, though, there are certain caveats:

The U.S. Open, for all its prestige, has recently given us Scott Simpson, Andy North, and Larry Nelson. This has to do with the way courses are set up by the USGA, not with the field. Indeed, the U.S. Open field is stronger than that of any of the other majors.

The PGA in the last decade has given us such champions as Wayne Grady, Jeff Sluman, and Bob Tway. The field for the PGA is weakened by the inclusion of forty club pros, but the main problem is the same as at U.S. Opens (if not always quite so extreme): course setups that tend to favor cautious, conservative play.

The British Open produces great champions: the last DP, Tom Watson, won five British Open titles during his reign. Recently, a local boy—Nick Faldo—has made the most of the home-court advantage.

Of the four established majors, the Masters correlates best with DP status: the last Nicklaus, remember, owns six green jackets. Unlike the U.S. Open and the PGA, the Masters tends to reward the big hitter, the daring shot maker, the more creative player. Therefore, when handicapping potential DP candidates, take a close look at their records in the Masters and how their game fits Augusta National.

An almost equally good test of a golfer's worthiness for consideration as an era's DP is his performance in the Ryder Cup Matches.

The last three Ryder Cup Matches were the most thrilling golf tournaments of the year since the 1986 Masters. For three straight days in 1987, 1989, and 1991, the Ryder Cup Matches brought together the best golfers in the world in head-to-head competition with enormous stakes—but no money—riding on every shot. Collectively, they made an open-and-shut case for the biennial event's consecration as a fifth major.

In a regular professional golf tournament, if a top player gets a little sloppy and doesn't shoot lights out on Thursday or

Friday, hey, that's no big deal: he just hangs in there, tries to make the cut, and hopes to get something going on Sunday afternoon. If he does, great: the worst that can happen is that he comes away with a check. If he doesn't make the cut, well, there's always next week.

Even in a major, if a top player makes a bad shot, or lets his concentration drift, or catches a piece of bad luck, the worst that can happen is that he lets himself down.

The Ryder Cup is different. The stakes are higher. *Much* higher. Friday is as important as Sunday. There is no next week. There's not even a next year. A player screws up and he lets his teammates down, not just himself. One bad shot could cost his *country* the match.

Just how much the Ryder Cup means to the game's top players was written on the face of Lanny Wadkins after his final match in 1991. He had just beaten Mark James three and two to give the United States a one-point lead over Europe with only the match between Hale Irwin and Bernhard Langer still undecided. Television and radio reporters poked microphones in Wadkins's face and asked him for his reaction. Wadkins cried.

You have to understand that Lanny Wadkins is one of the grittiest, toughest, nerviest competitors on the tour. At the time, he was a hardened veteran with twenty tour victories, including the 1977 PGA Championship, who had seen and done just about everything in golf. But this Ryder Cup match was so charged with meaning for Wadkins, the pressure so intense, that once it was over he could not find words, could no longer hold back his emotions.

Lanny Wadkins in tears tells you all you need to know about what the Ryder Cup has become and why it must now be considered professional golf's fifth major.

It's pretty clear there's no Next Nicklaus standing on the first tee somewhere, waiting for the applause to die down so he can stack up five or six wins and a couple of major titles every year for a decade. Or if there is, he's sure keeping his game under wraps.

But what about half a loaf? What about a Tom Watson or a Lee Trevino or even a Johnny Miller to step up and cast his shadow over golf for a couple of years or so? Isn't there anybody out there whose name we can slap on this era in golf?

Among the usual suspects, Seve Ballesteros is a very old thirty-six, Payne Stewart has a chronically bad back and a wandering attention span, Curtis Strange let the fire go out somewhere on his way to the bank, and Greg Norman is now only the second or third best Australian in the game.

John Daly? Please. Keep in mind that coming into the 1993 season, he had won exactly two golf tournaments. But because one of them was a major, and because he was only twenty-five at the time, and because he hits the ball farther than God, he was immediately hailed as the next Nicklaus. (At the same age, the first Nicklaus had won eleven tournaments, including three majors. This information is offered as a public service to keep discussions of John Daly in perspective.)

Daly spent the year after the 1991 PGA making personal appearances, collecting huge appearance fees at overseas golf tournaments, doing corporate outings on Mondays and Tuesdays, signing endorsement deals worth $10 million, being disqualified from two tournaments, missing cuts at a third of the events he entered, and leading a tabloid off-course life—just about everything, that is, except working on his game. You have to believe that Jack Nicklaus would have spent that time on the practice range.

The 1991 PGA champion did finally manage to get himself and his game under control at the end of 1992. He won the B.C. Open with four near-perfect rounds, he showed signs of settling down with his new family, and he actually seemed relieved to have his "PGA year" behind him. But then things turned sour over the holidays, and he opened 1993 in a substance-abuse rehab clinic. Stay tuned.

Fred Couples? Between the end of September in 1991 and

the first week in April in 1992, Fred Couples won the Masters and four other tournaments, starred in the 1991 Ryder Cup Matches, and gave every indication that *he* was the era's Dominant Player. But then Couples went back home to Palm Beach, far from the madding crowd, where he could sit around, watch television, avoid people, and not answer the phone. ("I'm always afraid there might be somebody at the other end" was the undisputed 1992 Quote of the Year.) His attitude: this winning majors is kind of neat, but not if it means being famous and having people expect you to do and say a lot of stuff. He tuned up for the 1992 PGA Championship by sitting at home watching TV.

Thanks, Fred. Let us know when you're ready to come out and play again.

No, at the close of business in 1992, the best player in the world was a golfer who is not even a member of the PGA Tour: Nick Faldo. He has won three British Open titles and two Masters championships since 1987, and he has come close in two U.S. Opens and one PGA. Nobody can touch his record in the majors in the last five years. Faldo didn't shine in the 1991 Ryder Cup, and he has the on-course charisma of an android. But another green jacket, maybe a U.S. Open, a strong showing in the 1993 Ryder Cup, and we'll have to start calling the nineties the Faldo Era.

Back on the PGA Tour, Fred Couples might figure out a way to handle all the hullabaloo. John Daly might grow up. Paul Azinger might put it all together. Davis Love III might win a big one and learn to smile. Phil Mickelson might turn out to have all the right stuff.

And if none of the above cuts the mustard, well, there's always Tiger Woods. We won't know for a few years, but the Tiger Era might well be worth the wait.

Let the Big Dog Eat

There's nothing I like better than sitting around, eating barbecue potato chips, and drinking Bud.

—Mark Calcavecchia

Maybe it's the way Mark Calcavecchia steps to the tee, hitches up his belt, sweeps back his driver, then nearly comes out of his shoes with a mighty lash that sends the ball rocketing into the distant sky.

Maybe it was the answer he gave, shortly after clinching a place on the Ryder Cup team for the first time, when somebody asked which would he rather win, the Masters or the Ryder Cup: "In terms of personal satisfaction, the Ryder Cup. It's a team deal. You get all wrapped up in pulling for eleven other guys. Just for pure enjoyment I think it'd be funner to win the Ryder Cup."

Maybe it's his taste in music: Allman Brothers, Lynyrd Skynyrd, Marshall Tucker, Creedence Clearwater Revival. And that to him the most important thing about a car is its stereo: "It's *got* to have good sound."

Maybe it's the attitude he carries to the first tee of every tournament—that he's starting off sixteen under because he's going to birdie all the par fives.

Maybe it's his gift for language: "gunch" is "rough," "skag" means "hit it poorly," "waffle" means "hit it well," "power lipout" is a putt that hits the edge of cup, makes a ninety-degree turn, and ends up outside the leather.

Maybe it's that he didn't think twice about pulling out his L wedge and taking an eight-inch divot out of one of the Old Course's giant double greens the first time he ever played at St. Andrews. ("I was about thirty yards from the hole, and I didn't think I could hold a putt on line that far." The Scottish gallery assembled for the 1989 Dunhill Cup was not amused. He did it again the next day.)

Maybe it's the way he puts things in perspective: "Golf is just a game," he said after failing to make the cut at a British Open, "and an idiotic one at that."

Maybe it's the rough edges, the plain talk, the sense that he's gone through hard times and paid some dues. (Everything is relative: in comparison to John Daly, Calcavecchia is David Niven.)

Maybe it's his attitude toward money: "If you want it, get it and spend it. It's only money, not something to worship. If you run out, go out and get some more."

Maybe it's his approach to the game: "I'm out there to win tournaments. Period. If I come to the tenth tee on Sunday and I'm ten strokes back, I don't have the patience to grind it out for a seventy-two instead of a seventy-four."

Or maybe it's his taste in snacks.

Whatever it is, and really it's all of the above and then some, Mark Calcavecchia is a piece of work, an original. He's one of the most charismatic golfers on the PGA Tour and—I may be the only person outside his immediate family to believe this—still a long-shot candidate to become the tour's next Dominant Player.

. . .

Mark John Calcavecchia was born on June 12, 1960, in Laurel, Nebraska, where his father managed a nine-hole daily-fee golf course and an adjacent eight-lane bowling alley. As a boy, Mark split time between the two facilities and became equally adept at golf and bowling. His father suffered from multiple sclerosis, so in 1973 the family left the cold Nebraska winters and sought out the warmer climate of West Palm Beach, Florida, where Mark became even more absorbed with golf.

Calcavecchia went to the University of Florida, where he majored in golf. He left school after three years and, shortly after his twenty-first birthday, turned professional.

After earning his tour card in 1981 at the PGA Tour's Qualifying School, Calcavecchia spent the next four years missing cuts, hacking around the mini-tour circuit, working on his game a little, bowling, drinking beer, and hanging out. This was not a prescription for professional success: during this period, he finished 134th, 161st, 140th, and 162nd on the money list. Calcavecchia went back to Q-School twice, but didn't bother again after losing his playing card again in 1984 for the third straight year. What the hell—he might not be going anywhere, but he was having a few laughs.

Turning Point No. 1 in Calcavecchia's golf career came in December 1985, when he switched to Ping irons and went to see master golf instructor Peter Kostis for the first time. For the next several years, the former move drew the most attention, but it was the latter that had the most profound effect on his game.

Kostis, then only a much-respected swing guru and not yet a TV golf analyst, replaced Calcavecchia's long draw with a power fade. He helped Calcavecchia gain a measure of self-discipline on the course. He showed him how to practice with a purpose, rather than just hit balls out of sight. Somewhere along the line he may even have reminded his raw young student that you drive for show, putt for dough. In the process, he helped Calcavecchia develop confidence in his game.

"I think I've got a lot of ability to play golf," says Calcavecchia. "Couple that with a lot of hard practice, and a good teacher like Peter Kostis, and that's why I got better so fast."

How fast was that? Well, in 1986, he caddied for his pal Ken Green at the Honda Classic; the very next year, Calcavecchia won the tournament and went on to earn half a million dollars. He finished tenth on the money list in 1987, the first of four straight finishes in the top 10. That's how fast.

It was at the 1987 Honda Classic that Calcavecchia arched eyebrows by repeatedly making iron shots back up on the green from lies that produced fliers for everybody else. After seeing one mighty Calcavecchia slash from particularly deep rough suck back toward the hole for a tap-in birdie, Tom Watson observed that, in all his years in golf, he had never seen a golf ball do *that* from *there*.

From that moment on, whenever the name Calcavecchia came up, the words "Ping" and "square grooves" were soon to follow. Was it the player or the clubs? Hey, Mark—don't square grooves give you an unfair advantage?

"That's bullshit," Calcavecchia answered, but the questions wouldn't go away. Exasperated, he traded in his Pings for a set of Tommy Armours in 1990. He did it not only to prove to the world that clubs don't make the man, but also to stay out of the line of fire in the pissing contest between the PGA Tour's Board of Directors and Karsten Solheim, the founder of Karsten Manufacturing Company and maker of Ping clubs.

"I gotta believe that if I grabbed Curtis Strange's clubs and threw them in my sack, and if I was swinging good, that I'd be scoring good," Calcavecchia said. The 1989 British Open champion had clearly had his fill of questions about square grooves. "It's me, the player, not the clubs. On the practice tee earlier, I was using Azinger's clubs and juicing them as good as always. Other players out here tell me I can play with anything. I can."

Calcavecchia is a big hitter, one of the biggest on the tour, but he's not one of the straightest. He's usually among the top 20 on the tour in driving distance; he rarely cracks the top 150 in driving accuracy. The key to Calcavecchia's success is his short game. A good if streaky putter, Calcavecchia is a virtuoso with his beloved L wedge in his hands, and he takes pride in his ability to make the ball boogie once it gets to the dance floor.

"I like making guys sick by hitting one out of the gunch and sucking it back over a hump," Calcavecchia said before the Masters one year, drawing on a language he and Ken Green have invented while contemplating the mysteries of golf. "I like juicing it in there while the other guys are hitting fliers off the back edge. It's like, 'Hey, take that!' "

Turning Point No. 2 in Mark Calcavecchia's life would make a swell TV sitcom. Let's sit in on the first story conference.

Okay, quiet down. Pass the muffins? Thanks. Now let's get started.

The hero is a big, good-hearted lug with a lot of rough edges: John Goodman would be perfect, but we'll settle for Randy Quaid. Street smart but not well educated. Good bullshit detector. Likes cars. Travels a lot, no fancy tastes. Loves rock music and bowling. He's a professional golfer.

A *what?*

A golfer. Look at the demographics: baby boomers turn forty, quit playing tennis, start playing golf. They'll eat him up.

But isn't golf boring?

Only in real life.

(Laughter.)

Okay, so he travels a lot, and one night he's at this club, you know, just hanging out, and he meets Madonna . . .

He meets *Madonna?*

Well, she looks like Madonna, like Madonna sometimes looks. Dark hair. Athletic. Italian. Tough. Smart. A dancer, maybe— no, I got it, an aerobics instructor.

Madonna? You think we could get Madonna? Jeez, if we could get Madonna . . .

Hey, no, forget Madonna. If we get her, great. But the story works without her. This isn't a Madonna show. It's about him, the lug, John Goodman.

I dunno. With Madonna, I get it. Without Madonna, I don't get it . . .

No, right, somebody *like* Madonna, then. Maybe that Annabella . . . whatshername? . . . Annabella *Sciorra*, the one in *The Hand That Rocks the Cradle,* the mother, not the crazy one, not Rebecca De Mornay. The mother. Annabella Sciorra.

She's good.

Right. And she's like Madonna, a little. But if not her, someone else. But it's not her show, remember, it's his.

Okay, it's his show. What happens?

They meet and fall in love . . .

Now, *that's* original!

. . . they fall in love, or actually he falls in love, but she's saying to herself, No way, this guy is a slob.

But a lovable slob?

Of course. But he's a golfer, on the road forty weeks of the year, a friggin' gypsy. They meet on Wednesday, he's gonna be gone Sunday night. Next town, next babe. She's attracted, but she's not into that.

So what's the hook?

The hook is that he only *seems* to be that kind of guy. After the golf tournament he leaves for the next town Sunday night. Only he's back Monday night, calling her up.

Where are they?

Out west somewhere. Arizona. Phoenix. Tucson. Somewhere pro golfers go to play golf. We can look it up. He grew up in Nowheresville, Nebraska. Not a farmer, but small-town. John Cougar Mellencamp. He lives in Florida now, that's where golfers live.

Where's she from?

From there, from Arizona. She lives there in Tucson or Phoenix, wherever they meet in the club.

Arizona? Nobody is *from* Arizona. People who live there, they *go* there. They're not *from* there.

Okay, you're right. So, we make her from the Midwest, Indianapolis maybe—no, no, I hate Indianapolis, I was there once—I got it, she's from *Minneapolis!*

Mary Tyler Moore!

Right!

Could we get her?

Who?

Mary Tyler Moore!

Christ, Mel, you kidding? She must be eighty! We need somebody who can pass for twenty-five!

Right, yeah. It's just I saw this rerun last night, and . . . boy, she was great, wasn't she? Great show. *Great* show. So a Mary Tyler Moore type then?

Yeah, okay, a Mary Tyler Moore type with a little Madonna, somebody like Annabella Sciorra.

Good. So they meet. He falls in love. She's not sure. He leaves town. He comes back. Then what?

Flowers. Dancing. Candy. Sunset on the desert. A full-court press. He's a sweet, simple guy, and he gives her this cornball courtship routine, and she loves him for it, falls like a ton of bricks. Old-fashioned, but hip. Maybe it should be Tucson. Hipper than Phoenix.

Then what?

He's a golfer, but she knows nothing, zero, *nada,* about golf, so we have some fun with that, with her learning about the game. You know, making fun of the clothes, making fun of all the stiffs on the tour, making fun of all the crapola.

I like it. Then what?

She caddies for him . . .

Yes! *Caddyshack!*

Great film. *Great* film. Yeah, well, she caddies for him because that's a way to get to know him better. Just practice rounds at first, but later, after their marriage, even after the baby, she carries his bag from time to time. During the Masters one year even, she caddies for him. She gets to know the game, gets to know *his* game.

Wait a minute. What kid? What marriage? They've just met. Go back.

Sure, right. Well, she doesn't know from golf, but she does know from aerobics and health, and he's a complete mess.

Like what?

The guy's fat. Eats junk food. Never works out. Sits around and watches TV all the time. Hangs out with the caddies at bowling alleys. Drinks too much beer. Wears a lot of polyester. A slob.

So since when did that become a crime?

Hey, nothing personal, Mel. It's just that she's not sure. Here's a guy who can't take care of himself so well. Plus he's got this attitude on the course. Sulks when things go wrong, yells a lot, blows up in the middle of a tournament if he hits a bad shot, breaks clubs. Generally makes an ass out of himself. A sweet guy, but a jerk sometimes.

So what else is new? You said he was a golfer . . .

Yeah, but this guy—Mark? Want to call him Mark? Let's call him Mark—this guy Mark is off the charts.

But she loves him?

Sure, sure, she loves him. Her name is Sheryl, with an *S.* Yeah, Sheryl is crazy about the big lug.

I got it! So they get married and she goes to work reforming him!

Now, *that* is original . . .

"She can see when my attitude starts hurting me," says Cal-cavecchia, who loves giving chapter and verse on how marriage to Sheryl Timms has made him a better man—and a better golfer.

"She'll just tell me, 'Stop acting like a big jerk.' She really puts the hammer down and sets me straight. Like when I miss a three-footer, and all I can think is 'It's not my fault!' I used to be good at that."

It was a couple of years ago, and Calcavecchia had been cornered after a practice round by a gaggle of reporters. He took the opportunity to reflect on his good fortune. "At the Bank of Boston Classic I was counting up how many times I was being screwed. It was never me, it was always something else. She got me turned back around. Fast."

At Pebble Beach in 1989, Calcavecchia started hitting balls sideways and got "really steamed." So steamed that he stopped talking to his playing partner, baseball player Gary Carter, after the fourth hole of the third round. So steamed that he started throwing his clubs in the general direction of his bag after a less-than-perfect shot. So steamed that he buried the head of his putter in the ground at the edge of the eighteenth green, in full view of a couple of thousand spectators, a Saturday afternoon TV audience—and Sheryl.

Back in the privacy of their room after the round, Mrs. Calcavecchia came out smoking. Mark would later recall her exact words: "She looked at me and said, 'Look at you. You just won $126,000 [at the Phoenix Open], and now you're acting like *this*? You embarrassed me. You embarrassed yourself. You really are a great asshole.' "

The distinct impression was that this was only the warm-up drill, that Sheryl had a few more things to say before the evening was out. There was also the impression that Calcavecchia was genuinely proud of his wife for having the guts to jerk a knot in him. This is a heartwarming family show, remember, and the big lovable lug is head over heels in love with the feisty little gal and vice versa.

The next day, Calcavecchia apologized profusely to Carter, then went out and played hard for the team, even though he had not made the cut. The team won third place in the pro-am portion of the tournament. Roll credits.

Golfers have a way of slipping into old habits, and Calcavecchia is no exception to the rule. When things started going bad for him in 1991, Calcavecchia reverted on occasion to his old, club-throwing, self-destructive self. A good guess is that this is a permanent condition, something that can be controlled but not cured. If there were a twelve-step program for temper tantrums, Mark Calcavecchia would be a prime candidate. You also have to figure that Sheryl clearly has her work cut out for her. Maybe that's what they mean when they talk about working on a relationship. In her case, it looks like a life sentence at hard labor.

Turning Point No. 3 in Mark Calcavecchia's golf career very nearly came in April 1988, when he walked off the eighteenth green at Augusta National on Sunday looking like a man ready for a nice new blazer, 44-long, please, in green.

Calcavecchia's final-round 70 at the Masters put him at 282, six under par and tied for the lead with Sandy Lyle, who was about to hit his drive back at the eighteenth tee. Lyle had started the day with a two-stroke lead, but had lost it at Amen Corner, and he now had to make a four on the seventy-second hole just to force a play-off.

No matter how you cut it, that was going to be a tough row to hoe, considering what the final hole at Augusta National asks a golfer to do. Having seen it on TV a zillion times, you know the drill: from a slightly elevated tee, you thread the ball down through a narrow canyon of mile-high trees and bend it to the right and up the hill toward the clubhouse.

Not too far right or you'll end up in Lonesome Pine Prison, the way Tom Watson did in 1991, when all he needed was a par to get into a play-off.

And not too far left or you'll end up in one of the two bunkers put in a couple of decades ago to prevent Jack Nicklaus and other big hitters from driving the ball through the fairway and onto a plateau where they would have only a short iron to the green.

In 1991 Ian Woosnam would solve the fairway bunkers problem by launching a rocket over them on his way to the par he needed to avoid a play-off. But in 1988 Sandy Lyle did exactly what he didn't want to do: he hit a one iron smack-dab into the middle of the first bunker on the left, about 170 yards from the green.

Up at the top of the hill, Calcavecchia fans started getting their party faces on—and with good reason. From where Lyle's tee shot landed, bogey was almost a certainty, up-and-down for par and a play-off virtually impossible. Longtime chairman and Supreme Being of the Masters Hord Hardin and avid bowler Mark Calcavecchia would soon be dressed like fraternity brothers. Or so it seemed for another couple of minutes.

"It all happened so fast," Calcavecchia recalled later. "After I finished, they took me over to the Bobby Jones cottage in a cart, and on the way somebody hollered out that Sandy had hit the ball in the bunker on eighteen. I walked in the door, and there it was on TV, him standing in the bunker. He made his swing and the camera stayed right with him after he hit it. Just looking at his eyes, I knew he must have hit some kind of startling, unbelievable shot. Then they showed the ball hitting the green on the mound above the hole and rolling back. I got a diet Coke and waited for him to sink an eight-foot putt. I knew he was going to do it. And he did."

So what did *you* do? "My wife cried, my friends cried. I just said, 'Hey, let's go party!' "

Calcavecchia said he thought about his near win a lot for a month or so and then let it go, at least until a month or so before the 1989 Masters, when reporters' questions got him to thinking about it again. By then he realized, "I shouldn't really have been disappointed at all. It's not like I'd gaffed a three-footer at the end to lose. *That* would have been a major bummer. But I got beat fair and square: Sandy hit a great bunker shot and made a great putt. End of story."

End of chapter, maybe, but you have to figure there will be

more to the story, that someday a green jacket or two will hang in Calcavecchia's closet. If ever a golfer's game and a course seemed suited for each other, it is Calcavecchia's and Augusta National. To win there, a golfer has to hit the ball long and high, he has to have a delicate touch around the greens, he has to be an exceptional putter (at least for four days), and he has to be able to stand the heat.

Mark Calcavecchia qualifies on all counts.

Turning Point No. 3 in Calcavecchia's golf career actually came, of course, at a drought-parched, pancake-flat slice of Scottish seaside known as Royal Troon Golf Club, bathed by hot, dry weather more reminiscent of Phoenix than Scotland. It was there, on the fourth hole of a play-off with Greg Norman and Wayne Grady, that Calcavecchia hit "the best shot of my life" to win the 1989 British Open.

The three golfers arrived at the play-off by different routes. Grady, the tournament leader after the second and third rounds, shot a steady 71, the first time all week he'd been over 70. Norman, seven strokes off the lead at the start of the day, blazed to a brilliant 64. Calcavecchia, three back when play began, birdied the seventy-second hole for his third straight 68. But he would have been on his way to the airport save for an outrageous bit of luck at the twelfth hole, where a semiskulled pitch from just off the green hit high on the flagstick and dropped straight down into the cup.

Norman began the play-off with the same panache that characterized his final round: a birdie from thirty-five feet. If this had been the Masters, the tournament would have been over then and there, because Grady and Calcavecchia made par. If it had been the U.S. Open, it would have been Monday and there would be seventeen holes to go. But the Royal and Ancient prescribes a much more sensible format for settling ties at its championship: a play-off of four holes, followed by sudden death if necessary.

Norman and Calcavecchia both birdied the next hole while Grady parred, so they came to the third play-off hole—the 273-yard par-three seventeenth—with Norman holding a one-stroke lead over Calcavecchia and a two-stroke advantage over Grady. But Norman bogied when his tee shot hit by the flag and rolled through the green, while Calcavecchia made par and Grady bogied. The trio went to the eighteenth tee—the fourth play-off hole—with Norman and Calcavecchia tied and Grady two strokes back.

Calcavecchia says that every now and then he sits back on his right side with the driver and that when he does, "I squirt a weak little fade off to the right." Everything's relative: a weak little fade by Calcavecchia goes about 240 yards, huge by hacker standards, yet a good thirty yards shy of what he averages on the tour. But the push-fade he squirted on the fourth play-off stopped shorter still after hitting a paying customer behind the ropes on the far, far right.

The bad news was that it was a heckuva time to hit his worst drive of the day. The good news was that if his ball hadn't hit the spectator, Calcavecchia wouldn't have had any kind of shot at the green.

Meanwhile, after watching Calcavecchia's drive disappear into the rough, Greg Norman did a very Shark-like thing: rather than play it safe with a three wood or an iron, he pulled out his driver and bombed his tee shot 335 yards into an "unreachable" fairway bunker. Norman's hallmark is aggressive play ("I'm even aggressive when I go fishing"), but this shot was more than aggressive: it was just about the only shot Norman might have made (short of a whiff) that would open the door for Calcavecchia to get back into the match.

Calcavecchia proceeded to kick the door down.

Television and golf are not a good pairing. The camera lens flattens everything out: no one who has not seen Augusta National in person can have any idea how hilly the course is. The camera also distorts distances and trajectories. I don't know about you, but everything on TV looks like it's going far right to me. And after about fifteen minutes of pan shots tracing a ball's flight in a clear, blue—and so far as I can see, empty—sky, I'm ready for a nap.

But the television camera does one thing superbly well in golf: close-ups. As Calcavecchia completed the follow-through on the startling 185-yard five iron he hit out of thin rough that would give him the British Open title, the TV camera came in tight on his face. It caught the face of a golfer who knows he has just struck the ball as well as he has ever struck it in his life, as well as he can possibly strike it. It caught the face of a golfer who had just hit a perfect golf shot. It caught the face of a man about to become a champion.

All that was left was for Norman to complete his by-now ritual act of self-destruction. The smart play—agreed everyone from TV commentator Jack Nicklaus to Aunt Edna taking her Pekingese for walkies—was to select a club with enough loft to get over the lip of the bunker and safely out into the fairway, thereby setting up a third shot to the green that would put pressure on Calcavecchia's birdie putt. The I'm-Even-Aggressive-When-I-Go-Fishing play was to go for the pin, catch the lip of the bunker, and dribble weakly into an impossible lie in another bunker in the middle of the fairway about 140 yards short of the green. The coup de main was a final blast from the second bunker that bounced beyond the green onto a pathway and out-of-bounds next to the clubhouse.

Another Norman choke job, right? Wrong. "Choke" is a stupid word to apply to anyone who's just shot 64 on the final round of a major championship and made consecutive birdies on the first two holes of a play-off. Norman made a bad chip on the third play-off hole. He took an unnecessary risk with his tee shot on the fourth play-off hole. And he made a dumb play out of the sand after he'd bunkered his drive. It's true that majors seem to be lost more often than they are won, and Norman did some things to lose this British Open. But choking was not one of them.

Calcavecchia, on the other hand, was not some passive bystander who caught the championship when Norman kicked it away. Standing in the rough, seeing Norman's ball in the bunker up ahead, Calcavecchia knew he had a shot at winning—but he had to *make* an incredible shot to take advantage of his opportunity. And when Norman's third shot bounced over the green and out-of-bounds, it took the pressure off Calcavecchia's eight-footer for a birdie, and he drained it. Who knows—if Norman had played it smart and gotten his third shot close to the hole, would Calcavecchia have still made his birdie?

Nobody knows. But we do know that all day the entire field made only five birdies at the eighteenth hole at Royal Troon— and that Mark Calcavecchia made two of them.

One major title isn't enough. Sure, it's more than the vast majority of professional golfers ever win. It brings a golfer respect and endorsements. It elevates him to another level among his brethren. It's often a stepping-stone to higher things: win one, the next is easier. But a single major title is not enough for its winner to get an era named after him. If it were, the post–World War II period would be known as the Herman Keiser Era.

The year after Mark Calcavecchia's first major title—his only one, to date—was a woulda-coulda-shoulda kind of year. He won a lot of money again, even more than he had won the year before. But he didn't win a single golf tournament. He had five second-place finishes, including three in a row, and four other top-10 efforts. Any time a pro golfer comes that close he can say, Shucks, if it weren't for a spike mark here and an unlucky bounce there and a bad lie over there, I could have had me three, four, maybe five wins.

Less easy to put a high-gloss finish on would be Calcavecchia's record in 1990s majors: tied for twentieth in the Masters, missed the cut in the U.S. Open, missed the cut in the British Open, missed the cut in the PGA Championship.

Nineteen ninety was one of those dreams where everything is going along really terrific until, just before the big, high-kicking

Hollywood finale, you wake up and can't remember anything except how great it almost was. Nineteen ninety-one, however, was an unmitigated, free-falling, Freddy's-back-in-town-and-he's-looking-for-you nightmare. In 3-D.

The first half of the year, Calcavecchia was nagged by injuries (tendinitis in his left elbow, broken big toe) and a shaky putter. He never got out of the chute in California and Arizona, which he'd taken by storm the two previous winters, and although he had two top-10 finishes in Florida, he never came close to winning. He had a good Masters, finishing just five strokes behind winner Ian Woosnam despite shooting 77 in the third round. But for the year, he missed seven cuts in the twenty-four tournaments he entered and earned half a million dollars less in official prize money.

The few times Calcavecchia did find himself in contention, he found a way to flub his chances, often because he blew a gasket. In the third round at Colonial, for example, he snapped the shaft of his driver by slamming the disobedient tool against the ground at the eleventh tee. On Sunday, he trashed any chance of catching eventual winner Tom Purtzer when he airmailed the eighteenth green into Crampton's Lake, took a double bogey, dropped from sole possession of second place to a tie for fifth, squandered $84,000 in prize money in the process, and nearly drove his fist through the scorer's table.

In the press room afterward, Calcavecchia was a little, ah, perturbed with his play: "I'm a mental basket case," he told reporter Gary Van Sickle of *Golf World.* "I have the mind of a twelve-year-old, a total waste of space. I can't get it on the green with an eight iron from the middle of the fairway. Disgusting, absolutely disgusting. I was just trying to hit the thing at the pin and hope for a miracle, and I hit a 125-yard duck hook. I've got the yips on my putts and the yips on my chips. I don't think I could win a Hogan Tour event now. I'd find some way to screw it up."

(Oh, Sherrr-yl!)

After that, it was all downhill. Tied for thirty-seventh at the 1991 U.S. Open. Missed the cut at the British Open for the second straight year. Tied for thirty-second at the PGA. And then things got *really* bad on the final day of the Ryder Cup Matches.

Calcavecchia had been a first-time member of the 1987 Ryder Cup team that lost to the European team at Muirfield Village. He had been a member of the 1989 team that hung on for a tie in England, which permitted Europe to keep the cup. All through 1989 he told one and all that his highest priority for the year was to win back the cup, higher even than winning a major. He won a major, but America didn't win back the cup, and Calcavecchia was one of five Americans to lose a singles match on the final day.

Professional golf is not a team game. There are a few international team events—notably, two international tournaments, the Alfred Dunhill Cup and the Asahi Glass Four Tours World Championship of Golf (try saying that with your mouth full of marbles). But those are mainly money games: nothing serious in the way of prestige or national pride is at stake.

Not so the Ryder Cup. The buildup for the 1991 Ryder Cup Matches at Pete Dye's new Ocean Course on Kiawah Island, South Carolina, was an echo of Operation Desert Storm. It was "War by the Shore," as *Golf World* proclaimed on its cover. It was payback time. It was Us against Them. And once the war started, Corey Pavin and Steve Pate even wore camouflage golf caps in their matches.[1]

Unlike most superhyped sporting events, the 1991 Ryder Cup Matches delivered the goods. The night after they ended, I ran into Ziggy, one of my regular golf partners, at a cocktail party on Manhattan's East Side. Both of us had watched all twenty-three hours of television coverage, and we proceeded to rehash

---

[1] For my money, the idea of 25,000 patriots drinking beer in the sun all day and waving flags is pretty disturbing. But the golf was *great.*

every minute—maybe a little more loudly than was absolutely necessary. Not only had no one else at the party watched even a minute of the matches, but a solid majority thought the Ryder Cup was some sort of horseman's protective device, and made rude remarks intended to silence us.

All it had been was the most exciting golf tournament I had ever seen on television, more exciting even than the 1986 Masters, when Nicklaus won his sixth green jacket at age forty-six. But for Mark Calcavecchia, then thirty-one, what took place on the final day of the 1991 Ryder Cup Matches came close to destroying him as a professional golfer.

Calcavecchia had won two of the three team matches he played on Friday and Saturday, but at the start of Sunday's singles matches the Americans were tied with eight points each: the Ryder Cup would be decided by the day's twelve singles matches.

Calcavecchia's opponent in the third match of the day was Colin Montgomerie, a twenty-eight-year-old Scot with a body like Mark had before Sheryl put him on a diet. A first-time Ryder Cup player, Montgomerie was one-one in four-ball and four-somes play the two preceding days. Now, in singles, he was being beaten like a tom-tom: after thirteen holes, Calcavecchia was four up with five holes to go.

In match play, four up with five to go means it's time to break out the champagne. Calcavecchia had a mortal lock on the match, and it was a good thing that he did, because up ahead of him Raymond Floyd and Payne Stewart were on their way to defeat by Nick Faldo and David Feherty.

But then Montgomerie won the fourteenth: no matter, Calcavecchia was still three up. But Montgomerie won the fifteenth, as well: still two up. And then Montgomerie won the sixteenth, and the two golfers went to the most frightening hole on the course with Calcavecchia one up and choking like a dog.

It happens. In every sport, in every walk of life (specifically *in*cluding book writing), choking happens. Certainly in golf it happens. The best ones admit it, get it out on the table. Curtis Strange will be the first to tell you he choked at Amen Corner in the 1985 Masters. Deal with it by being open about it. Recognize it and fight it. In golf, especially in golf, it happens at one time or another to everybody.

Not always, thank God, the way it happened to Mark Calcavecchia on the seventeenth hole of the Ocean Course. The seventeenth is a 192-yard par three to a narrow green angled sharply toward a lake that stretches all the way back to the tee. It's a terrifying hole, even if the Ryder Cup is not at stake.

With Montgomerie safely on the green, Calcavecchia stepped forward with a three iron in his hand. His face was ashen. He looked as if he were in shock. Lose this hole and they would go into the eighteenth dead even. He had been four up with five to play. But that was years ago.

Calcavecchia hit it into the water. No, he *shanked* it into the water, about twenty-five yards short of the green. He called it a "snap slice" later, but the shot barely got airborne, and it sure looked like a shank to us hackers. (With due modesty, we qualify as expert witnesses on the subject of shanks.) Then Calcavecchia went to the drop area, hit another into the water, and the two golfers moved on to the eighteenth dead even.

What happened next was even more amazing than Calcavecchia's collapse: somehow he managed to reach down, get control of his emotions, and match Montgomerie's par on the final hole to halve the match.

If Calcavecchia hadn't recovered to halve the match, if his collapse had continued and he had lost the final hole to Montgomerie, then the United States and Europe would have tied the Ryder Cup Matches at 14-14 and Europe would have retained the cup. In effect, Calcavecchia's match with Montgomerie provided the winning margin in America's 14½-13½ Ryder Cup victory.

Try telling that to Mark Calcavecchia. It's customary in Ryder Cup play for golfers who have finished their matches to go out on the course and root for their teammates. But Calcavecchia was too shattered to do that. He broke down completely and fled from the course. For three quarters of an hour, he walked the beach with Sheryl, convinced that he had let teammates and country down, that he had single-handedly lost the Ryder Cup.

Calcavecchia finally returned to the eighteenth green, face flushed and eyes swollen, just in time to join in the victory celebration when Bernhard Langer's six-foot putt to tie his match with Hale Irwin slid by the hole. The day had drained everyone's emotions. Irwin looked like a dead man, Lanny Wadkins cried from sheer nervous tension after his match. And they were on the *winning* side.

Payne Stewart tried to console Calcavecchia. Your half point won it for us, big guy, your half point did it. Calcavecchia nodded and smiled weakly. Champagne corks popped, people yelled and cheered and carried on, and Mark Calcavecchia looked like he'd swallowed a Titleist. Maybe he knew in his head that Stewart was right, but his pride and self-esteem were sending out a different message.

Winning the Ryder Cup meant more to him than winning a major, Calcavecchia had said repeatedly for a couple of years. But that was before he knew the emotional price he would have to pay for victory.

Just a few years ago, the golf world was talking about Mark Calcavecchia in terms used most recently for John Daly. After being paired with Calcavecchia for the first time in the 1989 Doral Ryder Open, Jack Nicklaus said, "He reminds me of me." Three years later, Nicklaus would say virtually the same thing about Daly. The British Open victory was just the first of many majors to come, many said: Mark Calcavecchia will be the game's next Dominant Player.

But when all he won in the next two years was money, the grumbling started. Too erratic. Too much of a temper. Too many off-course distractions. Not hungry anymore. In a *Golf*

Digest article in 1991, Tom Weiskopf said that Calcavecchia had a lousy swing. (This was the same article in which Weiskopf accused Fred Couples of being an underachiever and lazy; Couples responded that Weiskopf was something of a "waste product" himself.) And then came the Ryder Cup. Would the experience strengthen Calcavecchia or scar him? Would he ever get over it?

Calcavecchia replied by winning a tournament early last year, but it was only Phoenix. Big deal. He set a course record with a 29 on the back nine on the fourth round at the 1992 Masters, but that only got him a tie for thirty-first. Big deal. He made the cut at the U.S. Open—that was a big deal, given his recent record in Opens—but finished eleven strokes off the pace, tied for thirty-third. Missed the cut at the British Open and the PGA. Moved up eleven places on the money list to thirty-ninth. Big deal.

The skinny is that he's turning out to be just another long hitter who hits a hot streak from time to time. Win one or two a year, maybe. Top quarter, maybe a little better. As good now as he's ever going to be. No big deal.

Maybe, but if you're a fan, none of that matters. When I go to a tournament, I still follow Calcavecchia for at least one round. I still run my eye down the fine print in Friday morning's paper to see what Calcavecchia shot the day before. I still check on Saturday morning to see if he made the cut. And if he's among the leaders, I leave Sunday afternoon open, just in case.

(Not Saturday. Unless it's a major, nothing in the world can induce me to watch the *third* round of a golf tournament on TV. You have to draw a line somewhere.)

And I still think he will win more majors. Not a U.S. Open or a PGA, with their tight fairways that favor singles hitters. Maybe a British Open, his record since 1989 notwithstanding. Most likely a Masters, which doesn't discriminate against home-run hitters, so long as they remember to bring along hot putters.

But what do I know? I'm a fan.

The Greening of the Golden Bear

You shouldn't be involved with things you really don't know about. It's taken me twenty-five years of being on the periphery of my business to learn that.

—Jack Nicklaus

The Golden Bear was grumpy. His back hurt. His golf game was shot to hell. He had a head cold. He was stuck in the middle of Ohio on business when he wanted to be in Florida to see a brand-new grandson. He was feeling every minute of his fifty-two years. And somebody had stolen his golf shoes and pants.

But Jack Nicklaus couldn't do what he dearly wanted to do this sunny day in September 1992, which was to slip back into his civvies, hop on his private plane, and hightail it back home to North Palm Beach. He had too much work to do. He was at the New Albany Country Club, a luxurious new golf club with a Jack Nicklaus–designed course that is the centerpiece of a high-ticket residential development near Columbus, to take part in a made-for-TV golf match created and produced by his company, Golden Bear International. There were sponsors to coddle, meetings and receptions to attend, and—almost incidentally—a round of competitive golf to be played.

As conceived by Terry Jastrow, head of Jack Nicklaus Productions, and Ken Bowden, long-time Nicklaus ghostwriter, the Wendy's Three Tours Challenge was a one-day, $650,000 tournament pitting stars from the regular PGA Tour, the Senior PGA Tour, and the LPGA. Wendy's founder and TV hamburger huckster Dave Thomas, like Nicklaus a proud son of Columbus, put up the main money and got the chain's name over the title. ABC signed on to broadcast the show on the Saturday and Sunday after Christmas. The hook to entice viewers was a format that brought together the top players from the three tours in head-to-head-to-head competition for the first time ever.

The Three Tours Challenge was only the latest in a growing series of made-for-TV golf exhibitions that began with the Skins Match, an event that had become Nicklaus's primary source of golf winnings in the last decade. But this one was Nicklaus's baby. If it worked, the Three Tours Challenge would become a star in Golden Bear International's crown. So there he sat in the posh clubhouse the day before the event, clad in only golf shirt, dress socks, and boxer shorts, while an attendant ran over to the pro shop to get him some shoes and pants.

Even for people who have paid only passing attention to the game of golf for the last three decades, the name Jack Nicklaus is synonymous with unsurpassed excellence: fifty-five wins on the PGA Tour, six Masters victories, five PGA championships, four U.S. Open titles, three British Opens, two U.S. Amateur crowns, eighteen international titles—and more *second*-place finishes (fifty-eight) than any golfer who ever played the game.

During most of that time, Nicklaus has worn another hat as CEO of Golden Bear International, Inc., the company he created to manage his financial assets and capitalize on his name. These are tasks that most name-brand athletes leave to professional managers and agents, but over the years Nicklaus has never been content to cash his endorsement checks and hand the proceeds to investment counselors. The game's preeminent specialist in course management has always believed himself equally capable of entrepreneurial management in the world of commerce, his ambitions in the business world no less lofty than his achievements on the golf course.

As a golfer who owned a business, Jack Nicklaus was without peer. But now he is in the final stages of becoming a business-man who plays golf, with different rules and new ways of keeping score. The transition has been a painful one, in part because he has been—and to some degree remains—a prisoner of his own glorious past.

For Jack Nicklaus, Golfer, the event the next day would be a meaningless exhibition, a nuisance at best, and potentially a source of further embarrassment in a year in which he had failed to make the cut in three of golf's four major championships. But for Jack Nicklaus, Businessman, it was a big deal indeed, a major new intitiative for a company that he was trying to build into a major player in sports business.

And that was why the Golden Bear now heaved himself to his feet, pulled on a tired smile, and prepared to give a clubhouse tour to a semi-awestruck *Fortune* 500 CEO who was pleased as punch to be talking to the greatest golfer in history, pants or no pants.

The image will live as long as grown men and women put on silly clothes and try to knock a small white ball into a hole in the ground: Jack Nicklaus, steel-blue eyes focused intently on the work still to be done that fine April Sunday afternoon, striding purposefully up the eighteenth fairway of Augusta National Country Club toward the final green of the 1986 Masters Cham-pionship and everlasting glory.

The more than 20,000 people wedged tightly together on the lush Georgia hillside saluted their champion's arrival with a tribute of cheers that rolled like thunder all the way back down to Amen Corner. Behind him, Greg Norman had just carded his fourth straight birdie to pull into a tie with Nicklaus, a tie he would blow with a bogey on the eighteenth. But the Shark was playing before a gallery of maybe fifty people; everybody else had rushed ahead to be with the Golden Bear.

It was a transcendent moment in sports history. After dominating the game of golf for two decades, Jack Nicklaus had in recent years become, in his words, a "ceremonial golfer." His last win on the PGA Tour had come two years earlier, his last major title four years before that. But now, at age forty-six, he was about to win his sixth Masters tournament, thereby becoming the oldest player ever to win a major championship.

For Jack Nicklaus, the greatest golfer of all time, it was his finest hour. But for another Jack Nicklaus, the business entrepreneur who had built a glittering empire of enterprises over the previous fifteen years, it was his darkest hour. At this moment of his greatest triumph, what a shock it would have been to the thousands gathered at Augusta National and the millions more watching on television had they realized that their beloved Golden Bear stood on the brink of financial ruin.

A top athlete has three things to invest: his or her athletic skills, the money those skills generate, and the residual celebrity that lives on after those skills have eroded.

The first investment is always the easiest. True, there are certain occupational hazards the rest of us never encounter—you don't even want to think about what Joe Namath's or Bobby Orr's knees look like, for example, and you don't have to see your life flash before your eyes as Roger Clemens rears back to throw a high hard one. Also, compared with other members of the work force, a professional athlete has the shelf life of a loaf of bread—the average career in the NFL and the NBA is less than five years, only slightly more in major-league baseball, and a tennis player is ancient history at thirty unless his name is Jimmy Connors.

But if you are born with great genes, run into some terrific coaches along the way, have a phenomenal amount of luck, work really hard, form no bad habits, and avoid serious injury, then you have an outside chance to succeed in your profession, i.e., make pots of money playing games that little boys and girls play for fun.

All too often, however, successful investment of athletic skills on the playing field fails to translate into investment success off the field. For every Gino's, the national chain of pizza restaurants founded by former Baltimore Colts star Gino Marchetti, there are a thousand boarded-up saloons and restaurants that once bore a famous athlete's name over the door. Marchetti's teammate, Hall of Famer Johnny Unitas, has gone to bankruptcy court more often than to the bank in recent years. One reason Kareem Abdul-Jabbar contemplated coming out of retirement in the fall of 1991 is that most of the many millions he made in his long career as an NBA star were dribbled away in bad investments. And tennis great Bjorn Borg, who used to make $10 million a year wearing short pants, lost his shirt trying to design, manufacture, and market them.

Jack Nicklaus turned professional in 1961, joined the PGA Tour in 1962, won five tournaments (including the U.S. Open) his first year, and quickly established himself as the second-hottest property in golf after Arnold Palmer. In the early years, Nicklaus managed his own business ventures—mostly endorsements and personal appearances—through Ohio Golf Exhibitions, Inc., a company he had formed with assistance from Columbus-area businessmen. But in 1968, Nicklaus finally succumbed to the blandishments of Mark McCormack, the first superagent in sports, and assigned marketing control of his name and fame to McCormack's International Management Group, today the largest and most powerful agency in sports. The marriage lasted only a year, however, because Nicklaus chafed at playing second fiddle at IMG to Palmer, McCormack's first and foremost client. In 1969, Nicklaus left IMG, changed the name of his company to Golden Bear Enterprises, Inc., and took nominal charge of running his own business affairs, i.e., for investing his own cash as well as his name.

In fact, though, Nicklaus was an absentee CEO who spent workdays chasing birdies. While he was away, aggressive managers under his employ guided the Golden Bear far from the fairways and greens he knew best. Nicklaus money and the Nicklaus name went into real estate developments, a Pontiac dealership, a shrimp farm, a financial services company, a travel agency, a radio station, an oil-and-gas exploration partnership, and dozens of large and small endorsement and licensing deals, to name just some of the seventy-odd ventures undertaken by his company's twenty-plus subsidiaries.

"We were an accounting nightmare," Nicklaus told *The Wall Street Journal* a few years ago. "I didn't know what any of the divisions did, and neither did anyone else."

Partly because of bad luck but mostly because of overextension into unlikely enterprises he and his managers knew little about, the house that Jack built teetered on the brink of collapse in late 1985, when two big real estate deals, one in California and one in New York, went sour almost simultaneously.

Bear Creek, a residential community built around a new Nicklaus-designed golf course seventy miles north of San Diego, came on the market about five years too soon: people weren't yet ready to buy pricey homes that far out in the boonies. (Today, Bear Creek is completely sold out.) St. Andrews, a condo development in New York's Westchester County a little over an hour from Times Square, featured a Nicklaus redesign of the oldest golf course in America but was plagued by major construction delays and flawed engineering studies that overestimated the number of units that could be built on the rocky, hilly site. In the end, only 94 of the originally projected 242 units were able to be constructed, so not even brisk sales could make the project profitable.

Between them, St. Andrews and Bear Creek spilled $12 million in red ink, while losses in other parts of the company—this was the time, remember, when people started trading in their Pontiacs for Toyotas—added another $9 million to Nicklaus's problems. "We're not talking about paper losses or contingent liabilities here," recalls longtime Nicklaus friend and business associate Tom Peterson. "We're talking about cumulative losses of twenty-one million dollars in *cash.*"

Even in our modern era of stratospheric salaries for otherwise unskilled young adults who can throw, hit, or catch a ball, $21 million is serious money. Golden Bear International, Inc., as the privately held corporation formed to manage Nicklaus's assets and market his celebrity was now called, teetered on the edge of insolvency. And if GBI went down, its founder and namesake would be wiped out as well, because Nicklaus had personally guaranteed large loans to shore up GBI enterprises now gone shaky. Guarantees made to protect the Nicklaus reputation now threatened to drag it into bankruptcy court.

Word naturally spread within the PGA Tour in the mid-eighties that Nicklaus and Golden Bear International were in trouble, although no one knew at the time the full dimensions of the financial crisis. But even if his fellow pros had known how close Nicklaus was to losing everything, no tears would have been shed. The fact is, Nicklaus's peers respect him—how could they not?—but they don't much like him. This is particularly true of the younger generation of golfers, but some of the older heads on the tour also grouse—privately, never for public consumption—at Nicklaus's quickness to speak (some would say pontificate) ex cathedra about anything and everything in the world of golf. That's why they long ago hung the nickname "Karnak" on Nicklaus: because he always has an answer even before there is a question.

His fellow pros do *not* call him Karnak to his face, but several did break silence in 1991 when there was speculation in the golf press that perhaps the greatest golfer of the century should be selected for America's Ryder Cup team. Payne Stewart and Mark Calcavecchia went out of their way to make it clear—publicly— that they felt he should *not* be selected. Team captain Dave Stockton allowed that he was interested in *making* history, not reliving it. And at a press conference shortly before the Ryder Cup Matches began, team member Lanny Wadkins made a point of noting that the American team had received telegrams and letters of congratulations from scores of golfers, including all past team members and team captains.

"Everybody," said Wadkins, "except one."

To some degree, this anti-Nicklaus feeling among his fellow golfers comes from good old-fashioned envy. Part of it has to do with his authoritative, somewhat imperial manner. But most of the resentment stems from Nicklaus's frequently blunt criticisms of the current generation of professional golfers. They don't like it one bit.

No doubt his manner might sometimes have been a little less lordly. Certainly he could have been more diplomatic along the way. Perhaps he should be a bit more understanding of the weaknesses and foibles of lesser mortals.

But what it comes down to is this: Jack Nicklaus is an intelligent, articulate, self-aware, supremely self-confident man who is accustomed to being in charge and who has a lot of very strongly held opinions about a lot of things. And he is generally willing to share them.

That's a potent mix. And it doesn't always go down well.

How could it happen that everything Jack Nicklaus had built up was on the brink of being washed away?

Nicklaus was generally regarded as the best golfer in history. He had the second most bankable name—Arnold Palmer was still the king—in the game that the American corporate Establishment loves the most. After nearly a decade of being resented as the upstart kid who toppled King Arnold from his throne, he was now almost as widely loved by American golf fans as he was respected. And by 1985 he was one of golf's most sought after course designers, with fees to match his fame and all the business his design team could handle. How did it come to pass that his business found itself poised on the edge of utter and complete failure?

The answer is that Nicklaus was nowhere near as good at running a business enterprise in the 1970s and early 1980s as he was at winning golf tournaments. (Had he been, he would have owned America.) Like so many other American business executives, he was spending too doggone much time on the golf course.

If only he had approached business the way he approached golf, he never would have gotten into trouble.

Out on the golf course, remember, Jack Nicklaus was always the master of the safe play. If a pin was unprotected, he would go for it. If not, he would play the prudent shot and take his chances with his putter. Let the other guy play the sucker's game.

But in business, at least through 1985, Jack Nicklaus was a freewheeling swashbuckler. And it almost cost him his shirt, if not his green jackets.

Assessing his business career recently, Nicklaus said, "Although I have 'missed some putts,' I'd say my success ratio in business has been eighty to ninety percent." Maybe. But the putts he did miss almost cost him everything.

Would Nicklaus have been wiser to have let professional business managers handle the investment of his celebrity? Hughes Norton of IMG, who makes sure that top clients like Greg Norman and Curtis Strange earn $10 off the golf course for every $1 on, thinks so. Norton believes that Nicklaus cost himself a small fortune over the years trying to juggle a golf career and manage his business interests. "It's very difficult to do both well," Norton told a Fort Lauderdale financial reporter three years ago. "I still think Jack should have a full-time businessman running his affairs."

But that was not in the cards, because the same competitive fire and unabashed confidence that drove Nicklaus to dominate the game of golf led him to believe he could call—and make— all the shots in the world of business as well as on the golf course. One of his greatest strengths as a golfer was his legendary ability to screen out all distractions and to concentrate on the task at hand. His main weakness as an investor of his own celebrity, at least in the early days, was the apparent belief that he could build a secure, successful business in his spare time.

That's not the way it works, as Nicklaus concluded when an ocean of red ink forced him to reexamine his investment philosophy. "You shouldn't be involved with things you really don't know about," he told a *Wall Street Journal* reporter. "It's taken me twenty-five years of being on the periphery of my business to learn that."

That insight became the driving idea behind a painful recovery process that produced a radically restructured Golden Bear International. Out went chief operating officer Charles Perry, an aggressive entrepreneur who had run Golden Bear for six years and had led the company into the big real estate deals. In came a new president and chief operating officer (Richard Bellinger, formerly GBI's controller), a new five-man executive committee, and an old and severely shaken CEO. Effective damage control kept the full magnitude of GBI's troubles from becoming public knowledge, as the new team moved urgently to scale down the operation, cut losses, reduce exposure, consolidate resources, slash overhead, and concentrate on the business the company knew best: golf.

The patient survived the operation, and today Golden Bear International is a smaller but infinitely more coherent enterprise with nine separate divisions:

○ *Marketing Services.* Endorsements (among them Lincoln-Mercury cars, Manville building products, Uniden cordless and cellular phones) and licensing (Hartmarx men's clothing, Bostonian shoes, and an array of international licenses for clothing and golf gear). Look for the Golden Bear logo.

○ *Golf Operations.* Nicklaus-Flick Golf School (with master golf teacher Jim Flick) held its first classes in 1991. Top quality, top price. Also, a joint development plan with Mitsubishi to create fifty golf academies in Japan. Nicklaus could give Detroit a few tips on doing business with the Japanese.

◦ *Real Estate.* Partnership with Tampa-based developer J. Robert Sierra to build exclusive, very high-end residential developments, each with a Nicklaus-designed golf course, called "Jack Nicklaus Communities." Business has been slow since the eighties ended.

◦ *Video and Television.* Jack Nicklaus Productions, Inc., headed by former ABC sports executive Terry Jastrow, produces instructional videos, television specials, and computer/video games. Only Jane Fonda sells more how-to tapes.

◦ *Daily-Fee Course Project.* Joint venture with Marriott Golf to build fifty upscale daily-fee golf courses around the country, each with the "feel" of a private club but open to the public, with greens fees in the $50 to $60 range. As of this winter, the $200 million project unveiled over two years ago was still looking for a financial partner (i.e., somebody to put up all the cash).

◦ *Publishing.* Over 3.5 million copies sold of fifteen books "coauthored" by the Golden Bear. Top titles: *My Fifty-five Ways to Lower Your Golf Score, Golf My Way, The Full Swing.*

◦ *Sports Management.* New venture launched in 1991 to crack the lucrative player-agent field. Signed on as consultants of Jack Nicklaus Sports Management: former Philadelphia greats Mike Schmidt and Julius Erving. Among first clients: baseball stars Cal Ripken, Jr., and Howard Johnson (for endorsements and investments only; both have agents for contract negotiations).

◦ *The Memorial Tournament.* One of the premier stops on the PGA Tour, and Jack's baby. Staged at one of the first courses he designed (with Desmond Muirhead), Muirfield Village Golf Club in Dublin, Ohio, north of Columbus. The Nicklaus touch on everything from course condition (traditionally the finest on the tour) to practice range (the largest and best) to sandwich wrappers (Masters green). Oh, and forget about grabbing a burger at a refreshment stand: Nicklaus doesn't permit cooking smells on the course during the tournament.

◦ *Golf Clubs.* After spending his entire career associated with

MacGregor Golf Company, Nicklaus teamed up with Nelson Doubleday in 1992 to form the Nicklaus Golf Equipment Company. The new line of Nicklaus clubs was introduced in January 1993 at the annual PGA Merchandise Show.

○ *Golf Course Design.* The largest and most important component of GBI—and the one upon which the success or failure of the rest of the company hinges.

The golf course design division, Jack Nicklaus Golf Services, accounts for 70 percent of the company's gross revenues. Nicklaus became interested in course design in the early 1970s; by the mid-1980s he was designing more courses than he was playing.

At the end of 1992, there were ninety-three golf courses bearing the Nicklaus name open for play in America, Europe, and Asia (seventy-six designed by Jack Nicklaus, seventeen co-designed or redesigned by him), and twenty-five under construction. Nicklaus's design fees—$1.25 million in the USA and Europe, $1.5 million in Asia, $2.1 million in Japan—are the industry's highest by a significant margin. As the course design business goes, so goes GBI.

It is a source of considerable pride (as well as marketing value) to Nicklaus that, alone among the ranks of professional golfers turned golf course designers, he is a member of the American Society of Golf Course Architects. And it is of considerable marketing importance to GBI to have the world believe that Nicklaus takes an active, hands-on creative role in every golf course project that bears his name.

While it is undoubtedly true that Nicklaus gives final approval to all GBI golf course projects and plays a genuinely active part in the design of many, it's also true that he has a team of forty-seven architects, engineers, project managers, and other professionals on staff to do the heavy lifting. How could it be otherwise? With a dozen or so projects in various stages of design at a given time, it's not credible that Nicklaus would be on top of the topographicals on all of them *and* find time to squeeze in a little golf.

And while Nicklaus usually pays a site visit or two for courses he is designing in this hemisphere, he does not typically do so for Nicklaus courses in Asia, whose developers are far more likely to stick the blueprints he furnishes in a drawer and build whatever course they like. After all, it's the name that carries the magic.

For a new business proposition even to be considered by GBI, says Dick Bellinger, it must clear a set of hurdles known inside the organization as "The Five Criteria," which for Bellinger have almost become a mantra:

1. No personal financial guarantees by Jack Nicklaus. (Once burned, twice cautious.)
2. No (or very little) investment of capital funds by GBI. (The company considers the Nicklaus name its capital equivalent.)
3. Minimum requirement of Jack Nicklaus's time.
4. Credibility, i.e., related to golf or other sports. (No more shrimp farms.)
5. Attractive rate of return.

So far, adherence to The Five Criteria has paid off. GBI currently racks up an estimated $50 million in gross annual revenues, about ten times what the boss won in tournament prize money in three decades on the PGA Tour. Officers of the privately held corporation will say of GBI profit margins only that they are "healthy," but *Fortune* magazine estimates that Golden Bear International earned $15 million in 1990.

We should all be so healthy.

One might expect Jack Nicklaus to be an active investor of his own personal funds. After all, he broke away from a highly rewarding relationship with the top management agency in the field to take personal charge of his own business affairs. Also, he has direct access to any number of corporate heads, all of whom hold him in awe and would be honored to provide investment tips. You figure someone like that at least to dabble in the equities market.

Not so. A new investment strategy for GBI was accompanied by a new investment strategy for Jack Nicklaus. At least since the mid-1980s, Nicklaus has viewed fliers in the stock market with the same distaste he feels for fliers from deep rough. All of Nicklaus's personal funds, including the money in the Nicklaus children's trust funds and his and Barbara Nicklaus's share of GBI's profit-sharing plan, are managed by an investments committee headed by Tom Peterson, now senior vice president of GBI. And these funds are managed very, very conservatively.

"Once we got things turned around after 1985, we decided the most important thing was for Jack to get some liquidity," said Peterson, sixty-one, a direct, no-nonsense banker from Fort Wayne, Indiana, who has been with Nicklaus since 1970, when he helped his fellow Midwesterner put together the deal for Muirfield Village Golf Club, still one of the brightest jewels in the Golden Bear's crown. To achieve that liquidity, from 1986 through 1991 Peterson dumped every bit of Nicklaus's spare cash into tax-free municipal bonds.

"Jack was quite vulnerable before," Peterson said late in 1991. "Now he has a nice big basket of munis."

At the beginning of 1992 Nicklaus gingerly reentered the equities market. Without touching the tax-frees, Peterson assigned new pools of cash to four money managers, each with a different specialty (i.e., fixed-income bonds; value-oriented equities; growth equities; and balanced funds). The children's trust funds and proceeds from GBI's profit-sharing plan have been in balanced funds (60 percent fixed, 40 percent equities); Peterson says he will slowly move some of those monies into specialty areas.

"We will closely monitor our money managers' performances," promised Peterson, "but we're not market timers. We're taking a patient, long-term approach. Our goal is a modest, twelve-percent growth."

The eighties are dead. Long live the nineties.

. . .

Jack Nicklaus's goal in restructuring his business affairs after 1985 was to create a company that didn't depend on him: "I don't want to see Golden Bear International operating as a company that revolves solely around me. While I'm sure a great amount of business will be generated through leveraging my name, it will not rely on me personally."

That's the business plan, but the management team's job would instantly become a whole bunch easier if the boss could pull just one final miracle out of his golf bag—say, his seventh Masters championship or another British Open. GBI executives remember what the Golden Bear's sixth Masters title in 1986 did for business, and they can be excused for fantasizing about what winning another major might contribute to the bottom line.

Remember the clunky, oversized putter that Nicklaus used that incredible April Sunday when he held off Seve Ballesteros, Greg Norman, and Tom Kite in one of the most dramatic sports events in history? If you are a golfer, you darned well *do* remember, because you probably ran out the next day and bought one of the ugly things. You weren't alone. In the calendar year *before* Nicklaus's stunning Masters victory in 1986, the company that manufactured the Response putter sold something like 13,000 putters of all shapes and sizes. In the year *after* the Golden Bear wielded his wide-bodied mallet to such miraculous effect, the company sold *160,000* Response putters.

Oh, and one more thing: that company's name was McGregor, owned at the time by . . . Jack Nicklaus.

The Golden Bear's 1986 Masters title did a lot more than add to his wardrobe and sell a few putters. In the next few months, says Dick Bellinger, inquiries from real estate developers interested in retaining Nicklaus's golf course design services increased by 25 percent. While Bellinger is not sure how many of those inquiries translated into actual commissions, he knows that the Golden Bear's mastery of Augusta National gave Golden Bear International a much-needed jolt of confidence (and cash) at a critical point in the company's history.

For Jack Nicklaus, Golfer, the days in the sun are mostly past, and he knows it. But he still believes in his heart that, for just a little bit longer, he can hold back the night.

If he can, it will be of inestimable benefit to Jack Nicklaus, Businessman.

As Jack Nicklaus's golf career winds down, his business career is cranking up. He survived one major crisis. Can he now nurture a business enterprise that capitalizes on his name and reputation without monopolizing his time the way golf once did?

"I've approached golf and my business in the same way," Nicklaus said last year. "I didn't burn myself out through my golfing career by playing thirty to forty events a year; I paced myself so that I could play well at the beginning of my career as well as toward the end. I'm fifty-two now, and I'm still competitive on the PGA Tour. As a businessman, I've tried to pace myself so that GBI will last a long time. I try to be as methodical going into a new business as I am preparing for a major championship."

No one has ever been more methodical in playing a golf shot or better prepared for competing in a major championship. Yet despite circumstantial evidence to the contrary, the golf course and the business arena are not synonymous. Nicklaus and Golden Bear International may not find it easy to create, in GBI president Dick Bellinger's words, "an organization capable of producing value independent of Jack Nicklaus, the golfer."

Among the obstacles to achieving that goal:

○The development of residential communities built around a golf course—the bread and butter of Jack Nicklaus Golf Services for the last fifteen years—has come to a screeching halt. The collapse of the S&L industry, which funded most such "golf communities," means golf designers will have to look elsewhere for commissions. Two thirds of the Nicklaus courses open for play are in the United States; but of the thirty-six under construction at the end of 1992, only ten are in this country.

○Internationally, Nicklaus holds a huge lead over other American golf course designers. But some international markets may soon become saturated (e.g., Japan), and competition will surely increase.

○The ambitious daily-fee golf course project, obviously a response to shifts in the domestic market, still had not found financing late this winter, over a year after it was announced. And even if the project goes ahead, there are no guarantees that golfers will pay the stiff greens fees needed to make it work. This is the nineties, after all.

○Sports management is a logical field for GBI to enter, given its CEO's reputation and success. But it will take time to establish a foothold in a highly competitive, often cutthroat, field. "Happiness is a positive cash flow" is the embroidered message on a throw pillow in Nicklaus's office in North Palm Beach, Florida; by that definition, it will be some time before Golden Bear Sports Management finds happiness. Asked whether the Golden Bear's entry into the sports management field had him worried, Mark McCormack answered, "About as worried as Jack would be if he saw me on the practice tee at Augusta National."[1]

○The Nicklaus-Flick Golf School, launched in 1991 at the height of the Bush Recession, offers absolutely top-of-the-line instruction headed by one of the best teachers in the game. But the price tag—$2,500 for three days of school and four nights at a spiffy golf resort—is the market's highest. Will that fly in the 1990s?

○In case you hadn't noticed, the public has a short memory. While it might seem unthinkable, given his stature in the game, it could be that Nicklaus's fame will no longer translate into sales—of golf gear, men's clothing, Lincolns, whatever his name

---

[1] Golden Bear Sports Management failed to land the first really big fish it went after when phenom Phil Mickelson was netted by another sports management firm, Cornerstone Sports, of Dallas. Golden Bear marketing people complained (anonymously) to *Golf Digest* that their CEO undermined their efforts by not playing the active recruiting role they had counted on. If true, this may bode ill for GBI's future in sports management.

now appears on—once he leaves competitive golf for good. And even if the name continues to move product, it may not be enough to support an enterprise of the size and scope the founder and CEO envisions.

○Marketing a line of Jack Nicklaus golf clubs is a natural for Nicklaus and GBI, but this is a very, very crowded field. Even the Golden Bear will have to scratch and claw to find a niche.

○The biggest challenge Golden Bear International faces is the size of its CEO's ambition. The organization currently has 120 full-time employees spread among its headquarters in North Palm Beach and in offices in New York, Chicago, Los Angeles, Tokyo, and Kuala Lumpur. That adds up to a lot of overhead to carry in lean times. (Arnold Palmer's golf course design firm, by comparison, has fourteen full-time employees. All of Palmer's endorsement deals and other business affairs are still handled by IMG.)

Jack Nicklaus wants to build an enterprise large and strong enough to become a thriving legacy for his five children. He wants to create career opportunities for them in the family business. He also wants to eradicate the memory of 1985, and in so doing to establish that he can be a big hitter in business as well as in golf. All that may be a tough row to hoe in the current economic climate.

The last green jacket he won paid rich dividends to Jack Nicklaus's business—enough to keep it from going under in the eighties. He may have to win another for his restructured business to thrive in the nineties.

Can he do it? Can Nicklaus, who turned fifty-three on January 21, 1993, make a little more history? Can he win again on the regular tour? Can he win another major?

Probably not. The odds against him are impossibly long. Nobody wins a PGA Tour event at his age, much less a major. That's why they have the Senior PGA Tour, to give fifty-something duffers a sporting chance. As Lee Trevino said when he turned the half-century mark and went over to the Senior Tour, "Why should I play against those flat bellies when I can play against these round bellies?"

But victories on the Senior Tour won't add a whit to the Nicklaus legend. On the oldies-but-goodies circuit, people expect the Golden Bear to win every time he tees it up. When he *doesn't* win, that's news. And that's why Nicklaus has kept the Senior Tour at arm's length: he has nothing to gain and plenty to lose by competing "against a bunch of guys I've beaten for the last thirty years," as he put it with more truth than tact the year he turned fifty.

"My problem is not getting motivated to play in a major golf tournament," Nicklaus said a couple of years ago. "My problem is getting motivated to *prepare* to play six to eight weeks beforehand. I go to the range and tell myself that I'm going to practice hard all day. But I just can't make myself do it."

From the start of the 1992 golf season, Nicklaus worked at his game more than at any time in the previous decade. Long hours at the range. An aerobics program to build endurance. Three hours a day of exercises to strengthen a back that has troubled him for years. ("Reporters used to ask me questions about the condition of my game," Nicklaus noted in the press tent at the 1989 U.S. Open. "Now all you want to know about is the condition of my health.")

The results were acutely disappointing. At the 1992 Masters, Nicklaus shot a solid 69 in the first round, ballooned to 75 the next day, came back with another 69 on Saturday, and struggled in with a 74 in the final round to tie for forty-second. Bad as that was, it was better than he did at the other three majors, in each of which he missed the cut. A third-place tie in the U.S. Senior Open was small consolation.

For Nicklaus the Golfer to give Nicklaus the Businessman a boost approaching that of the 1986 Masters, it won't be enough for the Golden Bear to win just any old tournament on the PGA Tour. After all, Ray Floyd has already won a regular tour event—

the Doral Ryder Open—at close enough to the half-century mark to be a gimme. The Businessman needs for the Golfer to win another *major*.

If the Golden Bear does manage to pull off one more miracle, it's most likely to occur at Augusta, where the course sets up perfectly for his game and where he is on a first-name basis with every blade of grass. He's already said that he will no longer play the British Open on a regular basis, and he will need a special exemption from the USGA—as much a certainty to be granted as you will ever find in life—to play in this year's U.S. Open. The PGA? Depends on how he does in the other majors. But Jack Nicklaus will keep on teeing it up at Augusta until they pry the putter from his cold, dead hands. He has a thing for green jackets.

Don't bet the family farm that he won't win another one. Sure, the man who for nearly two decades was the odds-on favorite to win every tournament he played is today the longest of long shots when he goes up against young bucks two decades his junior. But we're not talking about just another round belly. We're talking about Jack William Nicklaus.

Daylight was fading in New Albany, Ohio. The 1993 Masters was still eight months away. And the Wendy's Three Tours Challenge had come down to the final hole, with the last threesome of the day on the tee.

The women of the LPGA were four under par and held a one-stroke lead over the PGA Seniors. The flat-bellies of the PGA Tour were out of it at one under. The event had turned into a one-hole, match-play contest between Dottie Mochrie, the LPGA's leading money winner for the year, and Jack Nicklaus.

Against all odds, the Three Tours Challenge had actually been a captivating golf match, mainly because of the quality of the participants. Representing the PGA Tour were U.S. Open champion Tom Kite, Masters champion Fred Couples, and Raymond Floyd, who three days later would turn fifty and the following week would play his first PGA Senior Tour event. The LPGA team consisted of U.S. Women's Open champion Patty Sheehan, Nancy Lopez, and Mochrie. And from the PGA Senior Tour, U.S. Senior Open champion Larry Laoretti and Chi Chi Rodriguez teamed up with Nicklaus.

"The idea is to have fun," TV producer Terry Jastrow told the players just before the tournament began. Spirited competition? You betcha. These people were pros, after all. And even for golfers in their tax bracket, there is a significant difference between splitting $300,000 (the winning team's share of the $600,000 pie) and trying to cut $100,000 (the third-place finisher's share) into equal pieces. But none, least of all Jastrow, had any illusions about the event. It was show biz, he assured them so "feel free to talk among yourselves, have a good time."

They would be miked all the time, said Jastrow, but no one should feel at all inhibited because "I will protect you," i.e., edit out language commonly used by every other golfer in America in the course of a round.

Lopez: "I might teach Raymond a few new words in Spanish."

Rodriguez: "He knows them all. He lives in Miami."

Ba-bump. But seriously, folks . . .

Has there ever been a golf sitcom?

Seven hours later, all the participants (not to mention the 5,000 spectators) felt as if they had just completed a miniseries. *Seven hours?* That's a long, long time for a single round of golf by municipal course standards, even if you factor in a one-hour lunch break. How could three threesomes of pros take that long? Granted, Nicklaus is a notoriously deliberate (i.e., slow) player, one of the slowest ever. But seven hours?

Blame it on TV. Staged in September, the Three Tours Challenge was scheduled to air after Christmas. Partly to facilitate editing and partly to hold down production costs, the match was taped sequentially rather than simultaneously. This meant that instead of hitting their balls, going to find them, and hitting them again, the golfers in a threesome would hit their balls, go find them—and wait. Wait while the next threesome played their shots. And then the next. Wait three, four, five minutes between shots. It only seemed like forever.

Even though nothing interrupts a golfer's rhythm more than having to wait between every shot, the players were stoical. Why not? It was still a pretty good payday. But Couples nodded off early into the back nine, Floyd was thinking about his upcoming birthday party on the Senior Tour, and Kite was merely steady, not spectacular.

For the LPGA team, all three women played solid golf, stayed in red figures all day, and held at least a tie for the lead from the first hole. Sheehan was two under par, Lopez and Mochrie each one under. They were buoyed along the way by vocal supporters in the gallery, not all of them women, who became increasingly excited by the prospect of an LPGA victory.

Of the seniors, only Chi Chi Rodriguez was sharp: his four-under 68 carried the team. Larry Laoretti made a lot of new friends by taking Jastrow at his word and having fun. He joked with the gallery and kept a stogie on fire under his nose the entire round, but the best score he could manage was even par.

Nicklaus, the unofficial team captain for the Seniors, was lucky to be at only one over. Despite his regimen of back exercises and conditioning program, he had suffered much of the year from sciatica, an inflammation of either of the long nerves that run from the lower back down the legs. "I can walk, and I can play golf," he explained before the tournament. "I just can't do both." And there was no way, *no* way, that Jack Nicklaus was going to let himself be seen driving up the fairway in a golf cart. By the end of the round, he was hauling his left leg along like an extra golf bag.

The good news, from Golden Bear International's point of view, was that the LPGA team was winning. In terms of publicity, nothing would be better for the Three Tours Challenge than to have the women win in a close match.

The bad news was that the boss, the Golden Bear himself, had a chance on the final hole to force the match into a play-off. If he did, the production was in the soup. Technical problems had delayed the start, the sequential taping had caused the round to run longer than planned, and the tournament was *literally* entering the twilight zone. By the time cast and crew reassembled for a play-off, they would have enough light for one hole. Maybe. Coming back to finish the next day would blow the production budget, and there was no guarantee that all six players on the PGA Seniors and LPGA teams could make it anyway.

By rising to the occasion and winning this final hole, Jack Nicklaus would create a nightmare for Golden Bear International.

The finishing hole at the New Albany Country Club is a long, tree-lined, dogleg-right par four with a creek that crosses the fairway twice. For the Three Tours Challenge, it had been set up by officials from the three tours to play at 450 yards for the PGA Tour team, 430 for the PGA Seniors, and 391 for the LPGA. (The governing idea was to approximate the course lengths played on the three tours so that the three sets of pros would be hitting approximately the same club on their second shots.)

Driving second on the final hole, Nicklaus hit a long, high fade to the right center of the fairway—the ideal spot for his approach to the green. Mochrie, driving last, pulled her drive into the left rough.

Back in the TV production trailer on the other side of the course, Terry Jastrow's stomach twisted into a knot.

From a tough lie, Mochrie slashed a five iron that came to rest in short rough fifteen yards below the green, leaving her a delicate chip to the pin. Nicklaus then ripped a seven iron that hit three feet beyond the flag but rolled another twenty feet past. (A couple of decades ago, of course, he would have used an eight iron and the ball would have stopped dead. That's why they call them the good old days.)

Back in the trailer, Jastrow popped a couple of Rolaids.

Limping, tired, the lines in his face etched deeper by the sinking afternoon sun, Nicklaus stepped onto the green and acknowledged the applause from the hometown gallery with a weary smile. Mochrie, a fierce competitor with a superlative short game, was too intent on the work at hand for more than a perfunctory nod in response to her cheers.

After carefully inspecting her lie and walking up to the green to determine precisely where she wanted the ball to land, she stroked a chip that was absolutely on line. But it checked up short, stopping a good eight feet below the hole. Her jaw tightened: she had expected better.

Back in the trailer, Jastrow ground his teeth.

Nicklaus watched impassively from the edge of the green while Couples putted out, then moved forward to line up his putt. As anyone who has ever watched him play a round of golf can attest, nothing—not fading daylight, not a solar eclipse—can cause Jack Nicklaus to abbreviate the painstaking routine he follows in sizing up important putts. He never rushes anything when he has a golf club in his hands, but particularly not putts. Never has, never will.

(More than any other professional golfer, Nicklaus has a lot to answer for with regard to the plague of slow play that is paralyzing the game in America. Monkey see, monkey do—and golfers who have grown up watching Nicklaus go through his pre-shot routine or eyeball a putt have made the five-hour round a norm at too many courses.)

The only difference this time was that Nicklaus's sciatica made it too painful for him to squat down to line up his twenty-three-foot birdie putt. So Jack William Nicklaus II, who caddied for his father back at the 1986 Masters and was carrying his bag again today, did it for him. Jackie looked, spoke quietly to his father, stood up, and looked again. They huddled. Finally, the elder Nicklaus walked up to his ball, shook his head, and said to his son, "I've got to putt it the way I see it."

If Nicklaus and Mochrie both made their putts, the match would be tied and the PGA Seniors and the LPGA would move on to a sudden-death play-off in the gloaming. If both missed and then made their next putts, same result. If Nicklaus made his and Mochrie missed hers, the PGA Seniors would win. And if Nicklaus missed his and Mochrie made hers, the LPGA would win.

Back in the trailer, Jastrow's eyeballs rolled around in his head.

The ball slid downhill toward the hole. Nicklaus had read the putt to break about a foot to the left, and halfway there it seemed as if it would do just that. But the ball hung up about six inches outside the cup and slid a foot past. Good speed, bad read.

"You were right, Jackie," Nicklaus said to his son as he walked up to tap in for his par. And he said it loudly enough so that everyone around the green would know that the old man and not the caddie had misread the line.

Now it was Mochrie's turn.

No break, slightly uphill, impeccable green without a single spike mark—a professional golfer couldn't ask for a more makable eight-foot putt. But no putt that means anything is easy, and this one meant a lot to the women of the LPGA team. Least of all, it meant a bigger payday. More important, it was a win: pros love to win anywhere, anytime, at anything, for any stakes. Most of all, in this first direct, head-to-head competition with their male counterparts in golf history, a win would be a landmark.

Watching from the side of the green, Nicklaus the Competitor wanted a chance to win in a sudden-death play-off. Nicklaus the Senior with Sciatica wanted to get off his feet. Nicklaus the Businessman wanted to avoid extra production costs. Nicklaus the Showman knew the TV package worked best with an LPGA win.

There was never any doubt.

Firmly struck, the ball rolled dead straight into the heart of the cup.

The LPGA had won!

Back in the trailer, Jastrow exhaled for the first time in thirty minutes.

On the green, Sheehan and Lopez embraced Mochrie, and the three of them jumped up and down as the gallery screamed.

And Jack Nicklaus, a half smile fixed on his face, limped slowly away, looking for the cart that would take him to the clubhouse. It wasn't Augusta National. It wasn't Pebble Beach or Baltusrol. It wasn't Muirfield or the Old Course.

For the CEO of Golden Bear International, it was just another day at the office.

How to Watch a Golf Tournament

Golf and masturbation have at least one thing in common: both are a lot more satisfying to do than they are to watch.

—Anonymous

Even if you are seven feet tall, have the vision of an eagle, can run like a cheetah, and are able to abide legions of unidentified Republicans telling you to "Shhhhhh!" all the time, watching a golf tournament in person just may be the single most frustrating spectator experience in the whole wide world of sports—and that includes the luge and curling.

For starters, showing up at a PGA Tour event and plunking down $75 and up for a week-long gallery ticket is no guarantee that you are going to see the game's top pros in action, because not all golf tournaments are created equal. Other than the majors, there are only a handful of tournaments that year-in, year-out manage to attract a solid quorum of the game's biggest stars. Most of the tour stops, particularly those in the last third of the season, must make do with a handful of contestants that everyone in the gallery has heard of and 140 other guys named "Who's That?"

The rule of thumb is that the bigger the name, the fewer the tournaments he plays. Greg Norman still commands bigger galleries than just about anyone in golf not named John Daly, despite the fact that he continues to be a little, uh, short in the major-title department. But he doesn't command *many* galleries, at least not in the United States, where he plays just enough to keep his PGA Tour card. The year after winning his second straight U.S. Open, Curtis Strange played in the Tournament of Champions the first week of January and didn't show up again on the 1990 PGA Tour until the Doral Ryder Open, seven tournaments and two months later. The Payne Stewarts and Fred Couples of the game play twenty to twenty-two tour events; the guys only their mothers could pick out of a police lineup play thirty-three to thirty-five; and there are many, many more of the latter than the former.

Most sports have precisely defined seasons—and the bigger the star, the more he plays. Michael Jordan didn't cut back his playing schedule to sixty regular-season games after the Chicago Bulls won their second straight NBA championship in 1992. Baseball players elected to the All-Star Game don't cash in on the honor by taking weekends off the second half of the season. But in professional golf, a full season is what each individual player says it is. That means that so long as the PGA Tour doesn't require its members to play more than a third of the forty-plus events it sanctions, then tournaments like the Bell-South Classic and the Canon Greater Hartford Open are flat out of luck—as are golf fans who turn up in Atlanta in May and Hartford in August hoping to see the Great White Shark devour a school of guppies. (Sorry, mate.)

Money is part of it. The brighter the star, the bigger the appearance fee for teeing up in Europe, Australia, or Japan rather than in one of the several indistinguishable Buick-sponsored events in America. The cash is guaranteed, the competition is nowhere near as tough—hey, why not? Also, playing in too many golf tournaments wouldn't leave a fellow time for all his corporate outings, where just about any pro who bathes regularly can triple his tournament winnings by giving clinics to awestruck, overweight hackers with terminal slices.

Still, money is not the only reason some tournaments get the cold shoulder from top names. After all, just about every stop on the tour doles out a million bucks or more in prize money these days. Yet while moolah from the Greater Milwaukee Open spends just as well as cash won at the Southwestern Bell Colonial, the latter event always pulls a stronger field than the former. Something else is afoot.

A tournament's tradition and history (or lack of same), the course it's played on, and his past performance in the event are all factors in a player's decision whether to play or pass. So is regional loyalty. Ken Green swears he'd rather win at Hartford, where he grew up, than win a major; Joey Sindelar always plays in the B.C. Open, just down the road from where he grew up in Horseheads, New York; and Texan Ben Crenshaw would as soon beat his putter into a plowshare as skip the Colonial, the Byron Nelson, the Houston Open, or the Texas Open.

Probably the most important determinant of the strength of a field is scheduling. If a pro is confident and secure enough to schedule a break in the first part of the season, the logical place to take it is at the end of the West Coast swing before heading for Florida—often at the expense of the tour stop at San Diego. No town in the country is more golf-crazy than San Diego, but fans there frequently don't get to see Payne Stewart or Paul Azinger or Tom Kite play at Torrey Pines because they're on their way home to Florida for a little R & R before Doral. Similarly, the Anheuser-Busch Golf Classic in Williamsburg will always have to make do with Virginia homeboys Curtis Strange and Lanny Wadkins and a supporting cast of Mike Hulberts so long as the tournament is in the slot immediately before the British Open. That's because most of the top American golfers cross the Atlantic a few days early so they'll have time to get over jet lag, practice their bump-and-run, and fill up on bangers and mash.

Sometimes scheduling works the other way, of course. Tournaments immediately preceding the Masters, the U.S. Open, and the PGA typically draw glitzy fields, with an especially strong turnout by top players from Europe. At the Buick Westchester Classic in 1991, for example, Seve Ballesteros, José-María Olazábal, and Nick Faldo turned out to tune up for the U.S. Open the following week. Last year, when the tournament fell the week *after* the U.S. Open, none of the foreign players were there.

(The field was still plenty strong, however, because the pros like the Westchester Country Club course so much. Open winner Tom Kite was there, along with Ray Floyd, Greg Norman, Fred Couples, Davis Love III, and Payne Stewart. John Daly canceled at the last minute when he and his caddie were thrown off a commercial flight for allegedly obstreperous behavior.)

In fact, just about the only time American golf fans do get to see the top Europeans play in the United States is at the three majors played here, the Players Championship, the World Series of Golf, and (sometimes) the regular tour events immediately preceding them. With the growth of the European tour in recent years, all the top European golfers now opt to stay home rather than accede to the PGA Tour's fifteen-event requirement. The Europeans' sudden discovery of a sense of loyalty to their own tour may have had just a little to do with appearance money paid by tournament organizers to insure a lustrous field. If you had to choose between getting a check for $75,000 no matter what you shot in the Foie Gras Classique or running the risk of not making the cut in Hardee's Classic, where would you tee it up? But even now, with appearance money and guarantees supposedly phased out, there has been no influx of top international players to the PGA Tour.

The purported basis of the PGA Tour's position is that the "integrity of the tour" must be protected, although it's not readily apparent how letting the top international players play whenever and wherever they please would do anything but strengthen professional golf in America. To a man, all the biggest names in the American show—Nicklaus, Watson, Stewart, Floyd, Kite, and company—are on record in opposition to restrictions that effectively keep the Europeans on the other side of the Atlantic: the best always want to play against the best, and these days a bunch of the best don't carry American passports. And while no sponsors of existing PGA Tour events will take a public stand on the matter for fear of rocking the boat, it stands to reason that all of them want the top international pros playing here on whatever terms. If you put up a couple of million bucks to get a golf tournament named after your business, you'd be nuts *not* to want Nick Faldo and Ian Woosnam and Seve Ballesteros "cherry picking" in your orchard.

But the plain fact is that Commissioner Deane Beman and the PGA Tour's board of directors don't give a chili dip about anything except the journeymen pros whose interests they reflect. The way Beman and his constituency see things, if making it easier for foreign riffraff to play here might lead to Kenny Logo finishing tied for twenty-eighth instead of tied for twenty-seventh, then it's obviously a heinous threat to life, liberty, and the pursuit of endorsements.

CAVEAT SPECTATOR

Okay, you've swallowed the fact that Seve and Nick are going to duke it out in Belgium or somewhere during the Greater Kalamazoo Dr Pepper Open back home, and that Payne and Big John are in Japan, and that Boom-Boom is back home in Florida watching soap operas.

Good. Fine. So be it. You're *still* set on seeing the pros in the flesh. But before you make the commitment to watch a golf tournament in person, you have to accept one other irrefutable fact: wherever you might be on the golf course at a given moment, you will be missing *most* of the action.

There may be some other sports where this is also true, but I can't think of any. Station yourself on the side of a mountain to watch a downhill ski race, and all you see is a goggled figure swathed in spandex on his or her way to certain death. (Remember what Erma Bombeck said about skiing? "I never take part in any sport in which there is an ambulance ready and waiting at the bottom of the hill.") But at least you're not missing something going on somewhere else, which is always the case in golf.

In golf, if you stand behind one green all day in order to observe the entire field in action, all you see is a periodic raining of golf balls onto the green from afar and a bunch of guys taking too long over putts that would be gimmes at your course. But if you follow one threesome around all day, you won't get more than an occasional glimpse of the other 153 contestants, plus you will constantly be reminded by roaring crowds elsewhere on the course that something exciting just happened over there. While some people wax poetic about standing on an Augusta hillside and being able to distinguish a birdie roar from an eagle roar, I don't believe those same people would claim any enjoyment at watching the Wimbledon finals while blindfolded.

The point is that in every other spectator sport besides golf, all the action occurs right there in front of you. In golf, by the very nature of the game and the size of the playing field, most of the action is always taking place somewhere else.

One way to overcome that problem is not to think of golf as a spectator sport but to turn it into a spectacle, the way a retired Canadian investor named George Harris and seventy-five or so golfing buddies do every year with the Masters.

Since before Arnold Palmer developed an affinity for green jackets, Harris and his friends have paid an annual pilgrimage to Augusta in April. Over the years, elements of the trip have been refined and there have been changes in personnel, but the basic format calls for them to leave Toronto for Columbia, South Carolina, on a chartered jet at 5:00 A.M. on Saturday morning, board chartered buses for the forty-minute drive to Augusta, spend the day watching the third round of the Masters, and fly home that night.

This is not, by the way, to be confused with a student charter to Europe. On the way down, Bloody Marys fuel a lively (and expensive) Calcutta pool and enough elaborately inventive side bets on the day's action to keep everybody awake. The chartered buses that take them to the golf course are parked just off the grounds behind the fifth hole, where food and beverages are available all day.

Harris, who has become the group's unofficial accountant and recording secretary, takes up a post near the big scoreboard adjacent to the first tee, from which position he is available to record creative flourishes and amendments to an exponentially expanding list of wagers.

From time to time Harris will stroll over to empathize with golfers confounded by the severe undulations of the ninth green, or perhaps he will walk down to the fairway bunkers on the left side of eighteen to watch approach shots to the finishing hole. Occasionally, when he spots one of his favorites making a move on the scoreboard, he'll follow him for a few holes. But mostly, Harris just hangs out. A member of the Royal and Ancient Golf Club who has played Augusta National as a guest many times over the years, he prefers to tour Augusta National when there aren't so many people milling around. Anyway, the whole point of the trip is *being* at the Masters, not *watching* it.

When play is over, the champagne is uncorked before the buses pull out of the parking lot. And on the flight home, the bets are paid off, the day's best (and worst) shots are replayed, and talk drifts to Sunday's final round, which the group will watch on TV at their golf club. And there are always plans to be set, calendars noted, and assignments made for next year.

Now, that approach might work very well with the Masters, a revered institution in world golf that always takes place on the same hallowed ground, the only one of golf's majors in which the venue never changes. But a ticket to the Masters has long been the single hardest ticket in sports, bar none, so that leaves most of us out in the cold.

If the average golfer wants to go to a golf tournament, he'll likely have to be satisfied with a plain, ordinary, garden-variety million-dollar event . . . like the Greater Kalamazoo Dr Pepper Open. And for that you need a strategy.

Monday

Why Monday, when golf tournaments begin on Thursday? Because there's a lot of good golf to be seen *before* the tournament begins. When you go to a baseball game, don't you get there in time for batting practice? Anyway, if you're going to take off Thursday and Friday, you might as well blow off the whole week.

Not much happens on Monday, but you will get a pretty good idea of how professional golfers go about their business. By midday, the journeyman pros who don't have a Monday corporate outing will start straggling in. Most will play nine holes, then go to the practice range. Unless you see someone you're really interested in heading for the first tee, plan to spend most of your afternoon at the range.

Pay special attention to the guys who are working on their short game. There's not much hackers can learn from a pro busting 270-yard drives. But it can be instructive to watch how a pro sets his feet and hands for chip shots and to note the arc and tempo of his swing from bunkers.

Tuesday

Practice day, with just about everybody entered in the tournament getting in at least nine holes. Some tournaments post a schedule of practice tee times, but most do not, so plan to arrive early and stay late to be sure of seeing your favorite golfers play. This is a *very* important day.

About the only time you'll ever see a pro relaxed and having fun on a golf course is during a practice round. Once a tournament begins, there's no kibitzing, no joking between players, practically no smiling. Not that a threesome of pros playing a casual practice round suddenly turns into Moe, Larry, and

Curly—they are still pro golfers, after all. But if you ever want to see Davis Love III smile on a golf course, a Tuesday practice round is the place.

My all-time favorite practice round foursome was Tom Watson, Lanny Wadkins, Greg Norman, and Ray Floyd at Jack Nicklaus's Memorial Tournament one year. The gallery was larger than for most Tuesday practice rounds even though the weather was lousy—there must have been 200 of us slogging around in a steady, light rain. But it was well worth getting soaked to observe these guys at work at close hand.

Whenever Floyd plays a practice round, there's always a little something on the match, so you can count on play in his group maintaining a competitive edge. After all, a practice round is just about the only time the pros ever play for their own money.

Floyd almost always plays practice rounds with older players. It's not that he's unapproachable or that he doesn't like the younger guys. He says it's because most youngsters—unlike players of an earlier generation—have never developed the habit of a friendly little bet to keep things interesting. And to Raymond, a practice round without a few bucks riding on the outcome is bacon and eggs without the bacon.

Among the (somewhat) younger generation of professional golfers, Lanny Wadkins and Paul Azinger strive to keep the flame aglow. And not just in practice rounds. Whenever the two are paired in a tournament, there's always something extra on the side. Like Floyd, and just about every hacker who ever pressed a $2 Nassau, Wadkins and Azinger believe a little action is an integral part of golf. Call it the olive in the martini.

Tuesday afternoon at most tournaments is golf clinic time for kids. If you have a kid who's even remotely interested in golf, by all means take him or her. If you don't, go anyway. A few of the pros who spend an hour watching kids hit balls and giving tips are stiff, but most loosen up and have fun. The best advice for a young kid just taking up golf? Forget about technique and hit the ball as far as you can.

Finish off the day back at the practice range. Unless John Daly is around putting on a show, stand behind a pro who is hitting short or middle irons. If Daly *is* around . . . what the hell, go ahead and watch the show; there's never been another quite like it.

Wednesday

Sleep late, have a nice breakfast, play a leisurely round of golf, take a nap, and catch an early movie—but whatever you do, stay away from the tournament, because Wednesday is pro-am day.

Pro-ams are integral parts of most professional golf tournaments because they bring in so much of the money that tournament sponsors funnel to local charities. (Only a handful of events—notably the majors, the Players Championship, the NEC World Series, the Tour Championship, and the Memorial—don't have pro-ams.) Without money for the charities, the tournaments wouldn't be able to recruit volunteers, and without the unpaid labor of volunteers (as marshals, ticket sellers, vendors, whatever), there wouldn't be any tournaments.

Consequently, the pros are expected by the sponsors and the PGA Tour not only to play in pro-ams but also to smile about it, i.e., to be courteous, friendly, and helpful to their amateur partners, and to do their best to make sure the ams have such a good time that they will come back next year.

Problem is, the pros hate pro-ams, although only the most churlish will intimate as much publicly. Hey, what's to like? Five and a half rounds with three anxious strangers who think bogey is a great score? They play in them because it's the only way to get in a practice round the day before the tournament begins— and because the PGA Tour's agreement with the tournament sponsors says they have to, except under extraordinary circumstances.

Although horror stories abound about pros whose only words to their amateur partners all day are "Hello" and "Good-bye," most pros grin and bear the pro-am. But that doesn't mean you have to. Unless you are actually *playing* in the pro-am, steer clear of it altogether on Wednesday.

After all, you can see a bunch of guys who look suspiciously like you and your friends play really bad golf just about anytime.

Thursday

Tournament play begins. The first two days, fifty-two threesomes will be going off the front and back nines beginning at around eight in the morning, so you will have lots of options to weigh. Arrive early, grab a cup of coffee and a pairings sheet, and block out your day. Okay, maybe it's not like planning the invasion of Normandy, but if you're not careful, you'll find yourself standing silently for hours—"Quiet, please!"—while Larry Mize lines up a putt when you meant to be jogging along to watch Lanny Wadkins slash five irons.

(If both were instruments for measuring time, Mize would be a sundial, Wadkins a second hand.)

In the morning, pick a promising younger golfer and walk nine holes, then lag back until an established star comes along and walk another nine. Or walk three holes with each of three threesomes on the front nine, the same on the back. Either way, you'll now have a sense of the course and the best vantage points for watching a couple of holes at the same time.

(A secondary objective on your morning route is to identify the most remote—and therefore most likely to be overlooked—refreshment stands and Portosan installations. A good field general plans ahead, and this information will come in especially handy on Saturday when the course is packed.)

In the afternoon, follow a golfer who's been hot the past few weeks. Big name or barely known, it doesn't matter. The idea is to get lucky and latch on to somebody who might shoot a really low number.

Golf is a streaky game at the pro level: if a guy has had a

couple of top-10 finishes in his last three outings, it usually means his putter's on fire, which in turn means he's primed for a win. On the other hand, golf is a streaky game at the pro level (is there an echo in here?): if your man starts bogey-bogey-bogey, it usually means the fire is out, so be prepared to drop him like a broken tee.

Friday

Today your selections will be governed by yesterday's scores. Remember that golfers who teed off late yesterday will go off early today and vice versa. Starting times aren't set according to scores until the weekend, so yesterday's leader might be going at the crack of dawn today.

Steer clear of established stars who had a complete blowout the day before. They'll deny it till the cows come home, but a lot of the guys at the top don't go out there grinding on Friday just to make the cut. If they don't have a chance of being in contention by Sunday morning, then they could be looking for an early weekend getaway.

If you want to see intensity, though, now is the time to follow marginal players, especially veterans who have bills to pay and need to play on the weekend. They may have no chance of winning, but they face a certainty of losing money for the week if they don't follow Thursday's 74 with a 68. You see some good golf sometimes with these guys under these circumstances; it's just not very pretty.

Forget the practice range until the end of the day, when it can be interesting to see what the guys who made the cut are working on.

Saturday

The leaders tee off midday, but you should go out with an early group, keeping a close eye on the leader board to see who has a hot hand.

Saturday is moving day. Marginal players who were relieved just to make the cut may have a letdown and drop like rocks. Better players who finished in the middle after two days know they need to make a move today to have a good shot on Sunday, so they may play more aggressively. Other things (mainly the weather) being equal, there are more really low rounds shot on Saturday than on Sunday. In the morning, you need to stay loose and be ready to move on at the drop of a birdie.

Once the last five groups have teed off, though, it's time to stop and let the leaders come to you. Remember the good vantage points for watching several holes at once that you identified on Thursday? Head to the best one on the back nine now. Wait. Watch. Congratulate yourself for good course management.

By midafternoon, the third round will have taken shape. If someone went out early and shot a 64, you were there. If one of the second-round leaders pulls away from the pack, you *are* there. You have done as well as can be expected at shaping thirty-five to forty independent events—the number of pairings during the third round—into a single, relatively comprehensible whole.

By the way, Saturday provides you the best chance of the week to provide a great public service that will ennoble you in the eyes of your fellow golfers. If you find yourself standing behind a tee next to the guy who follows the big hitters around and shouts "You da Man!" at the top of his lungs, stuff your program down his throat. And if you should be elbowed aside by a zealot with a religious message printed on his T-shirt pushing his way into camera range, drive a putter through his heart.[1] Thank you.

---

[1]One exception. At the 1992 U.S. Open, a group of Nicklaus fans wore white T-shirts with JACK 3:16 emblazoned on the front and FOR GOD SO LOVED THE WORLD HE GAVE US . . . JACK on the back. Let them live.

Sunday

Stay home and watch the final round on TV.

No kidding: if you really care about the tournament as an athletic event, if you want to know not only who wins but how, if you want to follow all the key action in the last nine holes, when most tournaments are won and lost, then TV is your only realistic option.

You will miss the flavor of being there. You will miss the crowd's roar three holes away in response to a great shot. You will miss the chance of being an eyewitness to extraordinary shots, such as Corey Pavin slam-dunking from 180 yards.

But chances are you would miss the extraordinary shots anyway, unless you've figured out how to be at more than one place at one time. If you're stationed in front of a TV instead of behind a green, you will be able to see *all* the great shots, at least as well and certainly more often, thanks to the miracle of instant replay, than if you were at the course.

In a tightly contested tournament that's going down to the wire, where several players have a chance to win, the only way to keep up with what's going on is via TV coverage. Take a cue from the ladies and gentlemen of the press, whose noble calling requires them to provide a fair, accurate accounting of the tournament's outcome in Monday's papers: unless the final round is a runaway, and they are afforded the luxury of going out on the course to follow the leader, they will always be inside the press tent.

Watching on TV.

On the Road Again

If you watch a game, it's fun.
If you play it, it's recreation.
If you work at it, it's golf.
> —Bob Hope

The baseball season lasts 162 games. Football runs from September through December, except for a lucky few who play in January. Basketball begins in autumn and ends in spring. Hockey season is . . . well, whatever it is, it's too long. But golf season—well, if you're a grinder on the PGA Tour, golf season never ends.

The term "grinder" doesn't have a very flashy ring to it, even though on the PGA Tour it can be a term of honor. Curtis Strange calls himself a grinder, referring to his methodical, steady, unspectacular style of play. Tom Kite will come in on a day when his swing has been off and admit he was "really grinding out there," trying to hold his game together until he could find something that would work. The greatest grinder of all time, a golfer whose legendary ability to maintain his concentration and hang in there and make pars while everyone else was breaking down, was none other than Jack William Nicklaus.

Players like Mark Calcavecchia, Greg Norman, and John Daly, on the other hand, never grind. Their games are all-or-nothing high-wire acts. If Calcavecchia is out of contention, he slashes and burns around a course like someone who's paying by the hour to play and is short on cash. Ditto Norman, the last man on earth you will ever find grinding hard on Sunday just to finish twenty-seventh instead of twenty-eighth. And Daly? If he's not in the hunt, he's a caddie's nightmare, because he stops caring where his ball goes.

Caddies love grinders. To the guys who lug the bags, the difference between twenty-seventh and seventeenth matters a lot. They hate it when guys quit on them and just go through the motions because they have no hope of winning. They love guys who grind away even when their games are sour and keep on grinding to finish as high as possible, even if it's low. That's how Strange, once the consummate grinder in the decade before he won the two U.S. Opens, got his nickname from tour caddies. They call him "Money."

But in addition to describing a style of play, the term describes a certain category of player on the tour. Grinders in this sense of the term are the offensive linemen, the utility infielders, the second-string centers of golf. They are the guys who spend their entire careers on the tour struggling vainly to get above the bottom half of the money list.

(The 1992 U.S. Open champion and all-time leading money winner in professional golf is not a "grinder," certainly not anymore.)

True grinders are the journeymen, the spear-carriers, the members of the chorus. They play in obscurity before galleries consisting mostly of friends and family and people waiting for Payne Stewart to come along. They have lousy tee times, either very early (when the course may still be wet with dew) or very late (when the greens are all chewed up), but never in the middle (reserved for the tournament's upper crust). And they play a lot, just to survive.

During the golf "season" there are forty-five golf tournaments where a player's winnings count toward the official PGA Tour money list, which in turn is used to help determine a player's right to enter tournaments in the following year. Eight of those forty-five have limited fields and/or restrictions that exclude most grinders. For example, the first tournament of the year—the Tournament of Champions—is restricted to tournament winners the preceding year, while the last tournament of the year—the Tour Championship—is open only to the top 30 on the money list. Some restricted field events (e.g., the U.S. Open, where there are regional qualifying matches for pros who are not otherwise exempt) are marginally easier to enter than others (e.g., the Masters, where there is a sign in front of the main gate of Augusta National that says "Private Property: No Peddlers or Grinders Allowed"). In effect, then, grinders have thirty-eight shots at rising above their station in golf's hierarchy.

A grinder will play thirty to thirty-two events, maybe more, just to be sure of keeping his right to play at all. Greg Norman frets about winning majors, but the grinder's worries are a little more basic—he's constantly worrying about falling out of the top 125 money winners and losing his tour card.

While the game's elite players focus their energies on the majors, the almost-majors, and the big, prestige tournaments in the first half of the golf year, the grinder's best hope for pulling himself up by his Foot-Joy–tops and out of the grinder's world comes in the second half of the season. It's a lot easier to score a big payday when the best guys in the game are somewhere else.

From late summer through early fall, when the biggest names in golf are off to Japan or Europe cashing appearance-money checks, or trying to win back the Ryder Cup, or just sitting home drinking champagne and watching the NFL on TV, the tour grinders have their best chance of breaking free of the pack by winning a golf tournament.

Frank Webb Gardner, Jr., is not exactly a household name. Not even as "Buddy," which is how he's known to everybody who knows him at all. Not even around his own household, which the thirty-seven-year-old veteran of fifteen PGA Tour campaigns sees only slightly more often than he sees a winner's check with his name on it.

Buddy Gardner is the archetypal grinder.

If Buddy Gardner turned the double play as well as he plays bunker shots, you'd have heard of him over morning coffee: "Gardner Inks Two-Year $2.2 Million Pact," the headline would scream. Instead, the only way you'll ever likely see his name is if you are addicted to the agate type in the sports pages. Yet, while he may not make many headlines, Buddy Gardner does make a living in sports. Problem is, the sport he makes a living in is golf.

At a fateful point during his formative years in Birmingham, Alabama, Gardner picked up a two iron instead of a Louisville Slugger, liked the feel of it, and set out in hot pursuit of fame, fortune, and birdies. To date, he hasn't shot enough of the last to earn him much of the first, although by ordinary measures he's made a decent amount of the second. By the standards of modern professional sports, however, Buddy Gardner makes peanuts. The $1.4 million in official prize money that Gardner has won in fifteen years on the PGA Tour is still a hundred grand shy of what the San Francisco Giants paid shortstop José Uribe *last season*—in exchange for which Uribe batted a lusty .241 with thirteen RBIs in just 162 at-bats as a part-timer.

This isn't to say that the nearly $162,000 Buddy Gardner has averaged each of the last three years is small potatoes. It's not. Four veteran high school teachers would need to pool their salaries to come up with as much. Also, Buddy's working conditions are excellent, and he doesn't have to buy his own tools. It's only when you compare their compensation with the wages of players in other sports that the Buddy Gardners of the PGA Tour look underpaid.

"Sure, I read about all those big contracts in baseball and football and basketball, and I wonder where all that money comes from," says Gardner. "But what can you do about it?"

O

If you're a professional golfer, you do what Gardner does: you grind. Every year, he plays thirty-two, thirty-three tournaments on the tour. Every year, he leaves home in early January and doesn't see it again until late February, when he may spend a day or so in Birmingham while traveling from the West Coast circuit to the Florida swing of the tour. And after that? When I caught up with Gardner in Miami last year he didn't expect to get back home until . . . well, he just wasn't sure; it all depended on how he was doing.

"The name of the game is winning," says Gardner, who has four second-place finishes but nary a championship trophy to his credit. "I want to spend more time at home, but if you're not here, you can't win."

Gardner did win a PGA Tour–sponsored tournament in 1991, his first in fourteen years of trying. But the victory came on the Ben Hogan Tour, a minor league set up to give younger players a chance to make enough money to cover expenses while they sharpen their skills and earn a place on the regular PGA Tour. Buddy played in the Hogan tournament that was held at a golf club he represents in Panama City, Florida, to lend support to a hometown event. The $25,000 check he received for winning came in handy, even if it doesn't count as official money on the regular tour.

But the Hogan win didn't get Buddy Gardner into the Masters, didn't earn him a two-year exemption, and didn't mean he could afford to cut back just a little on his playing schedule. He's still out there almost every week, a regular on the Grinders' Tour.

A tournament victory on the PGA Tour is worth $180,000 and up. It gets you into the Masters, the U.S. Open, the World Series of Golf, and the following year's Tournament of Champions, where there is no cut and last place is good for $11,000. It usually (though not always) lifts you into the top 30 on the money list, which means an invitation to the year-ending Tour

Championship, where last place is good for *$32,000.* It bumps up your corporate-outing fee. It earns you a two-year exemption on the tour. And a tournament victory gets you respect from your peers.

But, as Mike Donald will attest, a single victory on the tour does not give a grinder a permanent address on Easy Street.

Donald earned the nickname "Iron Mike" in the 1980s because he played more tournaments than anybody, averaging thirty-five events a year, albeit without a single win. Only once did he crack the top 50 on the money list. Finally, in his tenth year on the tour, he won the 1989 Anheuser-Busch Golf Classic. He finished twenty-second on the money list that year and finally, at age thirty-four, seemed to have raised himself to another plateau.

The following year Iron Mike enjoyed fifteen minutes of fame when he lost a play-off to Hale Irwin in the U.S. Open, finished thirty-sixth on the money list, and seemed to have put his struggling days behind him. But in 1991, the second year of the two-year exemption that came with his only tour win, Donald won only $88,248, plummeted to 142nd on the money list, lost his card (he was a player director on the PGA Tour policy board at the time!), and had to go back to Qualifying School, where he finished out of the top 50 and failed to get his card back.

So much for job security on the PGA Tour.

Last year Iron Mike's exempt status was reduced to that of "Past Champion," about the equivalent of write-in candidate in a presidential election. He had to scrounge to get in enough tournaments through sponsors' exemptions to have a chance to fight his way back. In the end, he managed to play in thirty-one events, a relatively light schedule by Iron Mike's standards, and he earned his card for 1993 by finishing 120th on the money list—by a margin of less than $8,000.

One more missed cut along the way and Mike Donald would have been back at square one—Q-School.

·   ·   ·

Unlike athletes in team sports, professional golfers must take care of their own road expenses—and they're always on the road. Gardner figures it costs him "two grand a week just to stay out here." A veteran like Gardner remembers all too well how much time and energy younger players can spend chasing an affordable room and a decent meal. Over the years, he has learned how to cut corners without making life unspeakably grim. And having his wife and young daughter travel with him now makes the road less lonely. But being a veteran doesn't make a professional golfer of Gardner's stature any less of a gypsy: if you've seen one Red Roof Inn, you've seen them all.

"I *hate* the travel," Gardner says, in a voice that brooks no doubt that he really means it, right down to his spikes. "I mean, I really *hate* it. That's the only thing about all this that really gets me down."

The tour's stars find complimentary cars waiting for them at the airport when they arrive for a tournament, but the Buddy Gardners of the game more often than not have to scrounge their own wheels. Then there are caddies to pay, airplane tickets to buy, and plenty of incidentals. Meal money? Sure, if you haven't exceeded your credit-card limit.

On the other side of the ledger, no golfer on the PGA Tour can even remember the last time he bought a sleeve of balls, none is exactly au courant on the retail price of a good set of irons, and none has to win the Masters to get a free pair of Foot-Joys when he needs them. But none of the above pays the rent, much less covers the kids' college tuition. And you can't eat golf balls, even if they're free.

Working weekends is a drag for most folks, but in golf, if you *don't* work Saturdays and Sundays, you don't get paid. Mark Rypien throws five interceptions? No problem: he still gets his monthly check with all those zeroes. José Canseco goes 0 for 30? No big deal: all he has to worry about is losing his driver's license. But if Buddy Gardner doesn't make a cut on Friday, he walks away from a tournament without a red cent.

And should a grinder wake up on a Thursday morning feeling a little under the weather, he can't afford to spend the day in the trainer's room, the way Rickey Henderson has been known to do. There is no injured reserve list in professional golf, no disabled list to go on when the old back starts acting up. It comes down to a simple equation: No Play, No Pay.

Gardner learned this the hard way. In the fall of 1981, he tore ligaments in his left wrist in a touch football game with some other golfers at a tournament. He tried to play through the injury, but ended up having his wrist in a cast for two months. By the time he got full strength and movement back, 1982 had come and gone, and he had $6,214 in winnings to show for it.

What kept Gardner's body and soul together, at least until recently, is what golfers on the PGA Tour count on more and more to double, even triple their income: a corporate deal.

"I was waiting for an elevator at a tournament back in 1986," he recalls, his face crinkling in a smile at the recollection of being in the right place at the right time. "The elevator arrives, the doors open, and there's Fuzzy Zoeller with a couple of guys I don't recognize. Fuzzy points at me and says to them, 'There he is! That's the man you want right there!' "

The guys were RJR-Nabisco promotion executives, and they took Fuzzy's advice: they signed Gardner to a personal-services contract representing RJR-Nabisco, thereby providing the financial cushion that has made it possible for him to keep on chasing birdies.

Presto! Suddenly, money started growing on trees—or so it seemed to a grinder whose highest finish ever on the money list was fifty-fifth. For the next several years Gardner "just about matched" his tour winnings by appearing at RJR-Nabisco corporate outings, mostly on Mondays.

"I'll fly into a place on Sunday night," he explains, "have cocktails and dinner with some really swell people, and then give a clinic and play golf with them the next morning. It's a great deal."

The golf Gardner plays on the forty or so corporate outings he undertakes each year is a little different from the golf he plays on, say, a Friday afternoon when how he plays a five iron from a tight lie determines whether he makes the cut.

"Mostly they just want to see a pro hit the ball a long way," says Gardner of the customers and corporate execs who attend the outings. "So I tee it up high and let it fly."

Other golfers with RJR-Nabisco contracts back then had names like Nicklaus, Zoeller, and Floyd, so Gardner was in pretty good company and mighty thankful to be there. He also knows that his Monday paychecks would grow if only he would end up at the very top of the leader board some Sunday.

He came close in 1989. After twelve holes on the final round, he was ten under par, three strokes behind the leaders, Bill Glasson and Mark Calcavecchia, who seemed intent on self-destructing three holes behind. But on the thirteenth, a 246-yard monster par three that had been devouring golfers all week, Gardner hooked a one iron left of the green into thick Bermuda rough. Four strokes later he had a double-bogey five and was out of the hunt.

Gardner eventually finished in a three-way tie for ninth with Paul Azinger and Ben Crenshaw. It would turn out to be his highest finish of the year. For his efforts that week, he earned a big check—$35,100—but no brass ring. It was a good payday for Gardner. Just not good enough to get him back home for a week.

Three years later, Gardner was still grinding, only now he had to grind harder. The RJR-Nabisco gravy train had creaked to a halt when the company ended its $5.75 million annual sponsorship deal with the PGA Tour in the aftermath of its famous leveraged buyout, which had saddled the conglomerate with a huge debt load. The forty-plus appearances Gardner had been making under contract now had to be replaced by whatever individual dates he could hustle. Early in 1992 he landed a TV commercial gig for Tommy Armour golf clubs, but that was small potatoes. Life for Gardner after RJR-Nabisco became a little harder, a lot more uncertain.

Maybe the pressure took its toll. Maybe he just caught a lot of bad bounces. Whatever the case, in 1992 the wheels came off for Buddy Gardner.

Guys like Gardner make a living by making cuts. If you spend too many Saturdays watching cartoons, you'll soon be looking for a new line of work. In the three golf seasons prior to 1992, Gardner entered ninety-five golf tournaments and made fifty-six cuts. That's a good ratio. Nothing like the eighty-six *straight* cuts that Hale Irwin made back in the mid-seventies, but pretty good, especially for a grinder.

Last year, though, Gardner teed it up thirty-two times and played on weekends just twelve times. The year before, he won $201,700 and ranked eighty-third on the money list. Making just twelve cuts in thirty-two tries dropped his earnings by $88,000 and his ranking on the money list to 124th, just one notch above professional golf's Mendoza Line.

If he falls below that line, Buddy Gardner has three options: (1) return to Q-School and butt heads with a small army of young studs fighting for the same handful of union cards; (2) try to claw back the way Mike Donald did; or (3) quit. Hauling that mental load around with you on the golf course makes for a tough day at the office. And it may have had a little something to do with Gardner's performance in the Texas Open last October, his last chance in the year to move up on the money list: he shot 75–80 and missed the cut.

But he made the top 125, if only barely, and so Gardner will be back again this year for another campaign.

He'll be trying to solve the mystery of a game in which a couple of lousy strokes a round—Vardon Trophy winner Fred Couples averaged 69.38 strokes per round last year, Buddy Gardner averaged 71.88—is the difference between the penthouse and the outhouse.

He'll be playing thirty-two or thirty-three events, hustling as many corporate outings as he can, trying to hold down travel expenses, hoping to catch lightning in a bottle.

And when he absolutely, positively, *must* make a shot to make a cut, he'll probably be squeezing the club a little too tightly, because what's at stake is survival.

Life on the PGA Tour can be pretty glossy and glamorous, *if* you are a member in good standing of the upper stratum. But for grinders like Buddy Gardner—and for every Fred Couples there are a couple of dozen Buddy Gardners on the tour—the game of golf smells a whole lot like a job. One they are constantly in danger of losing.

Home on the Range

A motorist is lost on the back roads of rural Georgia. He stops to ask for directions at a ramshackle wooden structure with a fading sign that promises Eat–Gas–Live Bait. "Beg pardon," the motorist says to an old gent in grease-stained overalls. "Can you tell me how to get to the Masters in Augusta?" The old gent squints, grunts, and lets fly a stream of tobacco juice. Finally he wipes his stubby beard with the back of his hand, and drawls: "Practice, practice, practice."

—Variation on Old Theme

Kidnap and blindfold me, throw me in the back of a van, drive to a practice range at a golf course early on a Monday morning when nobody else is around, and fifteen seconds after you remove the blindfold I'll be able to tell you whether a pro golf tour was held there that weekend. How? By looking at the divots on the range.

A hacker makes a horrible mess of the grass on a practice range. Maybe it comes from banging so many balls off plastic mats at driving ranges where hitting fat causes the club to bounce rather than excavate, but a hacker—and here I dare to speak for us all—is perfectly capable of turning a grass-turf range into a freshly plowed field.

A pro can spend all afternoon clipping two irons off the grass without leaving a trace of his presence. And if he happens to be working on his short irons and does take divots, he does it neatly and precisely. Note what the pro does after he takes a divot at the practice range: he carefully rolls the next ball right to the edge of the bare spot so that the succeeding shot will barely widen the original divot. Sometimes he'll fuss over the ball's placement for several seconds, rolling the ball with his club head until it's just so, to make sure that he displaces the absolute minimum of turf.

A hacker whose timing is just slightly off wields a nine iron like a backhoe. After a couple of hours, the ground around him looks like a newly opened strip mine. In the same amount of time, a pro creates a tight little circle of bare ground that looks for all the world like a case of male pattern baldness. (One difference: the grass grows back.)

When it comes to divot making, pros are to hackers what a brain surgeon is to a hog butcher. If both were dancers, pros would be Fred Astaire, hackers Chubby Checker.

No wonder they're better golfers than we are.

Jimmy Demaret was right: the only activities in the world you can enjoy without being any good at are golf and sex. But that's still no excuse for not practicing, which is just one of the reasons why the pros are better than we are—they practice a lot more.

Most hackers are like my pal Okie, who thinks that a couple of hard practice swings to break the adhesions in his shoulders and a single, soul-cleansing passage of wind constitute ample preparation for a round of golf. While the other members of our foursome are spasmodically jerking putts on the practice green just before tee time, he's standing off to the side smoking a cigarette. So far as I know, Okie has never set foot on a practice range except to pick up a ball he knocked there from an adjacent fairway. If his shoes are tied, he's ready.

Some hackers are more like Michael, another member of my foursome. Michael does try to get in a few licks at the practice range before teeing off, provided there's plenty of time after a leisurely breakfast. His practice "routine," though, is to step up to the tee without so much as a single bend or stretch and start flailing away with his driver at top speed, which in Michael's case is very fast indeed. Several shanks, toe hits, snap hooks, boomerang slices, worm burners, pop flies, and topped dribblers later, Michael will make semisolid contact with an unsuspecting range ball and pronounce himself ready to play. He's not, but that's never deterred him yet.

There's a contrarian in every crowd, and in my foursome, that would be Lee, who would rather practice than play. Unless physically restrained, he will hit so many buckets of range balls before a round that he is pronounced arm-dead by the seventh hole.

Any of this sound familiar? Probably. In our eagerness to step up to that first tee and get on with the game, most American hackers unwittingly echo an attitude once articulated by Walter Hagen: "What a shame to waste those great shots on the practice tee. I'd be afraid to stand out there and work on my game like that. I'd be afraid of finding out what I was doing wrong."

Maybe it's part of our national character, this business about not practicing. Consider: *Golf* magazine calculates that there are only 2,500 commercial driving ranges in America to serve 24.5 million golfers, while in Japan there are over 5,000 ranges for only 11.5 million golfers. (For many Japanese golfers, of course, given the cost of playing and difficulty of getting a tee time should they have the yen, the *only* place they hit balls is at a practice range.)

First it was portable radios. Next it was cars. Now it's driving ranges. Where will it end?

"You'll never learn to play golf on a golf course."

Lee Trevino was standing on the practice tee at the Stadium Course at TPC-Sawgrass. It was the Monday before the 1989 Players Championship. He wasn't playing in the tournament; later in the week he would do color commentary for NBC. Today he was just hanging out with Tom Watson at the far end of the range, banging balls and talking golf.

"The place to learn how to play golf is on the practice range," Trevino said. Next to him, Watson was hitting balls methodically. Trevino would hit an occasional four iron, but mostly he was just talking—to Watson and whoever happened by. "That's where you learn how to maneuver the ball, how to get it in the air, how to hit it low, how to make it dance for you."

He stopped for a moment and took a couple of the quick, looping swipes that have become so familiar to golf fans over the years. One after another, two balls rocketed into near identical trajectories, starting slightly left and correcting in midflight, finally bending back softly to the right about 190 yards away. They ended up about five feet apart.

"Except for driving," Trevino returned to his lecture. He was the teacher; this was his classroom. "The worst thing you can do is hit a driver on the driving range. You need to practice driving on the golf course. Get yourself a couple of dozen brand-new balls, go out to the tightest fairway, and try to keep all of them in play."

Somebody asked him about the Masters: Would he go back again if invited once he was out on the Senior Tour? He sidestepped the question by saying for the umpteenth time that he liked the tournament but not the course because "it makes me have to do this all the time." And he turned and hit a long, gentle draw. "*That's* not my game," he said. "*This* is my game." And he turned and hit a long, gentle fade.

"When I'm working hard on my game," said the game's greatest talker, "I'll hit three hundred to four hundred balls on the range, listening to the radio, talking golf with whoever's around. Then I'll have lunch. Then I'll hit three hundred to four hundred more balls. And *then*, after everybody else has stopped, I'll go out and play nine holes by myself."

Meanwhile, Watson continued to work, his divot pattern a neat rectangle about the size of a small hand towel.

The practice range at a golf tournament is a show within a show. During the week, most pros spend as much time there as on the course. Some spend even more. Others should.

Tournament week at a PGA Tour stop is like the circus has just come to town. Hospitality tents spring up like Mighty Mouse and Snoopy at Macy's Thanksgiving Day parade. Grandstands go up. Riggers scamper around the TV towers, making sure they are stable. Marshals in brightly colored jackets fan out over the course. The aroma of hamburgers and hot dogs sizzling on the grill fills the air. (Unless, of course, the tournament is the Masters or the Memorial, where the burning of animal flesh is prohibited by local religious authorities.)

But the center of tournament activity from Monday until Thursday morning is the practice range. Players and caddies congregate there, of course, but they constitute a minority of the milling crowd behind the ropes. Reporters from local and regional newspapers scurry about, notepads in hand, trying to get a usable quote from last year's winner or this year's hottest hand, the obvious choices for a pretournament feature. Radio and TV guys brandish their microphones and minicams, hoping to elicit a usable sound bite for the 6:00 sports report. Stars' agents in silk shirts by Armani and sunglasses by Carrera stop by to see if their meal tickets need any pampering. Three reps from the BellSouth Classic—identically decked out in orange blazers, blue trousers, black-and-white golf shoes, and Rotary smiles— wander around, checking to see if golfers who have signed up to play in Atlanta need any special arrangements and trying to sign up those who haven't. (Note to BellSouth: Your advance scouts do a swell job, but they should lose the blazers.)

The largest contingent of nongolfers inside the ropes at the practice range is made up of sales reps and techies from the club manufacturers. The ones from the bigger companies, whose equipment trailers are parked just beyond the range, are there to service their clients. Need a little more loft on that wedge? Want to try that one iron a little more upright? No problem: they just step over to the trailer, which comes equipped with a complete workshop and enough spare clubs to launch a Nevada Bob's franchise.

The sales reps from the smaller companies, the ones without

the blue-chip endorsements, have the much harder task of trying to persuade rising young stars and established players who aren't locked up in long-term equipment contracts to try their wares. Usually it's a driver because, next to putters, that's the club touring pros experiment with and change most frequently. Even some guys already under contract might be persuaded to try a new driver. So the sales rep goes from player to player on the range, smiling, making small talk, and hoping and praying with all his soul that Kenny Logo will love the new beryllium shaft and kryptonite head he's just been given—love it enough to go out and win several majors with it.

Outside the ropes, fans can get closer to more golfers all at once than at any other time during the tournament. Sometimes you're close enough to eavesdrop on conversations, other times to be included in them if a pro is feeling gregarious. It's like hanging out behind the batting cage before a baseball game, only better: pro golfers are infinitely more civil than baseball players.

A full spectrum of golf swings is on display for anyone to study, from Tom Purtzer's (the best on tour, according to his peers) to Leonard Thompson's (cover your children's eyes). A patient fan gets to see touring pros practice what teaching pros preach: putting a club on the ground parallel to the line of flight as a constant alignment check, hitting each club in the bag and not just their favorites, working on their short game. One will set up a videocam, hit a few balls, then come back to review his swings, looking for explanation of that 74 last week. Another will stick a flexible, six-inch wire in the ground a foot behind the ball and inside the target line to monitor his swing path.

My first thought on watching pros go through long, tedious practice drills was similar to my reaction on seeing lean, hard, obviously fit people running in the park. If you're in such good shape, why run so much? If you can play golf as well as you do, why spend so much time on boring practice drills? And then it dawned on me: maybe there was a connection.

The best practice facilities on the PGA Tour are at Muirfield

Village in Dublin, Ohio, site of the Memorial Tournament. This is Jack Nicklaus's event, and he designed the practice range with the touring pro in mind. The range's teeing stations wrap halfway around a large, manicured hitting area, permitting players to practice with the wind coming from varying angles. There are several practice greens for practicing bunker and chip shots. Near the clubhouse and the first tee is another putting green, one that receives exactly the same attention and is cut precisely to the same length as the greens on the course.

The worst practice facility on the tour is at Pebble Beach. A lot of the older golf clubs that stage tournaments have practice ranges that are inadequate by contemporary PGA Tour standards (e.g., Colonial in Fort Worth; Westchester, just outside of New York City), but at least they have ranges. Pebble Beach doesn't. What Pebble Beach has is a polo practice field that is jerry-rigged for the week to accommodate the small army of pros, ams, and celebs that turns up every winter for the AT&T Pebble Beach National Pro-Am (still "the Crosby" to golfers of a certain age).

Whatever the size and shape of the range, the range *balls* are always the same: none of the striped rocks that we hackers pay six bucks a bucket for, but brand-new, never-been-hit Titleists. The balls are donated by Titleist in exchange for "promotional considerations." After the tournament is over, the range balls are redonated to local junior golf programs. Each year, the pros on the PGA Tour go through *300,000* balls. Just for practice.

The best shows on the range are put on—big surprise—by the biggest hitters. When Greg Norman, Davis Love III, Mark Calcavecchia, Fred Couples, and other long knockers haul out the heavy artillery, the gallery snaps to attention. People gape in awe at the towering height of Norman's five irons. They give each other "How does he do that?" looks when Love launches 225-yard, wind-cheating two irons. They nudge each other and say, "He swings as hard as me" when Calcavecchia rocks back to uncork one. They marvel at Couples's slow, easy tempo and vow silently to swing easy the next time they play. (And they always break that vow on the first tee . . . don't we?)

Since the 1991 PGA Championship, of course, the biggest practice-range draw on the tour has been John Daly. Seve Ballesteros, Nick Faldo, and Payne Stewart could be standing on the range buck naked comparing the grooves on their niblicks, and the entire gallery would desert them the moment John Daly ambled into view.

"Grip it and rip it, Big John!" the faithful cry out in unison as Daly flips away a cigarette butt and reaches for his mammoth warstick. Big John is only too eager to accommodate them. And that, say critics, is something Daly is going to have to overcome if he is to become a complete player, i.e., his willingness to cater to his fan club's insatiable craving for breath-grabbing drives at the expense of other parts of his game. "He ought to think about working on hitting it short," said one pro last summer as he listened to the crowd cheer for the Mighty John Daly Show. "He already knows how to hit it long."

And how. At the Memorial in 1992, Jack Nicklaus had to quietly ask Daly to cease and desist when Big John started launching rockets at cars parked alongside a road a good 350 yards away: he was coming too close.

The first sign that John Daly is maturing as a golfer will be the day at the practice range when he hits more knock-down seven irons than full-bore drivers. As Buddy Holly said, "That'll be the day."

It was late in the afternoon of the second day of the 1990 Tournament of Champions at La Costa Country Club in Carlsbad, California, and Tom Kite was hitting balls at the practice range.

After finishing his morning round, Kite had paid a ritual visit to the press room, where he answered the usual questions about blowing the 1989 U.S. Open ("It still hurts") and about being named PGA Tour Player of the Year in 1989 ("It feels great").

Then he had lunch with Christy, his wife. Then he videotaped a couple of interviews for local TV sports shows. But there was still some daylight left in sunny Southern California, so where else would anyone who had followed his career expect to find Tom Kite, three hours after completing the day's round, but at his office, working?

You've got to understand that nobody works at the game of golf more than Tom Kite. Nobody. You want to see Tom Kite in his element, you go down to the practice range. Sooner or later he'll show up, and dollars to divots he stays there longer and hits more balls and wastes less time gabbing with reporters and other idlers on the range than anybody who ever wore spikes, with the possible exception of a fellow Texan from another generation by the name of Hogan.

Never mind that Kite had shot a couple of big numbers in the first two days of the first tournament of the 1990 season and was so far back in the pack that his chances of winning were only marginally better than mine. Never mind that most of his colleagues were logging more hours in La Costa's spa getting loofah rubs and herbal body wraps than at the range banging balls. Never mind that the Tournament of Champions, whose field consists exclusively of winners of tour events in the preceding year, has no cut to be made and hands out a check in the low five figures to the guy who finishes dead last.

Never mind any of that, because all you need to know to understand Tom Kite is that here he was, the all-time leading money winner in the history of golf, less than a week after the end of his greatest year ever, putting in hours at the practice range after two lackluster rounds in a tournament he had no chance of winning, doing everything he possibly could to make sure that the new year would be even better.

Tom Kite knows what got him to where he is. He knows what it will take to keep him there.

Shot after shot, more five irons soared into the fading sunlight than you and I will hit in a season. They followed the line of a fence that runs perpendicular to the tee and came softly to rest in a cluster that would fit inside a good-sized gazebo. But once he'd noted trajectory and line, Kite ignored the final half of the ball's flight and began setting up for the next shot. If I had hit any one of those five irons, which I might do about once every hundred swings, I would stand and gape in open admiration until the ball stopped rolling. That's why people look at eclipses: they don't happen that often.

Kite, of course, has hit enough golf balls in the last quarter century to have a pretty good idea where they're going to end up. Anyway, he had another agenda—all he was concerned about today was clearing his left side.

The sun began to sneak below the series of ridges that block sight of the Pacific Ocean about three miles away, and finally it became too hard in the failing light to follow the line of the ball, as deep shadows crept up the steep hills behind the range. But Kite still wanted to hit a few wedges, and he decided to make a game out of it.

"A bull's-eye and we'll go in," he told caddie Mike Carrick, who had been watching Tom's left hip for the last two hours, speaking up softly when it had been late in turning by so much as a nanosecond. Carrick nodded: a bull's-eye and we go in.

The target was a range marker set at exactly 115 yards from the afternoon's teeing area, a big red disk the size of a poker table on a white tee with white numerals. "C'mon, Tom," those of us in the small group standing around him said silently to ourselves. "Hit the bull's-eye so we can all go in."

Wedge after wedge landed close. If the marker had been the flagstick on the eighteenth hole at Pebble Beach, Kite would be looking at a lot more eight-footers than eighteen-footers. He is probably the best wedge player in the game, and he was demonstrating it. But this wasn't horseshoes, and close wasn't good enough, not today. Kite wanted to *hit* the marker. He *really* wanted to.

Remember when you were a kid late on a summer afternoon,

shooting baskets in the backyard after all the other kids had gone home? Just you, the rest of the world completely shut out, playing a game inside your head? Okay, ten straight short jumpers and then I can quit ("Glen Alan, dinner's ready!") . . . rushing your move because dusk is being outhustled by dark ("Glen Alan, you come in here right now and wash your hands!") . . . shooting by feel rather than sight ("Glen Alan, I mean it!") . . . until finally, exultantly, at the buzzer . . . *ten!*

How many times when Tom Kite was a kid did he stay out there on the range until, by God, he *did* hit that marker? Stay there, hitting wedge after wedge to the green on the seventy-second hole of the U.S. Open, until whoever was in charge ran him off, temporarily suspending pursuit of his dream? ("Get on home, Tommy. You're gonna be late for supper.")

It's the same deal now. Only now, as a grown-up, he understood that it was getting late and cold, and that there was a TV crew waiting anxiously to squeeze a little Q/A into the last few seconds of twilight, and that he wouldn't be running out onto the range to scoop up a few last balls to whack, the way he used to at the old Austin Country Club when he was a kid.

Time was running out, and so were the range balls. He had brought out the wedge when the bucket of new Titleists was three-quarters full, about thirty balls ago. He was now down to three. One, two, three strikes and you're out, right? Gotta hurry. Don't rush. Kite set his feet for the next shot, bent slightly at the waist, thrust his butt out, peered at the bull's-eye through saucer-sized spectacles, gave a final waggle, then triggered the smooth, compact swing that the season before earned him three tour victories and $1,395,000 in official prize money, the most anyone has ever won on the PGA Tour in a single season.

But little boys don't dream about being the leading money winner, no sir, they dream about winning tournaments, and right now that red marker out there was the eighteenth hole at Augusta, and Tom Kite was by God going to win the Masters with this very swing.

Cleck! The ball ascended into the gray-blue sky in a parabola identical to that followed by its predecessors. This time he had it for sure. It was dead on line. It couldn't miss. But it did, dropping four feet short.

"Only two left," Kite said to the handful of onlookers huddled around the only golfer left on the range. *Whish!* He'd barely completed the follow-through on his next swing when he said, "Only one chance now." He knew while the ball was still only quail-high that it was off line. And so it was, by a good eight feet. Close, but no green jacket.

The last ball. Except for a bit of nervous foot shuffling to relax tensed muscles, the little gallery was dead silent. Most of us had been there an hour or more. We were into it.

Everything now rested on one final swing. After the last two shots had come so close but still failed, hope had clearly faded. Suddenly it seemed unlikely. Oh well, it really was only the practice range at La Costa, not the seventy-second hole of the U.S. Open. Anyway, the idea is to get birdie-close with your wedge, not hole out.

C'mon, Tom, it's almost cocktail time.

Kite made the same smooth, precise, controlled swing at the last ball of the day that he had already applied to hundreds of its predecessors. This time, he followed the ball's flight as intently as the rest of us. As the ball rose into the dusk, Kite suddenly turned into Carlton Fisk in the twelfth inning of the sixth game of the 1975 World Series: he gave the wedge shot a little body English, a tight dip of the knees, and a shrug with his shoulders.

And just as Fisk's gyrations had worked in Fenway Park fifteen years before, sending his fly ball over the Green Monster and giving the Red Sox a victory, so Kite's body English worked now on the practice range at La Costa.

Clunk!

"Yes!" exclaimed someone in the hard-core group that had waited for this moment. "Yes!" said Kite in unison as he pumped the air with a clenched right fist, about the only sign of triumph he ever permits himself on the golf course.

A broad smile now creasing his freckled face, Kite turned away from the range and handed the wedge to Mike Carrick—who only then stepped back to reveal the extra ball he'd been hiding behind his foot. If Tom had missed, Mike was going to give him another "last one."

After all, as Mike knew better than anyone, buried deep in the soul of his middle-aged boss lived the dreams of a ten-year-old boy.

They say that hackers can't really learn anything from watching the pros, who play an utterly different game. They are wrong. Ever since that chilly January afternoon back in 1990 when I stood for nearly an hour watching Tom Kite hit shots into the Southern California twilight, my practice-range divots have been neat and compact.

Just like a pro's.

The
Hacker's
Game

It's All in the Wrists

The most exquisitely satisfying act in the world of golf is that of throwing a club. The full backswing, the delayed wrist action, the flowing follow-through, followed by that unique whirring sound, reminiscent only of a flock of passing starlings, is without parallel in sport.

—Henry Longhurst

A golfer who claims he has never, ever, not once in his entire lifetime thrown a golf club is like a candidate for president under fifty years old who swears he has never, ever, not once in his entire lifetime smoked a little grass.

At worst, the guy's a cold-blooded psychopathic liar who will someday go down to the local Wal-Mart, pull an Uzi out of his golf bag, and spray the checkout line.

At best, he's one of those weirdos you'd run into back in the late sixties, early seventies, usually at a big party in somebody's basement. You know the kind of party: bowls of clam dip, candles and incense, all the Boone's Farm varietals, Creedence blasting, strobes flashing, joints going around, a plate of brownies that caused everybody to laugh a lot. And there'd always be some guy eyeballing a tightly rolled cheroot someone had given him, holding it disdainfully at arm's length like it was a dog turd or something, and then passing it on, untoked, with a smugly superior look that foreshadowed Nancy Reagan after she quit the pills.

Either way, liar or psychopath, the golfer who claims he has never even *experimented* with club-throwing is not somebody you'd ever want to share a golf cart with. Or vote for, if ever he decides to run for political office.

But isn't it written somewhere that golf is a game of self-control, discipline, and restraint . . . a sport where untoward displays of temper are proscribed by a gentlemen's code . . . a noble activity not to be sullied with plebeian outbursts of commonplace emotion?

Sure, and pigs have wings.

Look, it's precisely because golf requires so much self-control that there needs to be a healthy, psyche-cleansing way for a golfer to flat-out lose it every now and then. When you've been slicing off the tee all day long, and you finally come to a dogleg right where a long banana will actually help, and then you proceed to snap-hook a blue darter into deep jungle—well, the emotion surging through your bloodstream at that moment is in no way commonplace.

Times like that, when the choice is between exploding and imploding, there is only one moral imperative: throw the bleeping club.

The immortal Bobby Jones, paradigm of all that is fine and true in the game of golf, launched many a mashie in his day. In the first round of the 1916 U.S. Amateur at Merion he threw *several* clubs. Of course, he was only fourteen years old at the time, so he couldn't be tried as an adult. But age didn't cure his temper. Five years later, at his first British Open at St. Andrews, Jones stormed off the Old Course midway through the wind-swept third round after posting a 46 on the front side and shooting double-triple to start the back side. (Yo, Immortal One—we've *all* had days like that.)

Jones would later swear off club-throwing and all other public manifestations of the volcanic rage that golf's frustrations are capable of igniting in the best of us. By the end of his startlingly brief competitive career, Jones was a paragon of gentlemanly behavior on the course. But by then the die was cast, not to mention any number of clubs. There's no escaping the fact that club-throwing helped make Bobby Jones the greatest golfer of his era. And if a little club-launching had helped the young Bobby Jones perfect *his* swing, who's to say it wouldn't do the same for yours and mine?

Great as Jones was, the all-time champion club thrower was the irrepressible Tommy Bolt. Golf fans who weren't even born the last time he launched a seven iron know this about the Tempestuous One. What Gerry Ford was to the shanked drive, Tommy Bolt was to the flying persimmon. Terrible Tommy. Thunder Bolt. The Man Who Threw Clubs.

From the reputation he's maintained all these years, you'd think Bolt never actually swung golf clubs, just threw them. The fact is, Tommy Bolt was a good golfer who won fifteen tournaments (including a U.S. Open) in over twenty-five years as a touring pro. Big temper? You betcha. Did it cost him a tournament here and there? Maybe. Would golf in his time have been a better game had he been as controlled and well behaved on the course as, say, Scott Simpson? No way.

For starters, Bolt insists his club-throwing was blown way out of proportion. "I never even threw a lot of golf clubs," he told *Golf* magazine contributing editor Mike Bryan a few years back. "I just got *credit* for throwing a lot."

Credit? As in advanced placement?

"Yes," said Bolt, "I only threw about six in my career."

Six? You mean per round, don't you?

What the hell, let's not quibble about numbers: the fact is, Bolt's reputation for club-throwing *was* far greater than his actual number of thrown clubs ever warranted. Had to be. Nobody could have airmailed as many clubs as popular imagination had him launching and still have enough sticks left to finish the back nine. Bolt regrets that his reputation for club disposal tended to obscure appreciation of his abilities, but he also recognizes that "that reputation made me a lot of money."

Drive for show, throw for dough? Something like that, at least for Tommy Bolt.

Well aware of what the crowd wanted, Bolt fed that reputation now and then by pretending he was going to fling one just to get a rise out of the gallery. Golf fans followed him around for the same reason that people go to car races (no matter *what* they say): to see a fiery crack-up. Because there was always the threat (or hope) that Tommy would oblige them, Bolt became one of the most popular figures in the game in the fifties.

A close friend and sometime student of Ben Hogan, Bolt was himself a mentor to younger touring pros, at least in the attitude department. When Arnold Palmer first came on the tour in 1955, he often traveled with Bolt. "He didn't know which way to throw his clubs!" Bolt recalled a few years ago. "He'd throw them backwards! I taught Arnold to throw them *forward* so he could pick them up on the way."

Bolt says Palmer was "vicious on the golf course" when he first started out. Ditto Sam Snead. And Bobby Jones was "the most temperamental golfer who ever lived." But who got all the ink for his ferocity on the fairways? Bolt.

What Tommy Bolt brought to the party was color, a transfusion of which the PGA Tour could well use today. His temper was only the flashiest part of a big, flaps-down personality that made for great entertainment. But the show also included some lights-out golf: for a while, the 1958 U.S. Open winner and two-time PGA champion was arguably the best player on tour. At least Terrible Tommy would make that argument, and who's going to argue with a guy with his kind of rep and a club in his hand?

This is going to sound cranky and old-fartish, but today's pros just don't seem to have a knack for throwing clubs. Petulance, pouting, whining, surliness—they're great at all that, along with any number of other ways to communicate anger and frustration at the most frustrating game ever invented. But they don't know diddly about throwing clubs. When was the last time you saw a member of the PGA Tour really cut loose and give an offending weapon the old heave-ho? It happens, but only rarely—and when it does, it's never on TV.

Remember a couple of years back at the Players Championship when Robert Gamez took an 11 at the seventeenth hole, aka the Famous Island Green? Plink-plank-plunk, he lobbed balls into the water with a consistency worthy of a 25-handicapper. But when Gamez finally landed one fairly on the putting surface, did he then take the next logical step and commit his contaminated stick to a watery grave? He did not. He handed it to his caddie, gave the TV camera a meek grin, waved lamely to the cheering gallery, and two-putted for his double quadruple.

In my book, that pretty much summed up what's wrong with the PGA Tour today: no imagination. Not to single out young Gamez, a decent fellow and a credit to his profession, but please: you drown enough balls to raise the water level in the lake by a good six inches, and you actually let the club that did it *live*? The cherry on the sundae for every golf fan who witnessed Gamez's ordeal that day would have been the sight of Robert's club tracing an end-over-end arc through the azure Florida sky on its way to burial at sea. And for those of us watching from the comfort of our own living rooms, there would have been the added attraction of instant replay.

How could Gamez have *not* thrown a club—*all* his clubs—into the water under those circumstances?

But even when today's pros do throw clubs, they try to make sure it's off-camera. That's a pity. At the 1992 Honda Classic, Paul Azinger—the PGA Tour's Tom Sawyer—drowned his driver, as did John Huston, the journeyman's journeyman. Zinger just shifted to a three wood, finished the round, and left town. Huston had second thoughts. He remembered that the club he had just disposed of was his favorite driver, so he went into the water to retrieve it. Up to his knees, then his waist, then his chest, Huston felt along the bottom of the pond with his feet until he found his driver—at which point he submarined down and fetched it up. Now, that move showed us something. Tour caddies, also impressed, immediately christened Huston with the perfect nickname: "Swamp Thing."

Was this amphibious mission shown on live TV? Did it appear in the next day's highlights? Or show up in *This Week on the PGA Tour* on ESPN? No, it most certainly did not.

Not to be overly paranoid, but I do think Oliver Stone ought to look into the possibility of a conspiracy by the PGA Tour to shield its dark underside from an eager public. There was *no* TV coverage of the Huston salvage operation, although reliable sources report that NBC did get the entire thing on tape. Why hasn't it been made public? Why have American golfers been deprived of the right to see a member in good standing of the PGA Tour behave exactly like them? Who is responsible for this cover-up?

You've got to figure there's a secret deal between Commissioner Beman and TV: no unflattering images, please. Hey, there's precedent. For instance, the PGA tour doesn't exactly have a formal policy against smoking. That would have been a little ludicrous during the years of its multimillion-dollar contract with RJR-Nabisco; not even the tour's image managers tried to convince anyone that the sponsorship dough came from cookies rather than cigarettes. But tour officials have made it clear, informally, that it's not good for the tour image for players to smoke when TV cameras are around.

Serious weed fiends like Ben Crenshaw no doubt find this nerve-racking. But a TV camera once caught Crenshaw copping a drag at a tournament back in the mid-eighties, and Gentle Ben allegedly got a call from the commissioner himself. Since then, Crenshaw has forsaken tobacco, at least on the course. As much as he smokes *off* the course, Crenshaw is probably ready to jump out of his skin by the third hole, which may explain the decline in his performance since winning the 1984 Masters.

. . .

Curtis Strange does not have a reputation as a club thrower. Perhaps when he was younger he launched a club or two, but none have been spotted airborne in recent years. One reason may be the size of the galleries that began to follow him after his first U.S. Open title in 1988: a prudent businessman, Strange must well have thought twice about throwing a club given the likelihood of hitting someone and the certainty of litigation if he did. Another reason may be the multimillion-dollar endorsement deal Strange signed with the Maruman club people of Japan in 1991.

A set of Maruman irons retails for $600 and up—*way* up, all the way up to $2,000, which is seriously up. Matching Maruman woods range from $155 to $700 per club. Now, if *I* manufactured clubs that sold for just under $5,000 per set, I'd want to have something in the contract with the guy I was paying several gazillion bucks to play with them that he ought not to fold, mutilate, or throw one every time he shanked a ball into the water, both on general principle and on the odd chance that it might be bad for sales. Is that too much to ask?

But if Strange is not a club thrower, he is most certainly a man of considerable passion, with the ability to express it in language every bit as salt-and-peppery as his hair.

Let me say here and now that I consider this a virtue, not a vice. Churchill was right: the language is poor enough without proscribing the use of certain words. And let me add that, in private, Strange is a genuinely funny, intelligent man whose candor and directness, along with his willingness to tell a joke at his own expense and his capacity for self-criticism, are altogether refreshing.

(In the interest of objective reporting, it must be noted that some veterans of the press corps remember Strange as a surly, ill-tempered jerk. Maybe he's changed.)

Sometimes, though, Strange's temper and mouth—combined with his celebrity—do get him in trouble. For instance, a few years back during the second round of the PGA Championship, he was lining up a little chip shot from just off the green when an accredited professional photographer working inside the gallery ropes began snapping pictures. That is forbidden: once a player has addressed his ball, a photographer with media credentials may not release his shutter until the shot is made. Strange stepped back, asked the photographer sharply but not discourteously to cease and desist, and stepped back up to his ball. The photographer clicked again, so Strange stepped back and spoke to him a second time, only this time his words were captured by an ESPN sound man with a field microphone and sent out live over the airwaves:

"If you don't stop snapping that bleeping camera, I'll shove it up your bleeping bleep." (Or words to that effect.)

Never mind that the photographer was in direct violation of an agreement he had signed upon receipt of the media credentials that allowed him to be there in the first place. Never mind that Strange was unaware that the ESPN mike was in the vicinity. Never mind that if the mike hadn't been there, only the photographer and about fifteen other people nearby would have heard Strange. (He said the words; he didn't scream them.) Never mind any of that, because a couple of million people had just heard the reigning U.S. Open champion use the f-word on national television.

Now, there are graybeards among us who can remember when it was rare and shocking to hear anyone say that word in mixed company. Guys said it—hey, we were *guys*—but not around persons of the opposite sex. And when a *female* said it, wow! Heads would turn. Ears would perk up. The air would crackle with an instant charge of anticipation. Coming from a female's lips at a polite social gathering, the word back then imparted a fresh, exciting, daring, sharp, sophisticated aura, like a movie with subtitles. Most of all, it was surprising.

(I know this must sound really quaint, incredibly stupid, utterly dubious in the Age of Rap. But yes, Virginia, there was really a time when that was the way things were.)

In case you lay down for a nap in 1958 and just woke up, you should know that times have changed—and I think we have the sixties to thank. Since shortly after Dylan went electric, there have been no gender rules regarding who can use what words. If you doubt it, try eavesdropping on a gaggle of eleven-year-old girls hanging out after school: it will singe your ear hairs. In one sense, this can be taken as a sign of progress, a victory for Churchill. In another sense, it's a pity, because the old f-word has long since lost so much of its shock value that you wonder why network television's hall monitors still bother clipping it out of movies and bleeping it from talk shows.

Some years ago, well after the language walls had come tumblin' down, I drove down from New York to a solidly middle-class suburb of Washington, D.C., to watch my teenage daughter play soccer. As a dutiful father, I had expected to spend a boring hour or so watching a covey of thirteen-year-olds squeal and giggle as they tried ineptly to kick a moving target. What I saw instead was an exciting athletic contest between two well-trained teams of skilled soccer players. I was startled.

(Okay, so report me to the enforcement division of NOW. Maybe I should have known better, but when I was growing up, the only sport young girls played was six-to-a-side basketball. The way I figured it, Babe Didrikson Zaharias, Louise Suggs, and Mickey Wright must have been born full-grown adults with the ability to hit a golf ball farther and straighter than most men.)

My consciousness significantly raised, I then had my ears blown off midway through the second half by the following exchange—reported here verbatim—between two comely, well-brought-up young girls who had gone down in a heap near the sideline after a particularly hard tackle:

"You little bitch!"

"You asshole!"

"Fuck you!"

"Fuck you!"

"No, fuck *you!*"

"No, fuck *you!*"

Parents on the sideline stood transfixed, but nobody seemed able or willing to step in and stop it, least of all the two male coaches and the male referees. Had the soccer players been boys, mind you, the coaches would have jerked them up short after the first fuck-yous. On all the sports teams I played on way back when, one of the cardinal rules was No Cussing. An umpire heard you cussing, you were out of the game. Period. But these were girls, and the male authority figures present were utterly helpless. Fortunately, the two young ladies finally ran out of gas (or maybe contracted laryngitis), and order was restored.

To parents of teenage kids these days this may well seem like no big deal: no harm, no foul. The words are just words. Let's worry about serious matters like safe sex, birth control, drugs, alcohol abuse, and that D in calculus. Forget about trivial stuff. The kids are alright.

But in Curtis Strange's case, there *was* harm (or at least the perception thereof) because it went out live on TV, thereby subjecting golf junkies—who else would be watching a golf tournament on cable on Friday afternoon?—to certain words they hadn't heard since, oh, the last time they played golf. Goodness gracious, something must be done, and what the PGA Tour did was fine Strange an undisclosed amount for "unprofessional conduct."

Consistent with standard policy, neither the amount nor even the fact of the fine was made public: the tour likes to keep its dirty laundry in the hamper. Strange, however, would have none of that. The father of two boys, then nine and seven, Strange insisted that the commissioner's office confirm publicly that he had been fined. Furthermore, he issued a public letter of apology in which he admitted his wrongdoing and expressed his sincere regret for the incident.

"I wanted the boys to understand that their father could make a mistake," he explained afterward, "and that when you make a mistake, you have to accept the consequences."

Screaming obscenities at the top of your lungs after a botched shot is, for my money, a whole lot worse than flinging the club responsible for the botching. Not because you might be playing on a course in a residential neighborhood populated by impressionable children watching a Madonna video on MTV, but because I might be within earshot lining up a downhill putt with a sharp left-to-right break. Who hears a club whistling through the air? My case rests.

There is, I am absolutely convinced, a place in golf for club-throwing—although that place is not necessarily when surrounded by a gallery, any one of whom might sue at the loss of an eye.

One golfer on the PGA Tour, Ken Green, used to throw a club after every shot—not because he was angry, but because tossing a club to caddie Joe La Cava was part of the show that Green liked to put on for the gallery. Like his hideous green shoes, the club toss was a Green signature, as much a part of him as the fiddle was to Jack Benny.

(La Cava now carries for Fred Couples, who *never* throws clubs.)

Green has, of course, always been a bit, ah, different. Once, when a sportswriter was visiting his house for an interview, Green opened the French doors of his rec room and started pounding two-iron shots off the carpet, through the open doors, out across the backyard, and over a small lake at the back of his North Palm Beach house. From time to time he takes potshots at Commissioner Beman, most recently on the issue of Bermuda shorts: "Why can't we wear them in tournaments? They do on the LPGA Tour." Currently, he is the only member of the PGA Tour—perhaps the most clean-shaven aggregation of males this side of Ross Perot's corporate headquarters—to sport a full beard.

Once shunned by established players, most of whom would rather handle snakes than tolerate a maverick in their midst, Green has at last earned respect for his game and his integrity and, along with that, greater toleration of his idiosyncracies. At a Ryder Cup team meeting on the night before the final matches in 1989, Green got up and said to his teammates, "You know, before coming here, there was a lot about you guys that I didn't like." Team captain Ray Floyd responded: "You know, Kenny, there was a lot about you that *we* didn't like." The room didn't turn into a sweat lodge and there was no tom-tom beating, but the team—including Green—did bond.

True, after an especially bad shot, a Green-to-caddie "toss" might have enough mustard on it to bear suspiciously close resemblance to a "thrown club" and thereby be grounds on the PGA Tour for a stiff fine. But anyone who follows Ken Green around a course for eighteen holes or so comes away with the distinct impression that here is a guy who, should he decide to throw a club, will really *throw* it. This is the golfer, after all, who every season drowns several putters, and each time it's for the perfectly good reason that "it was time for the club to die."

Mind you, I'm not advocating wholesale club-throwing: if abused, the fine art of club-throwing would suffer the same fate as the f-word and lose its ability to surprise. Also, if most of us threw a club after all our bad shots, we'd have to go in for rotator cuff surgery after every round. But if you do throw a club, and you will, you should at least do it the right way. You know what they say: if a thing is worth doing, it's worth doing *well.*

Perhaps the *worst* way is to skitter the offending club along the ground with a wristy toss while holding your arm close to your side in a pathetic attempt to disguise the fact that you are actually throwing it. A noted writer from *Sports Illustrated* once did that in my presence after a poor second shot from the eighteenth fairway at the Old Course in St. Andrews, in full sight of the Royal and Ancient Clubhouse! What could he have been thinking? That Old Tom Morris wouldn't see him?

You also want to be careful *where* you throw a club. Ben Crenshaw once flung his putter straight up after stubbing a three-footer, and the club came down on the back of his head, knocking him to his knees and drawing blood. Divine retribution? No, I prefer to think of it as poor technique.

But where is one to learn *proper* club-throwing technique? Not once in all the thousands of (mostly contradictory) instructional articles in the golf magazines do you read a word about club-throwing. Ditto the scores of golf books and tapes that come out every year. The golf schools are silent on the subject, and no teaching pro will admit to any knowledge of it. Go back to when Old Tom Morris was young, go back to when Hell Bunker and the Principal's Nose at the Old Course were sheep burrows, go back as far as you want in the history of golf, and what do you find written about proper club-throwing technique? Nothing, that's what: it's all word of mouth, hearsay, trial and error.

Until now, that is. Now, for the first time, I am proud to offer a primer on how to throw a golf club.

CLUB-THROWING TECHNIQUE 101

1. **Aim.** Always throw the club up the fairway, never behind you or to the side. This will save time in retrieval. And never, ever throw the club straight up. (See Crenshaw incident, above.)

2. **Proper Alignment.** The initial impulse to throw a club will come at the end of your follow-through, when your feet are still (presumably) on a line running toward the target and your body is turned at the waist with your belt buckle facing in the same direction. This is *not* a good position from which to launch a club. Instead, bring your right foot forward and square it with your left on a line perpendicular to the intended line of club flight so that your body is facing directly up the fairway. (Left-handers, bring your left foot forward.)

3. **Grip.** While some favor the two-handed throw (either interlocking or overlapping), the release requires finely tuned tim-

ing that may be beyond the capability of the casual club thrower. Unless both hands release at precisely the same time, the throw will go seriously—and embarrassingly—off line. Instead, grip the club firmly but not tightly in your right hand, with the V formed by your thumb and forefinger pointing toward your right shoulder. (Left-handers, of course, reverse these directions.)

4. **Forward Press.** The forward press in the golf swing is slight, almost imperceptible. For the club throw, it is definite and pronounced. Stride forward with your right leg, making sure to place your right foot at a forty-five-degree angle to the intended line of flight to facilitate your body turn. (Left-handers . . . aw, the hell with it: learn to throw righty.)

5. **Load and Fire Your Right Side.** With your right foot planted at an angle, let your lower body continue to move forward as you swing your left leg toward the target. At the same time, your right arm (club in hand) goes straight back and your upper body rocks slightly toward the rear as your right side "loads up." Your right leg, bent slightly to maintain balance, now uncoils and your right arm whips forward.

6. **Three-Quarters Overhand.** More-experienced club throwers will sometimes opt for the straight overhand throw, but beginners and intermediates will find that a three-quarters overhand throw is easier to control. In addition, a three-quarter motion places less strain on the thrower's shoulder.

7. **Caution: No Sidewinders!** The notorious Ewell Blackwell Sidearm Hurl, long ago prohibited by the R&A and the USGA, is exceedingly dangerous and should never be used. A sidearm throw causes the club to rotate in the air parallel to the ground like a scythe, endangering everything in its path. Moreover, the slightest miscalculation of the proper release point could cause the club to shoot out sideways rather than forward and maim a member of your foursome, thereby incurring a one-stroke penalty.

8. **Plant and Release.** The club should be released as the left

foot is planted (with left leg flexing at the knee to absorb the forward thrust of the body) and at a point when the extended right arm is at approximately two o'clock. (Ten o'clock for left-handers.) While baseball imagery can generally be useful in visualizing the proper club-throwing technique, it is misleading with regard to the release point. A club must be released much higher than a baseball, lest the twirling club head strike the ground too forcefully and snap off at the hosel. The idea is to throw the club, not destroy it.

9. **Keep Your Eye on the Club.** Particularly important when there is a gully, creek bed, or stand of trees along your target line. Nothing is more embarrassing than to throw a club and then have to ask a playing partner where it went.

The third hole (formerly the twelfth) at Stevens Park Municipal Golf Course in Dallas, where I misspent so much of my youth back in the fifties and early sixties, is a treacherous, tricky, essentially unfair 300-yard dogleg-right par four: 170 yards to an out-of-bounds fence, then a ninety-degree right turn 130 yards straight up a steep hill to a crowned green framed by trees. "Mount Sinai," my brother Henry used to call it when he played the course in the thirties, only he turned Mount Sinai into a 235-yard molehill by following the hypotenuse of the right triangle.

In non-Euclidean terms, that means he would take out his three wood and wallop the ball high and over the hillside trees guarding the front right of the green. When he made it, he was putting for an eagle. When he didn't, he was chipping from just off the green for a chance at a birdie.

After he told me about this approach, I had to try it. Sure sounded more promising than my way of playing the hole, which was either (a) to drive it too far and have the ball roll out-of-bounds or (b) to drive it too short and leave myself an impossible pitch over the trees. What did I have to lose?

The last four balls in my bag, for starters, because the first time I played the hole Henry's way, I slashed every drive into a thicket short and far, far right of the green. (Did I mention that my brother was a two handicap at Stevens Park? Well, he was. And I wasn't.)

But the four balls weren't all I lost that day. After my fourth tee shot had disappeared into the thick brush, I had by God had it. The minute I saw the ball disappear, I gave a mighty yell and threw my driver—actually an old Tommy Armour brassie that had been my father's favorite club—straight up into the air as hard as I could. Up, up, up it went, up to the top branches of a tall oak tree next to the tee. My playing partners and I shrunk back, looked up into the noonday sun, and shielded our heads as best we could. We needn't have bothered, because it never came down. We looked and looked, but we never saw it. It's as if the club disappeared into thin air. For all I know, that old brassie with the scarred persimmon head and the stiff steel shaft and the binding held down with a piece of white tape and the worn, smooth leather grip that my father had once wrapped his long, powerful fingers around is still up there in that tree.

And, believe it or not, in the thirty-four years since I tried to climb Mount Sinai the hard way, I have never thrown another golf club.

At least not that far.

A Craftsman and His Tools

Man is a tool-using animal.
Without tools he is nothing,
with tools he is all.
                    —Thomas Carlyle

Golf clubs aren't only tools.
They're totems. The game turns
on illusions.
                    —Frank Hannigan
                    (former executive
                    director of the USGA)

Remember the TV ad where an overnight delivery service transforms a pitty-pat short hitter into Long John Daly minus the mousy mustache? You know, the one CBS runs after every fourth putt during the third round of the Wal-Mart–Andy Rooney Greater Kalamazoo Classic. Doesn't ring a bell? Let me refresh your memory.

The scene is the first tee of Gnarled Pine Lakes Hills Country Club, U.S.A. In the foreground, a guy looks anxiously around, as if he were expecting somebody, then steps up to his ball and gives a nervous little waggle. Over his shoulder we catch a glimpse of his playing partner, a guy with a big, confident grin splitting his face. Then a voice calls out from the pro shop: "Mr. Hagen, your new graphites just arrived." "Yes!" our once anxious protagonist hisses exultantly as he bolts off the tee to sign for the delivery.

"On Saturday?" asks his nonplussed playing partner, suddenly uneasy about the number of strokes he's giving up. And worry he should, because when our hero steps back on the tee, brandishing his newly delivered driver, he looks six inches taller and fifty yards longer.

Cut to real life.

A couple of years ago, four of us had a Saturday morning tee time at Cranwell, a course in the Berkshires in western Massachusetts. Despite the imposing manor house that lent the course its name, the course was a scraggly dog track hacked out of the forest surrounding a once great estate that has long since been reborn as a conference center. But it didn't matter to us that we weren't teeing it up at The Country Club in Brookline. It was summer, it was a weekend, and it was golf.

The other perpetrators in the foursome were Michael, a more than usually wild lefty who tends to follow every mishit (and there are always several) with a full-throated scream ("You stink!"); Okie, whose signature tee shot is the "Thumper," in which his driver hits the ground about three inches behind the tee before dealing the ball a glancing blow; and Lee, whose swing looks beautiful to the untrained eye but whose short fuse typically produces a low-yield nuclear explosion by the seventh hole.

One thing united us: we stunk.

We were also crazy about the game. Literally crazy. This was the foursome's Manic Period, and we were insatiable. We played everywhere and anytime we could, but never enough, so each outing inevitably took on the significance of a fifth major. For two or three days before a match, everyone would be thinking ahead about the upcoming round the way a teenager who's just had sex for the first time looks forward to his next date.

(Everyone but Okie, that is. He never thinks about golf until he's on the first tee. Maybe he's not so crazy after all.)

This may help explain what transpired late on Tuesday night

before the Saturday outing, when Lee discovered the answer to his most fervent prayers: a sure cure for his slice. There it was in black and white, staring out at him from a small classified ad in the back of one of the golf magazines. A driver, a special driver, a *magical* driver, specifically designed to straighten out the most deviant slicers. Handcrafted from well-seasoned persimmon by a custom clubmaker somewhere in Winesburg, Middle America, the Magic Wand[1] was made in limited quantities and was not available in pro shops, golf discount stores, or catalogues. Mail order only, please, direct from the artisan; no credit cards; personal checks accepted; $335 plus shipping; allow three weeks for delivery.

Three *weeks?* But we were playing in three *days!* So the next morning Lee got on the phone. The more he talked to the clubmaker, the more convinced Lee became that he had to have the Magic Wand—and by Saturday morning. Yes, the craftsman finally admitted, he did have a club available to send, but it was his practice to allow sufficient time for a customer's check to clear before shipping; surely Lee would understand. Of course, said Lee, which is why I will send you a *certified* check by overnight mail, and you can send me the Magic Wand by overnight delivery so that I will have it in time to use Saturday, okay?

Okay. Had the clubmaker been greedy, he could have said at this moment, "Ooops, my mistake. The only Magic Wand I have in stock is a special-special edition at two thousand dollars." Money, by this time, was no object to Lee. The Magic Wand was the *only* object. But the clubmaker refrained from taking advantage of the situation, perhaps figuring that Lee had enough problems already.

So it came to pass that a bright, shiny new driver stood proudly in Lee's bag when we stepped up to the first tee that Saturday—and stayed there, untouched, when Lee startled us all

---

[1] That wasn't its real name. Its real name is lost to history. But that's okay because all too soon, as you will see, so was the club.

by teeing off with his three wood. Lee explained that he might be nuts, but he wasn't *crazy*. The course had no practice range, and Lee figured his first swing of the day was not going to be with a brand-new club. Better to leave it in his bag until he got warmed up, then bring it out only on certain holes. No need to rush things.

Intelligent golf strategy is not exactly a hallmark of our foursome's approach to the game, so perhaps we didn't fully appreciate the magnitude of Lee's restraint—even when, at first, it seemed to be working. His initial drive with his three wood sailed to the right, but fortunately it wasn't struck solidly enough to reach trouble. His tee shot on the second hole had a more pronounced banana bend, but he had aimed so far to the left that the ball stayed in the fairway. So far, so good—but not for long.

The third hole was a short, wide-open par five with no trouble anywhere off the tee except for a stand of trees far to the right. That, unfortunately, was precisely where Lee's tee shot landed. Several inventive expletives later, the three wood was banished rather abruptly to the bag. "Mulligan," he announced. At the time we followed a fairly generous mulligan policy—one per side plus one wild card plus one under "special circumstances"—so he was well within the Rules of Golf, as amended. And out came the Magic Wand.

It's important to explain that just to the left of the third tee—not at all in play—was a swamp. Home to every biting insect known to exist in New England, the fetid bog was choked with long grass, thick shrubbery, a variety of snakes, and skinny, stunted, water-logged trees. But not in play, remember.

At least it wasn't until Lee gave his second ball a mighty lash with the Magic Wand. He got all of it, his most solid hit of the day, but a pronounced outside-in swing path, a weak grip, and a wide-open club face on impact somehow imparted a right-of-right flight plan. *Far* right. Like a Darryl Strawberry home run, Lee's drive soared into the stratosphere, only it was going foul by at least one time zone. This was the Godzilla of slices, a high-flying top banana that went deeper into the woods than Little Red Riding Hood. And *now* the swamp to the left of the tee came into play.

Without so much as a pause at the top of his follow-through, Lee planted his left foot and yanked the club back to a fully cocked position. Then he fired his right side and brought the club down again at breathtaking speed, sweeping the club head forward even faster than before. And, just as Harold Connolly used to unleash his hammer in the Olympics, Lee released the Magic Wand at exactly the point in the swing's arc that would impart maximum thrust.

As majestic a sight as the long, powerful slice into the woods on the right had been, the Magic Wand sailing deep into the swamp sharply to the left was even grander. One reason was the surprise factor: we'd all half expected to see the two-dollar ball go right, but none of us was prepared to see the $335 club go left.

Another reason we all stood there dumbstruck with awe was the beautiful spontaneity of the act. Throwing a club is usually a semiconscious response to a terrible shot; that microsecond of calculation is what sometimes makes a club throw seem so ugly a thing on the course. But Lee's heave was, in contrast to either of his drives, utterly unpremeditated and instinctive. One moment the club was in his hands; the next moment it was simply gone.

Long gone.

Lee put on his rain suit—including the jacket, for protection from bugs—and sloshed into the bog in the general direction his new club had taken. We let two foursomes play through while he searched, but when he emerged twenty minutes later, his shoes ruined by slimy water and soaked to the skin with sweat, he had nothing to show for his troubles but insect bites on every square inch of exposed flesh. His custom-made, limited edition, overnight-delivered, $335 (plus shipping) Magic Wand belonged to the swamp.

There are undoubtedly several morals to be drawn from this

story, but the most useful one may be this: it is the poor crafts-man who blames his tools.

I know. We all know. And yet we continue to feed what has become a $20-billion-per-year business, figuring that if we can just get our hands on the right clubs, our game will be miracu-lously transformed.

To play basketball, all you need is a ball, a pair of sneaks, and access to a public park with a court. For touch football or soccer, it's more or less the same. Baseball and softball, ditto. Tennis? Even the most expensive racquet can't touch the outlay for top-of-the line golf gear.

In the eight years since I fell off the wagon and took up the game again, I have purchased two complete sets of woods and irons, four drivers, two "utility" clubs, and one putter. (I am particularly proud of the restraint I have demonstrated in the putter department.) In addition, I have bought three golf bags, four travel bags (I'm on the road a lot), one pull cart, dozens of gloves, five pairs of golf shoes, and one sleeve of balls.

Sound like a lot? No way. If the golf boom depended on me for survival, it would have gone bust a long time ago. The fact is, I'm a piker compared with most golfers when it comes to spending money for new golf equipment. At least that's what I tell my wife.

We throw good money after bad like lemmings going for a swim because we are mortally convinced that somewhere there exists a driver that will give us twenty extra yards, a long iron that we can get off the ground, a fairway wood that won't top the ball, a chipping iron that contains no chili dips, a wedge that will drop a ball softly on the green just over the trap, and a putter that will sink all four-footers for par.

For a barometer of the madness that has overcome America, wrangle a pass some January to the annual PGA Merchandise Show in Orlando.

Ten years ago, it was virtually a family affair—a couple of

thousand people, tops. Now upwards of 28,000 club pros, sales reps, and manufacturers from thirty countries descend on Orlando to inspect the wares displayed by 700-plus exhibitors in 2,600 exhibition booths spread out over 270,000 square feet. Every year the numbers grow; every year one wonders how—and why.

Dog-and-pony shows starring the likes of Greg Norman and Curtis Strange and Payne Stewart lend celebrity to the affair, but the main event is always whatever is *new*. New clubs, new shoes, new putters, new anything that pro shops and discount stores can grab up to feed the endless craving by golfers for quick fixes of bad swings.

Figured out a new dimple arrangement for your ball? Have a new glove that absorbs sweat and turns it into gin? Created a new club-head design that reduces wind resistance, accelerates to Mach 2 through the hitting zone, and hums the "Ode to Joy"? Built a new club that straightens out hooks, bends slices back into the fairway, adds twenty yards to your drive, and gives you a deep oil massage? The PGA Merchandise Show is the place to introduce it.

At the 1992 show, for example, the Ping people announced that their new Zing irons were ready to ship. Just *announced it*, mind you: they didn't show up with a model or even so much as a picture of the things.

They wrote orders for 40,000 sets.

There is, to be sure, much more to golf equipment than clubs and balls. There is also golf *stuff.*

Every December, just before Christmas, a good friend calls to recite an itemized list of golf stuff that she is *not* giving me as Christmas presents. Thus far, Kathleen has not given me bar glasses, coffee mugs, ashtrays, coasters, cocktail napkins, key chains, pens, pencils, swizzle sticks, statuettes, salt and pepper shakers, commemorative plates, or photos and prints (suitable for framing) if they bear so much as a hint of a golf leitmotif.

Not that I have escaped completely unscathed; no one who ever admits to playing an occasional round of golf ever does. On my desk are three frosted-glass golf ball paperweights and a plastic golf ball ice bucket currently in use as a receptacle for spare change. In a drawer are *three* range finders. Over in a corner sits a ten-pound box of monogrammed tees. All gifts from well-meaning nongolfers.

But were it not for good-taste rangers like Kathleen, I'd be up to my niblick in clever golf plaques ("Golf Is Not a Matter of Life and Death—It's *Much* More Important Than That"), bookends in the form of golf bags, and caddie statues to station on my front lawn, if I had a front lawn.

Eternal vigilance is the price of liberty from golf stuff. The following items, culled from a couple of the major golf stuff catalogues, are just the tip of the iceberg:

○GRIPTUBE. For only $9.95, a patented poly-bristled grip scrubber that "restores grips to like-new condition by scrubbing away dirt, oil, and flaking rubber." So *that's* my problem—flaking rubber!

○KRIS KRINGLE GOLFERS' SHORTS. As in underwear. Just $12.95 a pair, with a jolly Santa golfing against a bright-green background. One-hundred-percent cotton and "sure to make you the talk of the bedroom or locker room." No argument about that in my bedroom.

○PAR-B-QUE. The perfect barbecue utensil set for your nine-teenth-hole cookout! Long fork and burger flipper have golf grip handles; sauce brush has handle in shape of a tee. A mere $25.99.

○CHOCOLATE GOLF BALLS. And now, for a little dessert, a double sleeve of regulation-size golf balls, four white chocolate and two milk chocolate. $13.95. Caution: do not confuse them with . . .

○. . . THE EXPLODER. "The always popular golf gag." You've seen it: guy tees up a ball, takes a mighty cut, and the ball explodes in a cloud of smokelike powder. You haven't? Here, take one of mine . . . Only $2.95 (three for $7.95).

○CRAZY PUTTER. Comes complete with a horn to clear the way, a candle for night putting, a lucky rabbit's foot, a level for accuracy, and a tape measure for distance. Just $19.95. "A great gag gift." You bet.

○LETTER OPENER. Solid pewter with finely detailed golf bag handle. It's no CRAZY PUTTER, but for $14.95 it will open your mail.

○GOLFER'S TOILET SEAT. On the top of the lid, a tasteful three-frame sequential drawing of ball approaching hole, hanging on lip, and dropping in. "The gift that won't be duplicated." Is that a promise? $29.95.

Even more insidious is the golf stuff that promises to improve your game. It's one thing to resist a pair of pajamas covered in jolly little golfers; it's quite another thing to pass up an item that might take a stroke or two off your handicap. Consider the following:

○POWER-STIK. A two-foot metal bar with sponge-covered twisting pads. The idea, demonstrated by none other than a seemingly embarrassed Tom Kite, is to hold the bar out in front of you and twist it, thereby building "those muscles that effect both power and control in your golf game, the wrists and forearms." Just look at the promised benefits: longer, more controlled shots . . . more control in rough and sand . . . improved touch around the greens . . . more flexibility in hands and fingers for putting feel . . . prevention of tennis/golf elbow. All that for just $33.95? Wow.

○BLAST-OFF TEE. A plastic tee, costing $5.79, that will give you up to 4 percent more distance. (Nearly six bucks for a *tee*? You've got to be kidding.) Bite your tongue: golfers *never* kid about more distance. This tee is special. According to a New York University professor of physics, "a ball struck from the 'Blast-Off Tee' will travel farther than an identical ball struck in an identical way from a wooden tee." How does he know? Computer modeling, of course. Look, this guy's not some flimflam artist who will say anything for a buck: he's a bona fide Ph.D.

who is only interested in the pursuit of truth, not in prostituting himself on the altar of commerce. Besides, the BLAST-OFF is "Custom Molded from a secret energy-releasing practice formula." Why *wouldn't* it add ten yards to my drive?

○GROOVER. With a hacksaw, cut through the shaft of your driver about a foot up from the hosel, then reattach the two pieces of the club with a hinge, and—presto!—you've just built yourself a GROOVER. If you are not handy with tools (which you most likely are not or your handicap would be lower), you can buy a GROOVER ready-made for just $99, complete with a video starring Scott Hoch that shows you how to use it to "groove the perfect swing." The GROOVER is a real club, but "because of its special design, you'll be unable to hit a ball with it unless you put a perfect swing on the ball." Take the club away too fast and it will "break" at the hinge; put it in the wrong position at the top of your backswing and it will "break" again. Swing with perfect tempo and a correct weight shift and you can hit balls with the GROOVER. Swing the way you normally do and you can coldcock yourself with a nob-knocker to the cerebellum.

○SWING LINK. Not to be confused with the SWING TRAC hawked by Mark Brooks, or THE CONNECTOR that Jimmy Ballard says is the key to scratch golf, the SWING LINK ($29.95) is an elasticized cloth harness that wraps around your upper body and arms, rather like the business part of a straitjacket. Developed by Guru-to-the-Stars David Leadbetter, the SWING LINK "links the arms and body together in a single unit, thereby keeping the body in control and the arms in the proper position to encourage the body pivot." It's also useful as a restraining device to prevent a golfer who has just hit three consecutive balls into the water from diving in after them—or at least for making sure that he drowns if he does. "It works for Nick Faldo," says the ad. "Will it work for you?"

Sure it will. How could you ever doubt it?

Golf in the
Asphalt Jungle

I love this dirty town.
—Burt Lancaster in
Sweet Smell of Success

New York, New York—it's a wonderful town. The Bronx is up. The Battery's down. Take a bite out of the Big Apple. Give my regards to Broadway. Remember me to Herald Square. Tell all the gang at 42nd Street that I will soon be there. Capital of the World. Gotham. If you can make it here, you can make it anywhere. The city that never sleeps. The city, its citizens are always quick to tell you, that has everything.

Well, *almost* everything, because there is one thing that New York most assuredly does *not* have, and that's a golf course.

Okay, okay—put down the phone: I know that, strictly speaking, this is not a precisely correct statement. As a matter of fact, within the boundaries of the official legal entity known as "New York, New York," which is a municipality consisting of five separate administrative units called boroughs, there are actually thirteen municipal golf courses.

But you have to understand something about New York no-
menclature and sense of place. When New Yorkers who reside in
the four "outer boroughs" talk about "the City," they aren't
talking about the streets where they live. And when people who
live in "the City" talk about "New York," they don't mean
Brooklyn, Queens, Staten Island, or the Bronx. All are talking
about the place that tourists visit, that songwriters immortalize,
that the Empire State Building and the Statue of Liberty symbolize. They're talking about what you're talking about when you
talk about New York. They're talking about my hometown for
the last three decades, the borough of Manhattan, an island
community of 1,487,356 troubled souls—and not one single
damned golf course.

Now, we all know that being a golfer in the middle of the
much-ballyhooed "golf boom" is not always a tap-in for a birdie,
particularly for the guy who can't spare the cash equivalent of a
new Pentagon weapons system to join a private club. Maybe
fewer people treat you like a leper these days if you should
happen to mention at a cocktail party that you're thinking about
changing putters again. Perhaps some of the guys who used to
look down their noses at you for not running five miles a day are
coming to you now for swing tips. But marginally greater social
acceptance is more than offset by five-hour rounds, half-day
waits if you don't have a tee time, and getting caught behind a
squadron of boomers who decided to take up the game the day
before yesterday.

Don't come here expecting a lot of sympathy, though. At least
you have a public course in your hometown where foursomes
can stack up three-deep at the par threes on a sunny Saturday
morning. Or a private club that you can join if the bank ap-
proves that home equity loan. You're lucky. Me, I got nothing.
If I lived in Manhattan, *Kansas* (pop. 37,712), I would have two
courses (one public, one private) to choose from. But *my* Manhattan remains the largest community in America where a golfer
has to leave town to play a round of golf . . . or even to get in
a good practice session.

. . .

For the average American golfer, getting in a little quality practice is a piece of cake. Need a little work on swing mechanics? No problem: go out to the garage, even in the dead of winter in the Snow Belt, and spend a couple of hours on taking it back low-and-slow. Want to loosen up while tending the barbecue grill? Easy: take the shag bag out into the backyard and smack seven irons into one of those nets you can buy for $79.95. Need to get in some serious work grooving the old power fade? A snap: throw the sticks into the trunk and head over to the driving range by the mall, where you can hit balls until your hands bleed.

For me, it's a little different. My backyard is thirteen floors straight down, it's made of concrete, and here they call it a city street. There is a garage nearby, but if I could afford to pay $365 a month just for a parking space, I would own a car. And if I owned a car, I wouldn't bother with swinging a club in my garage or hitting balls into a net in my backyard: I'd throw the sticks into the trunk and join you at the driving range by the mall.

(Whenever you try to explain to people who don't live in Manhattan why you don't own a car, they look at you sort of funny and take a step back, as if you were advocating the abolition of mulligans or something. You're just going to have to trust me on this one: it may be un-American not to own a car, or even several cars, depending on the size of your family and/or the needs of your ego, but in New York only the very crazy and the very rich would even consider it.)

No garage and no backyard—so where does a New York golfer practice?

Well, the roof of my apartment building, sixteen stories up, offers plenty of open space for someone to swing a club without having to put up with sniggers from bystanders, and I could probably even rig a net up there. But with a northerly wind ripping off the Hudson in the winter, it's a little chilly for much off-season work. And in the summer, it's so hot your feet sink into the blacktop.

Besides, if anybody spotted me from the window of a neighboring building, I could count on the cops being called and having to explain to them that no, this is not some arcane suicide ritual . . . and no, I most certainly was not looking into that lady's window while she was dressing . . . and yes, I really do believe the problem is an outside-in swing path.

What about Central Park? Smack-dab in the middle of Manhattan, readily accessible, open to the public, a lot of wide-open space—why not?

Okay, just for the sake of argument, let's say you carry a shag bag full of balls and a wedge over to the park for a little short-iron work. And let's say you find a swath of green that isn't choked with sunbathers or volleyballers or softball players or parents pushing baby carriages. But then you start thinking, what if I shank one and conk a jogger or somebody's pedigreed pooch and get slapped with a $10 million lawsuit? You may push such thoughts aside, depending on how desperate you are to improve your work around the greens. But my guess is that fifteen minutes of worry and as many fat hits later, you give it up as a lost cause.

Once upon a time in New York, getting in a little practice wasn't so tough. Bob Hope first met Bing Crosby in New York back in 1932, when both were working in vaudeville at the Capitol Theatre. Hope was master of ceremonies, Crosby sang, and the two developed a patter that they later took on the road. But life wasn't all work and no play, even though they were doing three or four shows a day. Between shows, Hope recalls in *Bob Hope's Confessions of a Hooker,* he and Crosby would race over to a driving range that then existed under the 59th Street Bridge and bang balls.

That driving range is long gone, and Central Park is not the answer for a New York golfer anxious to keep his golf swing from ossifying. And neither are the indoor ranges that have opened in the city in the last few years as adjuncts to those stupid computer-simulated golf games that let you "Play Pebble Beach!" just around the corner from your office.

Pardon me, but the last time I looked, golf was still an outdoor sport: not even I am desperate enough to go into a large room and hit balls into a net. And those simulated golf games where you pull-hook a drive toward a poor-quality image of the first hole at Pebble and the computer says you sliced it OB to the right? Please. Give the technology another five years and call me again. Better still, let's all wait for Virtual Reality to be perfected so that we can go to Pebble Beach in the comfort of our own face masks.

Fortunately, there recently opened—practically in my own neighborhood—a bona fide *outdoor* driving range where I can now go to try to reason with my slice. After all, without practice, how can one hope to be perfect? Or even to break 90 consistently, which I consider an acceptable alternative?

That's right. Manhattan may not have a golf course to call its own, but we do now have a driving range nearby. How nearby? Very. In fact, from the rooftop of my apartment building on a clear day, I can almost see the Port Imperial Golf Driving Range about three miles away. (That's only about sixty city blocks!)

It's a new (1991), well-appointed operation, open seven days a week until 10:00 P.M., with forty-five tee stations, twenty of them in all-weather stalls, and with the structural steel to add twenty more. And you don't even have to have a car to get there. You do, however, have to cross a state line and one of the nation's great rivers, because the answer to my prayers is not in New York at all. It's across the Hudson in New Jersey.

Port Imperial is the brainchild of a New Jersey developer named Vincent Imperatore, who in the 1980s acquired a narrow stretch of riverfront wasteland directly across from midtown Manhattan. At that time, the flat, featureless wedge of barren land at the base of the Jersey Palisades contained nothing but rotting piers, an empty warehouse or two, the old roadbed of an abandoned railway spur, barren soil carved from the nearby cliffs by the Hudson, mounds of brick, concrete, and rusting metal that had been hauled in from construction projects up and down the river and illegally dumped, acres of weeds, a few stunted trees, several burned-out automobiles, the unmarked gravesites of lesser wise guys, and great views of Manhattan.

Imperatore saw something else. He saw a new city of luxury riverfront condos. He saw smart shops and swell restaurants with views of the Empire State Building. He saw a new ferry system linking New Jersey and New York, turning the Hudson once again into the great highway it had been in the nineteenth century.

What he didn't see was the collapse of the economy, the Savings & Loan debacle, and the banking crisis that brought the building boom to a screeching halt. He didn't see the day when twenty-six-year-old bond traders and investment bankers couldn't drop half a mil on a two-bedroom apartment. He didn't see the eighties turning into the nineties.

Even so, Imperatore did manage to get the ferry system up and operating, and traffic has grown steadily since Port Imperial boats started crisscrossing the river in 1988. By the end of 1992, thousands of people were using the service on weekdays. On the New York side of the river, there are terminals in midtown and lower Manhattan, with free buses to shuttle passengers to the main commercial districts. On the New Jersey side, there are the main terminal, a swell restaurant that nobody goes to, plenty of parking lots—and a driving range?

Right. Somebody had the bright idea that all those car trunks in the parking lots probably contained a fair number of golf bags, what with the golf boom and all, so why not turn a piece of Imperatore's huge vacant lot into a driving range? Eureka!

As building projects go, not many are simpler and cheaper to construct than a driving range, even if you do get fancy and build in heaters to keep golfers from freezing in Northeastern winters. The big cost is the land, and Imperatore already had plenty of that just sitting there doing nothing.

Nor are driving ranges complicated or costly to operate. Your two biggest worries are keeping the range balls picked up and finding a wheelbarrow big enough to carry the cash to the bank—in Port Imperial's case, about $12,000 a day in the summer.

Why don't I ever get ideas like that?

Hey, wait a minute, you're probably asking right about now, what's going on here? A guy moans and groans about how tough it is being a golfer and living in New York and then he tells us there's a state-of-the-art practice range that's open all year round just a few miles from his front door? What's he got to complain about? What is his problem?

Just this. Here's the quickest, most straightforward route from my home to this Manhattan golfer's "local" practice range:

○Enter Interborough Rapid Transit subway station at 96th Street and Broadway. Persuade hostile clerk who is busy stacking quarters to sell me a token. Apologize to little old lady I knock to floor with golf bag as I turn toward turnstile.

○Stay calm when golf bag gets stuck in only functioning turnstile. Smile lamely at people screaming, "Get out of the way, asshole!"

○Arrive on platform just as train doors close. Smile lamely at conductor as train sits in station for another minute. Scream at him when train pulls out of station without opening doors.

○Eleven minutes later, next train arrives. (In summer, add two minutes of waiting time for every degree above ninety degrees in subway tunnel. Remember to bring Gatorade.)

○Make mental note to go at rush hour next time, when trains run more frequently. Make another mental note to remember previous mental note made several years ago never to travel on subway at rush hour ever again for as long as I live, even if doing so would turn me into scratch player and retard aging process.

○Disembark at 42nd Street/Times Square Station. Put on game face.

○Walk on 42nd Street toward Eighth Avenue. Ignore catcalls and derisive abusive remarks about golf clubs. Decline offers to party. Do not make eye contact. Resist temptation to forget golf, pop into movie house, and check out promising double bill, *Wet Teen Sluts* and *Back Door Susie.*

○At corner of Eighth Avenue and 42nd Street, don't bother running to catch Port Imperial shuttle bus that's pulling away from corner; there will be another in fifteen minutes.

○At ferry terminal at 38th Street and the Hudson River, don't bother running to catch ferry that's pulling away from dock; there will be another in fifteen minutes.

○Finally on board, check pulse rate and take several slow, deep breaths. As Dan Rather used to say, "Courage."

○Buy a round-trip ticket ($8) for the ferry across the river to Port Imperial. (Option: abandon job and home, become a golf vagabond, and play your way across America.)

○Take seat on upper deck of ferry. Once under way, relax and take in panorama of Manhattan skyline spreading from George Washington Bridge all the way down to Statue of Liberty. There's no view in the world that can touch it. Smile smugly. Sing few bars of "New York, New York."

○When ferry docks, go to ticket window in terminal and ask clerk to call driving range and request transportation. When pickup truck arrives, throw clubs in back, hop in cab, and make small talk with driver during three-minute ride to Port Imperial Golf Driving Range.

○Pay $12 each for two "jumbo" buckets that would barely qualify as "large" anywhere else in America, find an empty pew, and get to work.

○Do stretching exercises. After coming this far, I don't want to pop a pucker string on first drive.

○Tee 'em high and let 'em fly until money is gone and/or square-groove irons are worn down to smooth.

○Pack swollen hands in ice and prepare for return trip. It's easy. Just go back the way I came.

Golf is not a city game. Basketball, handball, baseball, stickball, boxing—those are city games. Golf is a suburban game, even a rural game, certainly a resort game. A *great* game. But not a city game.

Sure, I could always go to suburban Westchester County and play Wykagyl (host of an LPGA event), Sleepy Hollow (host of a Senior PGA Tour tournament), Westchester Country Club (host of a PGA Tour event), or the noble Winged Foot (host of four U.S. Opens). Or perhaps Shinnecock Hills, National, or Maidstone out on Long Island. Even Baltusrol and Ridgewood Country Club (host of a Senior U.S. Open) are within easy driving distance in New Jersey.

Problem is, nobody has asked me—and I have to tell you, I'm not holding my breath. None of these private clubs is as hard to get into as Cypress Point on the Monterey peninsula. (Neither is Heaven, for that matter. Bob Hope said once that "Cypress Point has just completed a highly successful membership drive. Forty members resigned.") Nonetheless, I have never received the call, even though my number is in the book.

But hey, who needs 'em? Not me, not so long as I have thirteen public golf courses in the four outer boroughs of New York to choose from. If Pine Valley calls, tell them I'm playing golf.

New York's public courses have often been called on to serve civic purposes other than golf. One of the Brooklyn courses is allegedly used from time to time by mobsters as a dumping ground for stiffs. When the moon is full, one of the four courses in the Bronx occasionally does double duty as a chop shop for stolen cars. Another was the site of several muggings about ten years ago, but none have been reported in recent years, probably because muggers have figured that golfers at muni courses don't carry enough cash to be interesting.

The real problem with municipal courses in my adoptive hometown is the classic double whammy faced by most big cities in the last two decades: a dramatic increase in use coupled with a dramatic decrease in maintenance. When New York's fiscal crisis bottomed out back in the 1970s, golf course maintenance budgets were all but eliminated. For a decade, they cut the grass, but that was about it. There has been some improvement in the past five years, but all the courses are desperately in need of major capital improvements that simply aren't in the cards.

(Nor should they be. Even a golf junkie can see that New York has more pressing problems to address. So does every other city in the country. Reality sucks.)

The number of golfers at the thirteen New York muni courses is staggering. Each of the five courses that stay open all year *averages* 70,000 rounds of golf. All told, *750,000* rounds of golf are racked up each year at New York's public courses. But the key number that tells you all you need to know about New York public golf is 5—the *minimum* number of hours it takes to complete a single round.

When it comes to design, the quality ranges from horrible to good—not surprising, when you figure that some of the courses were laid by professional golf course architects with adequate construction budgets while others were cobbled together by the Parks Department with leftover petty cash.

There is a solution to New York's—make that Manhattan's—golf problem, and it's been sitting here right in front of our noses for 125 years. Imagine 840 lovely, wooded acres of mostly undeveloped land. Enough to accommodate four wonderful eighteen-hole golf courses, each designed by a different world-class golf course architect. The site has everything: varied terrain, plenty of mature trees, a couple of big lakes, numerous streams, easy access, and—get this—what would instantly be heralded as the grandest nineteenth hole in golf, Tavern on the Green.

○

I'm talking about Central Park.

Just imagine what Pete Dye, Tom Fazio, Rees Jones, and Tom Doaks could do with a piece of land like that! When he was given the commission to build the Ocean Course on Kiawah Island, Dye said it was the greatest natural setting for a golf course he'd ever been privileged to work with. I've got to figure he'll change his tune when he gets a close look at what someday could be Central Park No. 1.

Why not? Sure, there would be political obstacles to overcome, some tree huggers to placate, the usual pesky problems with security to handle. It might be necessary to leave the zoo and the skating rink in place in order to placate the naysaying crowd that is always ready to stand in the way of progress. Naturally, you want the courses laid out so that adjacent fairways in the middle of the complex could be used from time to time for Paul Simon concerts. And there are a few other minor details that will have to be worked out, such as where to relocate the free theater program, Shakespeare in the Park.

(No problem. What about Shakespeare in Grand Central Station? It's pretty empty at night, and there would be no rainouts.)

What it comes down to is vision and guts. If we can put a man on the moon *and* figure out how to operate a VCR, we can damned sure turn Central Park into the best golf complex this side of Pebble Beach. What Frederick Law Olmsted started in the nineteenth century, we can finish in the twentieth.

The Best Golf Teacher
in the World

A teacher who can arouse a feeling for one single good action, for one single good poem, accomplishes more than he who fills our memory with rows on rows of natural objects, classified with name and form.

—Goethe

A lean, fit, white-haired man who looks about fifty but is actually a dozen years older sits forward in a folding chair, his back to the practice range where we have been pounding golf balls for the last three days. He has a driver in his hands as he speaks, clearly and in a strong voice, about feeling the club, about proper alignment to the target, about keeping our arms loose. We sit in a semicircle in front of him, notebooks open but not taking notes, because he is summing up principles we have already committed to heart. Then, still seated and with his back to the range, he turns to his side and with a smooth turn and effortless swing drives a golf ball 250 yards straight down the middle of the range.

And that's only for starters.

Next he stands up, back still to the target line, takes a bead on the ball teed up at his side, and smacks another 250-yard drive.

And then another, this time kneeling on a towel but in otherwise "normal" address position. Finally, standing on one foot ("This one is a little tricky"), he booms yet another drive as long and straight as its predecessors.

Trick shots? You betcha. But trick shots with a point: to illustrate the importance of "feel" in swinging a golf club . . . to demonstrate that the golf swing is generated by the arms swinging, not the body turning . . . to show that it is a fluid motion rather than a mechanical act.

The shot-maker is Jim Flick, the best golf teacher in the world.

A true son of the middle border, James Myron Flick was born on November 17, 1929, in Bedford, Indiana. His parents were of sturdy Pennsylvania Dutch stock; Jim was their only child. His father, first a pole linesman and later an executive of the Indiana Public Service Company, died of cancer at the age of fifty-one, when Jim was twenty-seven years old. A strong, physically imposing man, Coleman Flick encouraged his son from an early age to participate in Indiana's state religion, basketball.

As a teenager, Jim Flick was a high school all-star in basketball; golf was just something he did for fun in the summers. He went to Wake Forest on a basketball scholarship, but by then he was good enough to play on the golf team, whose star player at the time was a long hitter from Pennsylvania named Arnold Palmer. Teammates Flick and Palmer became friends, and if one of them had been able to make correct change, there would have been no "Age of Palmer" in golf, no Arnie's Army, no Arnie.

"Arnold and I were selling tickets on one side of the stadium at a Duke–Wake Forest football game," Flick explains, "and our roommates were on the other side of the stadium doing the same thing." It was one of those jobs that the athletic department gave to scholarship players to let them earn a little extra spending money. At the end of the game, Palmer and Flick couldn't get their money to match up with the number of tickets they'd been assigned. It didn't amount to more than $300, and they were only something like $10 off, but their roommates finally got tired of waiting and decided to go on over to Duke for a dance, leaving Palmer and Flick behind.

"When we finally got the money settled, it was too late to go to the dance," Flick says quietly, "so we went to a movie and then played some pool. We didn't learn about the accident until the next morning."

Palmer's roommate was a talented young golfer named Buddy Worsham, Arnold's best friend and kid brother of 1947 U.S. Open Champion Lew Worsham. Flick's roommate was a basketball player from Indiana. Exactly what happened to them on the road to Duke that night was never determined, although police surmised that the rider in the passenger seat may have leaned over to light his friend's cigarette and that the flare from the lighter may have temporarily blinded the driver. In any event, the car swerved off the road, plunged down a steep incline, and crashed into a creek bed. The two occupants were trapped inside the car, probably unconscious; a fire broke out in the interior. The vehicle was not discovered until the following morning. Both young men were dead.

After the accident, Palmer and Flick roomed together for about three months. Emotionally shattered by the loss of his best friend, Palmer eventually left school at the end of the semester and joined the coast guard. Four years later he turned pro; a year after that he won his first tournament on the pro tour; by 1960 he commanded an army.

Did Palmer show flickerings back then of the megastar he would become within a decade?

"Oh, he was good, all right," Flick remembers. "But there were a lot of good golfers in that region at the time: Harvie Ward, the amateur champion, Art Wall, Mike Souchak, Jim Ferree, and a lot of guys you never heard of who went on to be good club pros and local PGA players. Arnold was at least as good as anybody else in that area. And I do remember making the statement at the time that Arnold would someday win the Masters. He didn't drive his ball very straight back then, but he hit it a long, long way. It was obvious to anybody who saw him play that he had the raw talent to be great. How great? Well, at that level you're never really quite sure."

Flick was graduated from Wake Forest with a degree in business administration in 1952, by which time golf had superseded basketball as his best sport. He then enlisted in the army and served two years in Korea, where he rose to the rank of sergeant. After his discharge, Flick turned pro and landed an assistant's job at an Evansville country club. A year later, he moved on to a bigger job in a smaller town, Connersville, Indiana. He stayed there until 1961, when he was named head pro at the prestigious Losantiville Golf Club in Cincinnati.[1] He would stay there sixteen years.

"That's where I really began to do some teaching," says Flick. Among Flick's students during the sixties were Susie Maxwell Berning, three times a U.S. Open winner; Hollis Stacy, who won eighteen LPGA tour events; and Burt Yancey and Ralph Johnson, from the PGA Tour. And as an increasingly prominent member of state and regional PGA organizations, Flick began to widen his circle of friends among tour players and teaching pros alike.

In 1971 master teacher Bob Toski, who had recently started putting together a series of schools for *Golf Digest,* invited Flick to come out to Silverado, the northern California golf resort, and watch him work. Flick was smitten: "I knew immediately that Bob knew a lot more than I did. He knew how to get people to respond in a more instinctive way to playing the game. That one visit made it instantly clear to me how much I had to learn."

[1]Losantiville was the second name of the town that later became Cincinnati. The original nineteenth-century settlement on the banks of the Ohio was called Porkapolis, presumably because of the hog-breeding proclivities of its early inhabitants. Just think: instead of the Cincinnati Bengals we could have had the Porkapolis Pigs.

When Toski subsequently invited Flick to work under him in the *Golf Digest* golf school program, "I jumped at it." Flick stayed at Cincinnati, joining Toski for a few schools a year at first, then a dozen, then twenty, until finally he left Losantiville to become a full-time professor of golf.

"Bob and I shared a lot of ideas in common," Flick explains. "And where we differed, we found ways to blend our ideas together. For example, I always put a lot of emphasis on position at setup, on how important a good setup is. Bob preferred to focus on free swinging with the arms. I began to understand how you needed both elements. We kind of played off each other, complemented each other well. To this day, I still feel that most of my concepts of teaching have evolved from things that Bob Toski introduced to me as a player."

Through the seventies and on into the eighties, the *Golf Digest* schools run by Toski and Flick came to be the standard against which all other golf instruction intended for ordinary folks like us was measured. Spurred by the *Golf Digest* success, other schools and golf academies were formed. Almost immediately, these new enterprises began to compete and countermarket on the basis of facilities and high-tech teaching aids, ranging from video to computer analysis and simulation of the "perfect swing." And as the golf boom of the eighties expanded, Flick began to believe that something fundamental to the game was being lost.

"The more good players I talk to," he says now, "the more I hear a recurring theme in how they play the game. It's the swinging of the arms that turns the shoulders on *both* sides of the swing, rather than a conscious effort to turn the body. I feel that's the one thing that sets schools of instruction apart: whether you approach golf from a mechanical standpoint, or from a motion-playable standpoint. My stimulus in learning to teach better is to help people play better, not just become swing freaks."

He believes that golf instruction—and particularly golf instruction in golf academies and schools—has gone off the deep end with computers and other devices to make people ultraconscious of swing mechanics, of "just so much weight shift at this point in the swing, and just so much at that point." By asking golfers to be so aware of swing mechanics, he fears, new-wave instructors are causing them to forget—or never even to learn— the importance of swing *feel.*

Says Flick: "People should not lose track of the simple fact that it's the club head that hits the ball. You've got to learn to have a relationship with the club head, to know where it's going and what it's doing, and how it's positioned throughout the swing. But most of all, *most of all,* you've got to feel the club."

Feel the club. If we heard that injunction once during our three days of higher learning at the PGA National campus in Florida, we must have heard it a thousand times. Feel is the keystone of Flick's philosophy of the golf swing, the alpha and the omega, the first principle—and it is what brought him and Jack Nicklaus together as teacher and pupil back in 1990.

Flick had first met Nicklaus in 1961 at the U.S. Pro-Amateur Championship in Cincinnati. The event was a scratch pro-am, which meant no fiddling with handicaps. The year before, Nicklaus played as an amateur and won; this time he played as a professional and won. As president of the Southern Ohio Division of the PGA, Flick met Nicklaus again in 1969 when the PGA Championship was contested at the NCR Country Club in Dayton. Thereafter, Flick and Nicklaus would exchange pleasantries when their paths crossed. But they never really got to know each other, not even after Flick joined Frenchman's Creek Golf Club in West Palm Beach, where from time to time he would watch Jack Grout and Gardner Dickinson work with Nicklaus.

The first time Flick and Nicklaus ever had anything approaching a serious talk about golf was at the Traditional in 1989, the first Senior Tour event Nicklaus ever played in. Nicklaus had been working with Peter Kostis for the previous few months, but he was still having trouble with his game, so he approached Flick and asked him what he saw in his swing.

"I told him I did *not* see Jack Nicklaus in that golf swing," says Flick. "He asked me what I meant. I said, 'Well, Jack, you don't feel your club head anymore.' He asked me how I knew that. I said that the speed with which he was moving his body was out of kilter for the old Nicklaus golf swing. One of his cardinal rules, one that Mr. Grout had taught him from day one, was that he must change directions from the ground up with his feet. And he was no longer doing that, he was initiating the change of direction with his body, and it was interfering with his swing. He was trying to work his body so hard that he had lost feel for the golf club."

Bells rang in Nicklaus's head, so they went to the practice tee and started working on it. "After having watched Mr. Grout work with him," Flick explains, "I didn't try to give him anything new. I just tried to come back and put him in the same concept that he used when he was playing his best golf. I just tried to help him find the golf swing that he'd played with for years. It happened to be the right information."

At the right time, too. Nicklaus and his colleagues at Golden Bear International were looking for someone to put together the curriculum and organizational structure for fifty golf academies that Mitsubishi wanted Golden Bear International to develop for them in Japan. Nicklaus knew Flick's reputation as a good teacher, but until they spent some time together working on Jack's game he didn't know, says Flick, "that we both believed in similar principles, concepts, philosophies."

Flick's approach is the antithesis of a quick fix. He resists giving golfers "keys" to think about. Simple is good, he says over and over, but not at the expense of accuracy. "Based on my experience with Toski, I believe that it is critical that I try to fix a student's mental misconceptions before I try to fix his physical and technical flaws. Turning a mental approach around takes a lot longer than changing a physical approach to the game. I can't give you confidence; you have to earn confidence. A major swing change is not a three-day deal."

Flick tried the pro tour briefly, but didn't pursue it because "I wasn't good enough." What he really means, he goes on to explain, is that a crippling—and painfully familiar—attitude prevented him from ever discovering whether he was good enough. "I was such a perfectionist that I would not allow anything short of perfection in my golf game," he says. "That attitude took away a lot of the natural instincts and undermined a lot of the natural talent I had, because from an emotional standpoint, I wouldn't accept anything but perfection."

A constant theme throughout his teaching career, Flick says, has been the importance of mental *and* physical preparation *before* a shot is attempted. "I think that ninety percent of physical problems that happen in golf have been caused prior to the swing. We either have the wrong approach emotionally, or we have the wrong approach conceptually (that is, we try to over-control the club or overpower the ball), or we fail to aim properly, or we bungle the grip and our setup. The errors that happen *prior to the club getting in motion* cause more problems than we ever recognize. We think the solution is fixing the swing, but ninety percent of the time it's fixing something prior to the swing."

Many times, Flick believes, the thing that most needs fixing is a golfer's attitude. "Six or seven years ago Davis Love and I were partners in a game against another couple of fellows, with some pretty good betting going on. I didn't do anything all day, not a single doggone thing to help us out. Got off with a couple of bad holes, and let 'em get to me, and my game went straight downhill from there. We came to the eighteenth hole in a flat-footed tie. Davis put his tee shot in a tough place. He had a shot at the green, but not a very good one, and I had a chance to redeem myself and help out the team a little. But I didn't. I hit a lousy tee shot, took myself right out of the hole.

" 'Well, partner,' I said to Davis, 'it looks like I've done it to you again, left the load all on you.' I felt like I'd really let him down. But he turned to me and smiled, and he said, 'You've got it all wrong. I should be *thanking* you. This is what I've been playing and practicing and working at my golf game all my life for, to have an opportunity like this.' And then he stepped up and put a smooth, easy swing on a long iron and got the ball up close enough for a birdie that won the match for us.

"My point here, Mr. Glen, is that Davis Love made that shot before he even took back the club. Are you with me, Coach? He had the right concept, the right attitude, and that let him make the right swing."

Remember your favorite teachers in elementary school? They all had one thing in common: the ability to make you feel that you were the center of the known world and thereby richly deserved their undivided attention.

That's the key to Jim Flick's pedagogical genius. When he looks at your pitiful swing, and calls you by your first name or "Coach," and tells you what he wants you to try next, it's as if you and he were the only people on the planet at the moment. In fact, there are twelve to fifteen students in a typical Nicklaus-Flick Golf School session, along with a couple of assistants monitoring the drills, televising your stroke, and helping teach the short game. But for three days, six hours a day, Professor Flick manages to make you feel as if you're the only matriculant.

"Mr. Glen," the voice rings out from the other end of the range, "I want you to bring your chin up so that your left shoulder can turn under it. Think tall, please, sir."

How does he do it? He's working closely with some other poor miserable hacker at the time, but still he manages to keep an eye on the rest of us as we struggle to practice what he preaches. It's uncanny—and it keeps you focused. The moment anyone slips back into an old, discredited swing habit, that clear, precise voice calls out a reminder: "Mr. Glen, I want you to feel the club in your hands. Close your eyes. Feel it. Now swing. You've got it, Coach."

It's a trick, this repeating-your-name business, but it keeps you awake. Give the average hacker a bucket of range balls and he'll bang away mindlessly until the bucket is empty, then walk away as hopelessly lost as when he started. Under Flick's watchful eye, every swing—well, just about every swing—has a grain of thought behind it, because the Professor always seems to be there to keep you honest: "Do you know where you were aiming that time, Mr. Glen? Okay, let's try it again."

Feel the club. Find your target. Feel the club in your hands. Turn those shoulders. Think about swinging, not hitting. *Feel the club.*

As happens with all great teachers, the Flick message sometimes goes way beyond the text. For instance:

o "Society has made us so aware of wanting instant results that people have forgotten the fundamentals that have to be under control before you can ever get successful results, whether it's in business or golf or whatever."

o "Golf is a game based not only on an intellectual understanding but also on sensitivity for the instrument. You can't bully your way to a good golf swing."

o "Too many people try to overpower the golf ball like they do their businesses. I get concerned about the philosophy of American business. We're no longer concerned with our customer and our product and our employee. We're only interested in the next quarterly report and our stockholders. As far as I'm concerned, stockholders should be taken care of last, not first. Business won't last without a good product, and it won't last if we don't take care of customers and our employees."

o "We get so concerned in the short term about having a positive quarterly report that we shortcut things that help us create quality in the long run. We have gotten away from things that made quality and integrity the most important factors in our society."

o "In the long term, people who have an instinctive feel for what they're doing are going to be better than people who don't.

I see that in business, I see that in the way we live our lives. I get concerned that we're losing contact with that instinctive feel for what is essential and valuable because of the increasingly fast and mechanical pace of our daily lives."

The current crop of Flick pupils on the PGA Tour ranges from rising stars (Tom Lehman, Andrew Magee) to solid players in the middle of the pack (Phil Blackmar) to young players struggling to keep their tour cards (John Adams, Ed Humenik, Ronnie Black). Their games are as varied as their success to date, which underscores a key factor that is relevant to hackers like me signed up for a three-day Nicklaus-Flick Golf School session: there is no "Flick Product." Jim Flick teaches individuals, and he adjusts his philosophy to the specific talents and styles of those individuals.

"One year a couple of my kids didn't make their card. They didn't have any money to pay me, so I told them, 'Don't pay me anything this year. If you have a good year next year, take care of me then.' "

Flick remembers that while he and Nicklaus were exploring each other's philosophies and trying to determine if their approaches were compatible, he once asked Nicklaus which of the younger tour kids' swings he liked best. Things got uncomfortably quiet. After a couple of minutes, Nicklaus said that he wasn't sure he liked any of them, that he thought most of them were too mechanical. Flick says he then followed up with the obvious question: What do you think is lost when you become too mechanical?

"Well," said Nicklaus, "you can win tournaments when you're mechanical, but golf is a game of emotion and adjustment. If you're not aware of what's happening to your mind and your body when you're playing, you'll never be able to be the very best you can be."

The morning of graduation day begins like the two preceding days: on the course. Baron von Flick's armored division, a dozen carts in all, rolls out onto the back nine of the Haig course at PGA National and splits into our three groups so that we can work on course management.

Course management? With a golf game like mine, I figure I've done a pretty good job of course management if I manage to get off the first tee without having to reload. Sure, I know the TV analysts have a little something else in mind when they talk about course management, even if they never make quite clear just what. But how in the dickens is a guy expected to "manage" a course when he's not sure which flight plan his ball is going to choose? Sorry, but I have more important things on my mind, such as whether I can please, dear Lord, get through this day without encountering an Abominable Snowman[2] or hitting a Perp[3] or carding an Okie.[4]

The time we spend on the course each day is relatively short, but it serves as a sobering reminder of the difference between range and course. (Try night and day.) It also provides Flick an opportunity to explain such matters as preferred target areas, weighing risk, and "reading" a course to identify the tricks and traps created by the course designer. We are given a primer on planning ahead on a par five so that the shot to the green employs the short iron the golfer is most comfortable with. And we are reminded—"Where do you want to hit the ball, Coach?

[2]An eight. Just think about it.

[3]A golf shot, usually from the tee, hit straight up and sharply to the right, i.e., perpendicular to the intended line of flight, no more than twenty-five yards; typically accompanied by a piercing scream of agony and, on occasions where it is the third or more such shot of the round, by a flying golf club that falls to earth just before the ball.

[4]An Okie, for those of you who do not play in my regular foursome, is derived from the patronym of a frequent playing partner of mine who has taken it upon himself to monitor adherence to the Rules of Golf, establish local variations, assign partners, determine the bets, and generally make a pain in the ass of himself before anyone has made so much as a practice swing. The term, which may well be known to you by another name, stands for the maximum number of strokes that one may take on a given hole, numerically expressed as two times par. Thus, on par threes an Okie is six; on par fours, eight; and on par fives, ten. The fact that this score, bad as it is, would have been significantly worse had the Rules of Golf been observed may well be the itsy-bitsiest of this world's small consolations.

Well, you're aiming about twenty yards to the right"—never, ever, to short-circuit our pre-shot alignment routine.

Later, back at the range, half of us groove swings that have improved demonstrably during the three days while the other half hit bunker shots ("Splash a little sand out for us, Mr. Glen"). Then there is chipping ("Your wrists have *got* to be quiet and your hands have *got* to stay in front of the ball"). And putting ("Speed is more important than line"). And more work on feeling the club during the full swing.

Three days, each minute filled with golf. Smart golf.

Late in the afternoon of the last day of class, Professor Flick is standing near the deserted practice range at PGA National. The sun is setting, and he is summing up the role he believes he can play in extending the legacy of Jack Nicklaus: "I truly want to be part of a legacy. Jack knows things about this game that nobody else knows. As much and as well as he has written about the game with Ken Bowden, I don't think there's any way to understand those things as well as through one-on-one instruction. That's what I'd like to leave to the game. I'd like to be part of the legacy that makes sure that the things that Jack has learned as a player and the things I've learned as a teacher don't get lost. Since those coincide, I feel secure."

And after three days with the best golf teacher in America, so do I.

Is Jim Flick *really* the best golf teacher in the world?

Beats me.

Most of my tutoring in the finer points of the game has come from the guys I play with: Lee, Okie, Mikey, Sudden Pete, Ziggy, Lennie, and Darrell. If we played as an eightsome, we *might* break 90 on our best ball. (Keep that in mind the next time you hear some educational reformer gas on about the virtues of peer instruction.) At this stage in my golf career, I still have not studied with David Leadbetter, Peter Kostis, Bob Toski, or Harvey Penick (though they are definitely on my list).

The reason I'm sticking with my story that Jim Flick is the best golf teacher in the world is that when he talks about the golf swing, something goes click in my brain. It's like a comic-strip panel where a light appears over somebody's head. Or like listening to someone new sing an old song and realizing that you are hearing the lyrics for the very first time.

Feel the swing. I don't know exactly why so simple an injunction strikes such a responsive chord, and I don't know for sure that somebody else doesn't have a better idea. But I do know that, for me, thinking of the golf swing as a fluid, physical, nonmechanical, athletic act has enormous aesthetic appeal.

Now, if only I could just get down into the low eighties and stay there, I would nominate James Myron Flick for the Nobel Prize.

School of Hard Knocks

In my school-days, when I had lost one shaft,
I shot his fellow of the self-same flight
The self-same way with more advised watch
To find the other forth; and by adventuring both,
I oft found both.

> —William Shakespeare
> on the Repeating Swing,
> from *The Merchant of Venice*

The Vs of both hands should point toward right shoulder. Flex at knees, keep back straight, bend at waist. Light grip, relaxed arms. Feel the club. *Tem-po.* Left foot slightly open toward target. Weight evenly distributed on insides of feet. Forward press. One-piece take-away. Turn shoulders, let hips follow. Early wrist cock. Stay behind the ball. *Tem-po.* Let left heel come up. Load the right side. Left arm straight, not rigid. Press body against imaginary board. Drop hands into slot. Fire the right side. Drive imaginary post into ground. Point heel of club at ball. *Tem-po.* Clear the left side. Keep eyes on back half of ball. Do not come over the top. Do not open up too soon. Do not pass Go. Do not collect $200.

Whoa, there! Wait a doggone minute. Now, just where exactly are the Vs in my hands?

Nothing has changed since caveman days when some Neanderthal in plaid pants first picked up a club and tried to groove an inside-out path. We're all still looking for a repeating swing that works.

The first golf instruction I ever received was from my father when I was eight years old. He had made a club for me by sawing down an old hickory-shafted spoon and wrapping the butt end with electrical tape. He then took me out into a freshly plowed field behind our house. There he knelt down, built up a little cone of dirt, and placed a golf ball on it. Then he stood up and told me something that, forty years later, I would hear Peter Jacobsen tell a bunch of boys and girls at a golf clinic at Pebble Beach.

"Go ahead," my dad said. "Hit it as hard as you can."

Fine, but at some point every golfer has to move beyond "Hit it as hard as you can," and that's when the wicket gets sticky.

Three out of four golfers are self-taught, and it shows. We scour the golf magazines for advice, devour the instructional articles, and study tips from Nicklaus and Trevino and Watson the way pagan priests once studied the entrails of goats. We parse instructions for how to draw (fade) the ball. We learn definitively how to cure our slice (hook). We try to keep straight what to do with uphill, downhill, and sidehill lies. We read how to play shots out of deep rough and sand, where we spend an inordinate amount of our time. We find out when to keep our weight back and when to keep it forward. We visualize. We memorize. And we realize every time we play how far we have to go.

We seek but never find, and so we ask for more. Both major golf magazines hear the same mantra repeated over and over by focus groups—more instruction, more instruction, more instruction. Who cares that Scott Simpson is a good family man, a born-again Christian, a martial-arts expert, and a rock-and-roll fan? Who cares that another new golf resort has opened in Arizona? Who cares why shafts made of polyurethane-anthracite are superior? (In a pinch, they can be used as fuel.) Just give us more tips.

So the magazines give us more tips, and what do we get?

Another day older and deeper in debt. And more confused than ever.

It is at about this point that the desperate golfer—and what golfer isn't at some level pathetically, hopelessly desperate?—begins to think about going to golf school.

"You're going to go *where?*"

That's the textbook reaction of unfortunate folk whose desolate lives are as yet untouched by the powerful moral and philosophical values inherent in the game of golf, and who cannot begin to understand why anyone would consider anything so ridiculous as golf school.

The first barrier to overcome, then, is ignorance. You have to be thick-skinned enough to survive the abuse you'll be subjected to when you mention the subject of golf school to nongolfing friends and family members, should you be so unfortunate as to have any of either. Funny how the loved ones who have been tolerant of your weekly disappearance for a day on the golf course, and of the palpable frustration and despair exuding from your every pore when you return, can get downright testy should you allow that you are considering—just considering, mind you—spending the family vacation at golf school.

"You've got to be kidding," the cleaned-up version of the common reaction begins. "Golf *school?* Are you out of your bleeping mind? Why don't you save your money and get a life?"

Your response should be measured, patient, and grounded in compassion for the pitiful ignorance that could prompt anyone to launch such an attack. Just because one does something for fun, you might suggest, does not mean that one should not try to do it as well as humanly possible, and thereby have even more fun. *N'est-ce pas?*

A golfer's single-minded pursuit of excellence in the most excellent of games, you might add, is not unlike the medieval knight's quest for the Holy Grail, an undertaking doomed to failure but awash in nobility of purpose. Or, if you don't feel like tolerating fools who ask you if you are really, seriously, thinking of going to golf school, you could say what I say: "Yes, god-damnit, and whatzit to ya?"

The second barrier to be overcome is the feeling that you really don't *need* to go to golf school, that you can learn all there is to know about the full swing and the short game and bunker play by reading the tips in the golf magazines and watching the pros on TV. Sure. Fine. And after you've mastered golf, you can move on to brain surgery with the help of the *New England Journal of Medicine* and reruns of *M*A*S*H*.

Nobody's giving me a scholarship for saying this (more's the pity), but *all* of us—at least that portion of us who live in the wide, wide world above 90—ought to drop what we're doing *right now* and enroll in golf school. If you've been playing golf more than a couple of years, and if you play at least twenty-five rounds a year, and if you have all your limbs and most of your senses, and if you are athletic enough to tie you shoes on the first try, and if you *still* can't shoot better than bogey golf on an average course, maybe it's time you woke up and smelled the coffee: you need help.

Take my friend Michael. A good athlete who played first base at the same Brooklyn high school that produced Sandy Koufax and Ed Kranepool, Michael is a crackerjack tennis player with a strong, accurate backhand and a solid baseline game. He's a devoted husband, loving father, and caring friend. A respected lawyer and head of his own firm, he has successfully argued several cases before the United States Supreme Court and is a specialist in the First Amendment. He has never been indicted for a Class 1 felony and has quit smoking innumerable times. He supports various charities, takes an active role in community affairs, and cleans up after his dog, the despicable Max. But when it comes to golf, Michael is a mess.

In many ways, Michael is your basic average golfer. He loves the game and plays maybe fifty rounds a year, most of them between May and October. He can get around the course, and because of his athleticism he does hit a good shot now and then. But he rarely scores better than the low 90s, and only then with the help of several mulligans and the occasional foot mashie, because he persists in swinging a golf club like a left-handed Jerry Lewis. But would Michael even consider going to golf school? Not on your life.

Michael will play anywhere, anytime. He'll buy a new set of clubs at the drop of a tee and he spends a fortune each year on golf vacations. But not a brass farthing will he invest in golf lessons, much less *school.* He has this crazy notion that just because he really, truly enjoys playing the game he shouldn't spend a lot of money, take a lot of time, ignore his clients, desert his wife, and bend himself all out of shape trying to get better. Go figure.

Let me tell you a true story about a multimillionaire Texas businessman—let's call him Jim Bob Mulligan (not his real name)—who had it figured a different way. When he lived in Los Angeles, Mulligan belonged to Riviera and played there regularly, where he took a lot of ribbing from his Hollywood cronies—and lost a small fortune to them—because no matter how hard he tried, he couldn't get below the high eighties. Finally, he got fed up. "In one calendar year," he announced at the nineteenth hole one day, "I will be playing par golf."

As you can imagine, everyone within earshot immediately whipped out his wallet. With enough money to buy a small country suddenly at risk, Mulligan faced a dilemma: how was a guy who only rarely broke 88 going to shoot par in a year?

Mulligan hired a pro. Not just any pro, mind you, but the guy reputed to be the best teaching pro in Los Angeles. And not just for a few lessons: Mulligan signed him to an exclusive personal-services contract. The pro's job: to be at Mulligan's beck and call, seven days a week, for a solid year.

You can write the rest of the script. Mulligan practiced and played, played and practiced virtually every day for nearly twelve months. His game would get better, then fall back, then get better only to hit a plateau. But still he persevered. He hit thousands and thousands of practice balls. He rolled miles and miles of putts on the putting green. He moved enough sand in the practice bunker to build a set for *Lawrence of Arabia II.* And then, just shy of a year from when he said he would, Mulligan went out to Riviera one bright, sunshiny Southern California morning and shot 71.

Par.

Only in Hollywood, you're saying to yourself. But wait—the sequel is even better. The following day, just twenty-four hours after pulling off the greatest feat seen at Riviera since Ben Hogan shot a record-shattering 276 in the 1948 U.S. Open, Jim Bob Mulligan gave away his golf clubs and quit the game. He has never played a round of golf since.

This is a *true* story, I swear it. The guy who told it to me knows his way around Hollywood, knows Jim Bob Mulligan (not his real name), and knows this sounds like a subplot for *Caddyshack III.* But he's sticking to his story, and so am I.

There are several morals to be drawn from this honest-to-God true story, the most important of which is this: You *can* teach old golfers new tricks.

A couple of years ago, when it finally penetrated my skull that a little higher learning might improve *my* game, I enrolled in a golf school. And then another. As of this moment, I have spent time at four different golf schools, and I can say this with authority: A little knowledge may be a dangerous thing, but it's a helluva lot less dangerous than the baggage I used to bring to the first tee.

As an errant grandson of a Southern Baptist preacher, I get a little itchy when people start setting down rules, particularly the ones that begin "Thou Shalt Not . . ." But I do believe the following general rules will be of value to anyone heading out in a search for truth, personal growth, and a better golf swing:

1. Shape Up Before You Ship Out. One of golf's most appealing qualities has always been that you don't have to be in particularly good physical condition to play it well. Consider: if God had meant for golfers to be in good shape, He wouldn't have invented golf carts. Still, there is something to be said for getting your body ready to hit more range balls in three days than it's seen in the last three years.

My hands are going to take a beating, I figured, so swinging a club half an hour a day for a couple of weeks before enrolling in golf school could help get them ready for the ordeal. So could the old Nolan Ryan Anti-Blister Remedy, i.e., soaking them in pickle brine.

I'll never know. Upon reflection, it dawned on me that as I was going to golf school to learn a new swing, spending the preceding two weeks burning the old one into my muscle memory didn't make a whole lot of sense. And I don't know how things are around your house, but pickled hands would make me *persona non grata* in mine.

Flexibility is crucial to success in golf, so I did plot out a comprehensive twice-a-day stretching program that would leave me limber as a preteen. If a 180-degree body turn is good, then 360 ought to be twice as good, right? The only problem is that in my first stretching drill I felt something go "ping!" in my rib cage and decided to take it easy for two weeks.

Jogging? Weight lifting? Yoga? Jane Fonda?

Let me ask a better question: What does any of them have to do with a snap hook?

2. The World Took Six Days. Your Golf Swing May Take a Little Longer. Repeat after me: "After just three days of golf school, I will not be playing scratch golf . . . After three days of golf school, I will not be playing scratch golf . . . After three days of golf school, I will not be playing scratch golf."

Say those words even though, deep down, you really believe you will. Not *scratch* golf, maybe, not for a while. But there in the back of your mind, just beneath the conscious part, you really do expect a minor miracle to emerge from golf school. Despite what your head tells you, you expect in your heart that a few days of high-level instruction and intensive practice will effect an immediate and dramatic transformation of your game.

I know I did. The first morning of class, I learned so much about the proper grip and the proper setup and the proper way to swing the club, and I hit so many good shots under close supervision of the instructors, that by noon I could hardly wait for class to be over so we could get out on the course for nine holes of spectacular golf before cocktails.

So, when class finally ended at 4:30, one of the guys from the school and I sprinted out to the first tee and proceeded to hit two balls each out of play. (One of the four didn't even make it past the ladies' tees, and you know what that means.)

What happened? That's easy enough to figure. For starters, we'd already played the equivalent of five rounds that day, in terms of full swings made on the practice tee, so we were maybe just a wee bit tired. But there was one other, rather more important factor as well: we were still horrible golfers.

This is not to say golf school doesn't help; it does. A lot. Even I made enough improvement in my short-game technique to shave three or four strokes off my normal score . . . immediately.

But common sense tells you that swing habits of a lifetime are not going to be transformed in seventy-two hours. Golf school *will* give you a new, better swing and, consequently, a new lease on life, but it will have a major impact on your golf *score* only if you spend the next six months practicing what's been preached to you.

The good news is that the higher your handicap going in, the more you can expect to gain from golf school. A golfer with a handicap between twenty and thirty can realistically expect to drop eight to ten strokes, provided he works at what he learned in school. The lower your handicap, of course, the fewer strokes you can expect to drop by going to golf school. If you're between a ten and a nineteen, you're looking at an improvement range of three to seven shots. And if your handicap is in single digits, to hell with you—I hate your eyes.

3. Warning: X-Rated. Unless you're a certified masochist, you've probably not spent a lot of time watching your golf swing on videotape. Be prepared for a shock, because at golf school you will, and it's certain to be a little unsettling. Remember the first time you saw *Psycho?* That was like *Mister Rogers' Neighborhood* compared to your first golf video.

In your mind, you may be Fred Couples. On tape, you're Fred Mertz. But don't look away in despair. Videotape is a great teaching tool because it shows you what the instructor is talking about. I have six videotapes made of me swinging a golf club over the last five years, and when I begin to wonder when I'm ever going to get any better, I pop in the oldest tape to confirm that I already have. A little.

4. Hey, This Feels Funny. Why shouldn't it? It took a lot of hard work to groove your old, bad swing, and it's as familiar as your old teddy bear. A new one is bound to feel uncomfortable. Funny, though, how swell your new, uncomfortable swing starts to feel after you've hit a few good shots with it.

5. Teacher Knows Best. Golf school is not to be confused with group therapy. You're not there to learn from your fellow classmates. You're there to learn from your teacher. Don't give or accept tips. Don't be competitive with anyone or anything. Don't show off. You're there with a group, but it's your job to wear blinders and keep things on a one-to-one basis. You and your teacher. This doesn't mean you can't have a few japes after class down at the Dairy Queen. It does mean that you're there for one primary purpose. To learn.

6. Do Your Homework. Be prepared to come home and practice what your golf school professor preaches. Otherwise, you're wasting your time and money. If you return from golf school, stick your clubs in the garage, and forget about them for three months, what's the point? You might as well have gone to bowling school.

Nobody's saying you have to quit your day job and spend all your time at the practice range, however appealing the idea. But you should hit a big bucket of range balls a couple of times a week to groove the lessons you learned in school. If this means playing a round or two less per month to make time for the practice range, so be it. Any pro will tell you that you do more for your swing in one hour at the range than in four on the course.

7. One Step Backward, Two Steps Forward. Lenin was wrong about world revolution, maybe, but he must have gone to golf school somewhere along the way to the Finland Station. "One step backward, two steps forward" is the way what you learn at golf school gets incorporated into your game. Not all at once. By bits and pieces. Back home, you will play some very weird golf for a while. *Very* weird. Some days you'll be Ben Hogan on the front nine, Harpo Marx on the back nine. Or even both on the same hole. Sound familiar? But in time you will notice a difference. A *good* difference. Just remember that you heard it here first.

8. Fun Comes Later. Class at a good golf school runs from eight in the morning until four in the afternoon. You'll be asked to concentrate on golf in a way you've never concentrated before. You'll hit range balls until your arms feel as if they're going to fall off. And you think that you're going to try to squeeze in nine holes after school? Think again. Remember: this is golf *school*, not golf *vacation*.

Work hard now, and you'll have more fun during spring break.

Playing the Mind Game
at Camp Granola

A man paints with his
brain, not with his hand.
—Michelangelo

You play enough golf, at some point you try everything. Instructional books. Videos. Tips from golf magazines. Tips from guys in your foursome who don't know their ass from a gin whistle. Tips from perfect strangers you collar on the street. Tips from Bobby Jones, who speaks through your neighbor's golden retriever.

You buy a new set of irons, have your woods regripped, change balls, use only white tees, get another putter (your fourth in five years, but who's counting?).

You leave the office early with a stomach virus—nobody ever challenges a stomach virus—and go to the driving range to hit balls. Suddenly, everything falls into place. You hit one good shot after another. You fix your slice. You feel confident. Life is good. But only until you get to the first tee.

You buy a large-screen TV to watch golf. Not just the Masters and the U.S. Open and the British Open and the PGA, but the

Freeport-MacMoran Classic and the Canon Greater Hartford Open and the Las Vegas Invitational. You watch Donald O'Connor and Foster Brooks and Gerald Ford at the Bob Hope–Chrysler Classic, and you think, Why them and not me, O Lord?

You go to tournaments and hang out at the practice range so you can watch Couples and Kite and Norman in person. You get as close as you can so maybe some of their karma will rub off. You stare until your eyes cross, trying to find the key.

You shave your head, paint yourself blue, dance naked under a full moon, sacrifice a live chicken, give up coffee.

Maybe you even get better. You catch yourself thinking about a shot before hitting it. You play a round without a single three-putt green. You occasionally identify the cause of a horrible shot and make the appropriate correction. Your handicap creeps down. You speak golfese more fluently.

But something is missing. You crave more. Your soul is restless. You find yourself engaged in an internal dialogue about the existential meaning of a perfectly struck three iron. You stand over a downhill, twenty-foot, left-to-right putt, too terrified to take the putter back, when suddenly it comes to you, as if by divine revelation, that you have the power to guide the ball into the hole with the force of your will. ("Go ahead and putt the goddamn thing," some oaf in your foursome always shouts and breaks the spell, just before your will gets up to speed.) You have an out-of-body experience in which you float weightlessly above the fairway. You walk down the street and hear yourself swapping golf yarns with Bobby Jones.

At this stage, you have two choices: take two aspirin every four hours, drink plenty of liquids, and give up the game; or enter the world of Zen Golf.

When Yogi Berra said, "Ninety percent of this game is half mental," he could have been talking about golf instead of baseball. And there's plenty of circumstantial evidence to corroborate Shaman Berra's testimony:

∘In 1991, the year Payne Stewart won the U.S. Open, sports

shrink Dr. Richard Koop of the University of North Carolina stayed with Stewart and his family at the house Stewart rented for Open week. Stewart's not the only PGA Tour golfer never to leave home without his shrink—at least not for a major.

○All the major golf publications feature regular columns by sports psychologists.

○In *no* sport, bar none, is visualization used more than in golf. Pick up any golf magazine at random and you'll find some teaching pro telling you to visualize the ball exploding off your club face like a kernel of popcorn popping, streaking into the sky like a heat-seeking missile, bending around that big tree guarding the green, and settling softly to the earth (pin-high) as if buoyed by an invisible parachute. After winning the 1992 U.S. Open at Pebble Beach, Tom Kite—yes, Tom *Kite*—explained that during the final round he was "seeing really good pictures" all day.

○It is a widely accepted truism that, with the possible exception of "inside the leather," no unit of measure is more important in golf than the eight inches between a golfer's ears.

So I figure maybe it's not really all that crazy to think that Zen Buddhism might lead one to the inner secrets of golf. And thus it came to pass that I found myself one summer at the Omega Institute for Holistic Studies, more familiarly known as Camp Granola.

The Omega Institute was founded in 1977 by Stephan Rechtschaffen, a medical doctor and charismatic oracle of New Age philosophy. Rechtschaffen is a protégé of Michael Murphy, author of *Golf in the Kingdom* and guiding light of the Esalen Institute in Big Sur. Since moving in 1982 to its current quarters, a former summer camp in the Hudson Valley near Rhinebeck, New York, the Omega Institute has expanded its curriculum dramatically and is now one of the largest learning centers in the country, with over 200 weekend and week-long workshops during its three-month summer season.

Anybody old enough to remember the movie *Bob & Carol &*

Ted & Alice? Well, Omega is not like that at all. True, there are workshops on Intimacy, Getting the Love You Want, and Couple Massage, but they are not what you might think. (Or not what I thought.) If you're looking for a touchy-feely singles weekend in the woods, you won't find it at Omega. (At least I didn't.)

What you will find is an extraordinary assortment of participatory workshops in five broad subject areas: personal health and development; relationships and family; arts, sports, and play; nature and society; and spiritual understanding.

At Omega you can take a Shamanic Journey, climb your own Personal Totem Pole, and accept (or decline) An Invitation to Ecstasy. You can explore The Way of the Dervish, study Drawing the Light from Within, and stroll down the Druid Path. You can learn how Freeing Your Inner Child and Radical Aliveness relate to Ultimate Self-Esteem.

Martial artists can choose from three schools of yoga (Astanga, Iyengar, and Darshana), get two perspectives on tai chi, or follow The Way of the Ninja. If you dig gardening, there is Soil and Soul. If you have dancing feet, there is Delicious Movement. If something has been bugging you, there is Gremlin Training. You can read poetry with Allen Ginsberg and Robert Bly, and you can write songs with Bobby McFerrin and Rosanne Cash. And, yes, you can spend the weekend beating tom-toms in a sweat lodge with A Gathering of Men.

(That's all well and good, you're probably thinking along about now, but what time do we tee off? Be patient. One of the things you'll learn in The Tao of Being is the interconnectedness of all life forces. Golf will come.)

Because of its focus on personal growth, spiritualism, holistic medicine, and oriental philosophy, Omega is sometimes referred to as Esalen East. Omega people prefer the nickname Camp Granola. But for me, it will always be the Om Country Club, the only place I know of where you play golf without a ball.

Omega founder Rechtschaffen is a sports freak: the man has

a basketball jones the size of Madison Square Garden. And so, at the end of each summer, Camp Granola features a sports weekend. Phil Jackson comes in to teach Beyond Basketball, which is really a New Age name for a brutally tough three-day basketball tournament. Bill "Spaceman" Lee teaches Baseball: The Spirit and Practice of an American Myth (he wears his old Red Sox uniform and a cap with CCCP on the brim). There is The Tao of Boxing: Exploring the Spiritual Ropes of Masculinity. There is The Dance of Tennis, taught by Jena Marcovicci.

And there is Zen Golf: Secrets of the Game.

The Omega Institute is located on eighty thickly wooded acres about two hours north of New York City. In an earlier incarnation, what is now Camp Granola had been a summer camp for kids. Since Omega bought it in 1982, it's been a summer camp for grown-ups.

The camp is built on a sloping hill that leads down to a small lake. There is a large central dining hall in a big, handsome frame building with a sweeping front porch that overlooks two full-size basketball courts. Half a dozen other smaller wooden structures serve as classrooms and meeting halls. Students are housed in a couple of dozen cabins, each sleeping eight people, and a dozen or so dormitories, each holding about thirty people.

On the accommodations chain, Camp Granola ranks somewhere between sleeping on a park bench and Motel 6. My dorm room was a ten-foot-square cubicle with no ceiling. The interior walls extended up only about seven feet, above which there was nothing until you reached the dormitory rafters: good news for the claustrophobic, bad news for the light sleeper. At the end of the double-loaded hall were a couple of toilets on one side and a couple of shower stalls on the other. The room itself contained a single bed, a folding chair, some shelves for clothes, and a sixty-watt light bulb screwed into a socket on the wall. There were two windows, both with torn screens, but mosquito season had passed so it didn't matter. The walls separating me from my neighbors were unpainted Sheetrock, the other walls were unfinished red pine—and all bore the written record of campers from yesteryear.

"Penni Loves Josh" (at least she did in 1979). Beth slept here in 1976. Claudia bumped her head here in 1977. Emily was here "1966–1971–?" (She obviously suspected in 1971 that she might not return. Did she, in fact, not come back? Did she stay in some other dorm? Did the family move away to California? Were her parents political activists who went underground? Did she sneak away from camp to go to Woodstock in 1969? Is she okay? Will we ever hear from her again?)

And then there was Jody, who wrote this poem in 1972:

> Beans, beans
> Good for your heart.
> The more you eat,
> The more you fart.
> The more you fart,
> The better you feel.
> So eat beans
> At every meal.
> Do it.

(I can't help but wonder about Jody. I figure she went on to Yale, where she took a literature course from Harold Bloom and thought for a while about going to graduate school. Instead, she got a job in advertising in New York, but left it after two years and went to Los Angeles, where she is an assistant producer of *Studs* and dates a former contestant on the show.)

The Om Country Club will never be mistaken for Pinehurst, but the graffiti are much better.

As someone who was raised on overdone pot roast, chicken-fried steak, cream gravy, and pecan pie, I long held to fellow Texan

Larry L. King's conviction that "if it ain't brown or it ain't gray, then it ain't food."

Not only that, but in Dallas County in the 1940s and 1950s, anybody with any weird eating habits—like using romaine instead of iceberg lettuce—came under suspicion of being a vegetarian, which could lead to your being reported to the House Un-American Activities Committee as a probable com-symp.[1] You couldn't be too careful in those days, what with Godless communism trying to undermine the cattle industry and weaken the moral fiber (*not* soluble in anything, thank you very much) of protein-enriched Texas boys and girls thereby diminishing their capacity to defend the oil-depletion allowance.

Exposure to an exponentially larger range of foods, a better understanding of nutrition, and a gnawing fear of death have, over the years, altered and expanded my eating habits. (When I was a child, I spake and ate as a child.) But even so, you can appreciate my apprehension that first evening at Camp Granola when three blasts from a conch shell at precisely 6:00 P.M. summoned one and all to dinner. My fears were confirmed when, as we walked down the chow line in the cavernous dining hall, it became painfully clear that not one of the large number of menu items arrayed before us had ever mooed, cackled, oinked, or even swum around without making a sound.

The Omega Institute is vegetarian. And not just garden-variety vegetarian, mind you. Omega is hard-core vegetarian. This means that not only was there no red meat or poultry or fish, but also no cheese or eggs, presumably so as not to take unfair advantage of hoofed or feathered toilers. There was, however, no shortage of legumes, tubers, leafy greens, fibers soluble, fibers insoluble, sprouts, grains, nuts, seeds, fruits, and tofu.

Lots of tofu. Scrambled tofu for breakfast. Curried tofu for lunch. Mystery tofu for dinner. Tofu ice cream for dessert. So

[1] For those readers too young to have served in the Cold War, "com-symp" was McCarthy Era shorthand for "communist sympathizer." And for those too young to remember who McCarthy was, you're lucky.

much tofu that I began to feel sorry for all the soybeans whose lives have been snuffed out in their prime.

Like many people in recent years, I've cut way back on red meat, grease, and the other finer things of life. No more double bacon cheeseburgers. No more sour cream and/or butter on the baked spud. Breakfast? Lemme see now, I'll have bacon and eggs with toast, but hold the bacon, hold the eggs, and make the toast whole wheat. And dry. Not too exciting, but it's been for a good cause: to live long enough to shoot one's age.

Even so, I was not fully prepared—emotionally or intestinally—for three meals a day of bean sprouts, bean casseroles, and beans. During my stay at Camp Granola, my fiber intake exceeded that of a mature Clydesdale. I even found myself grudgingly willing to entertain the proposition that George Bush may be right about one thing: broccoli. By the third day at Camp Granola, I was having fantasies about skinless chicken breasts. (Broiled. Plain. Raw.)

Put it this way: if I get a vote, the Omega Institute can kiss that third Michelin star good-bye.

Each day at Camp Granola began at 6:00 A.M. with a one-hour class in tai chi or yoga—or, for late risers, thirty minutes of meditation starting at 6:30. Three blasts from the conch shell signaled breakfast at 7:00, after which there was free time until the morning class session, which ran from 8:30 until noon. The lunch break lasted from 12:30 until 1:45, but you could squeeze in a class in dance movement from 12:15 until 1:00 and still have time left over for a quick tofu burger. The afternoon session ran from 2:00 until 5:00, followed by another tai chi class, cocktails, and dinner.

(Just kidding about the cocktails. The strongest beverage at Camp Granola is carrot juice. Served up or on the rocks.)

After dinner each evening, there was a full and varied program of lectures, concerts, and videos, all of them relentlessly uplifting and consciousness-raising, and most of them genuinely interesting. There was also a New Age sock hop called Barefoot Boogie, but I took a pass. Instead, I went to a session of Global Action Plan—and came away feeling abjectly dejected.

Global Action Plan turned out to be a quickie overview of something called the Household Eco-Team Program, a six-month plan to bring one's household into environmental balance. The program distills a mountain of environmental information into six sets of actions to be implemented, one a month, at the family or neighborhood level. The components are garbage reduction, water efficiency, energy efficiency, transportation efficiency, ecologically aware consumerism, and neighborhood empowerment.

A single one-hour session was all it took to plunge any sane person into a pit of guilt and despair at what we humans have done to the planet. We are systematically turning the only home we have into a polluted, poisonous garbage dump, unfit for human habitation. The situation is desperate. Given the utter lack of political leadership in halting this pell-mell march to self-destruction, we ordinary citizens must build a grass-roots movement to save the earth from ourselves.

My conclusion: with so much to be done and the planet's very survival at stake, what in the world was I doing at a three-day session on Zen Golf? And then I remembered: to get down into the mid-80s and stay there.

How were we going to learn about golf, Zen or otherwise, when there was no golf course, no practice range, no clubs, and no golf balls? That question surfaced the first morning shortly after we walked into the classroom.

The matter had not crossed my mind before then because I had been worrying about another question: was I going to have to sit on the floor with legs intertwined like strands of spaghetti, eyes closed and forefinger-tips touching thumb-tips, and chant Ommmmmm all day? My problem is that at 6'3" and 200-and-none-of-your-damned-business, I am not what you might call

○

ideally constructed for sitting on the floor in the lotus position for several hours. If you want the truth of it, I had this vision of not being able to get up and of having to sit in place all weekend, and I was too damned embarrassed to inquire whether the classroom was equipped with block and tackle.

Not to worry. Our classroom was a large, light, airy barn-size space with a gymnasium floor, high ceilings, and dozens of big windows. And smack in the center of the polished wood floor, arranged in a circle, were two dozen folding chairs. My first-day-at-a-new-school jitters abated.

Our teacher, Mike Hebron, was a further source of calm and of confidence in what lay ahead. One of only twenty-four members of the PGA of America to hold the title Master Professional, Mike runs a golf school at a club on Long Island. For years I'd seen his tips and articles in various golf publications, and *Golf* magazine had recently named him as one of the top 50 golf instructors in America. In his mid-forties, Mike is athletically and compactly built on the order of a second baseman (he'd played baseball in college), but riveting, pale-blue eyes are his most distinctive physical characteristic. They are key elements of his intense but understated charisma.

Mike had his work cut out for him, because as we went around the horn giving a little bio sketch of ourselves, it became clear that we were a motley crew indeed. Two of my classmates claimed single-digit handicaps, five of us shot in the 80s and 90s, an even dozen (most of whom had only taken up the game in the past few years) had never broken 100, and three had never played golf at all. (My favorites: a pair of newlywed yups who were "looking for a sport that we can do together" and who hugged and nuzzled each other throughout the three days.)

Twenty-two students. Experience Range: from a lifetime playing golf to never having touched a club. Ability Range: from a seven handicap to infinity. One teacher. Good thing he was a Master.

Okay, let's get started, I said to myself. (Anything to do with golf, I'm not the most patient individual in the universe.) Which way is the range? Let's start banging balls.

I'm afraid there has been a little misunderstanding, Mike said. We won't be hitting balls.

What? But the catalogue said we should bring our clubs!

Well, Mike said, as you know, I was brought in to teach the class after it had been set up, and the people who put the catalogue together made a mistake. The fact is, there is no range here.

Oh, yeah? Just when exactly did they discover that? Did it come as a big surprise? What about the range at the state park down the highway about twenty miles? Can't we go there?

No, we couldn't. Mike had already checked, and the Institute said no: lack of transportation, too much travel time, not enough insurance, unlikelihood of state park agreeing to give over driving range on Labor Day weekend, celestial disharmony, you name it—there were plenty of reasons why twenty-two golfers and wannabe golfers were going to spend a long weekend working on their golf games without benefit of golf clubs, golf balls, golf range, or golf course.

At least we had mops.

That's right, mops. Over in one corner of the room were two dozen lightweight, plastic-handled, regulation-length mops. In lieu of golf clubs, rag mops. But not immediately. We would get to the mops later.

Mike began to talk. He talked about the laws of learning and that he would not *teach* us golf but that we would *learn* it. He talked about physiology and neurology and psychology as they pertained to the golf swing. He quoted philosophers and theologians. He told us that a sound swing has the geometry (shape and motion) of a circle and the physics (power and action) of rotation. He talked about right-brain and left-brain differences. Using a slide projector, he flashed aphorisms and wise sayings on the screen, solemnly read them aloud, and paused silently for a moment as they sank in. On and on he talked, and the more he talked, the less it seemed to matter that we weren't going to be hitting balls this weekend: the guy was good.

Trust, Mike said at one point, is crucial to your golf game. You must trust your eyes and sense of touch. Once you learn certain basic techniques, you must trust that your body can—with regular practice—employ them. Most of all, you must not let your trust be interrupted by fears and doubts, such as "This is an impossible putt" or "I never play this hole well."

To drive home this point about positive visualization, Mike read from an essay he had written about learning golf: "The brain cannot tell the body anything by using words. Muscles do not understand the language of words, so when you say to yourself 'don't hit the ball into the lake,' all the brain can communicate to the body is 'hit the lake.' We should learn to trust the automatic system we all have—and imagine the ball hitting the green."

(Ah-ha! So that's all there is to it!)

But the main message of the first morning in class was summed up by Mike in the following triad:

THE BRAIN CONTROLS THE MIND.

THE MIND CONTROLS THE BODY.

THE BODY CONTROLS THE CLUB.

But as I was contemplating those interlocking propositions and trying to visualize strokes dropping from my score, my mind wandered back a couple of decades to a syllogism I once saw carved into a desk in a college lecture hall:

GOD IS LOVE.

LOVE IS BLIND.

RAY CHARLES IS BLIND.

RAY CHARLES IS GOD.

Funny, but after all these years, I still can't find anything wrong with that reasoning.

. . .

Ladies and gentlemen, grab your mops.

Brimming with excitement about the new precepts that would transform our golf game, we filed out of the classroom midway through the afternoon session and marched smartly across the compound. We passed the tennis courts where Dance of Tennis students were not dancing but hitting tennis balls with tennis racquets. We passed a big field where Bill Lee was leading the students of Baseball: The Spirit and Practice of an American Myth in spirited baseball practice, complete with bats and balls and gloves. We passed the basketball court where Phil Jackson was teaching Beyond Basketball matriculants the finer points of the old give-and-go, using—you guessed it—a basketball.

And what were we Zen golfers doing? Looking around for an unused patch of flat, unoccupied turf so that we could . . . could what? *Mop* it?

We finally stopped at a piece of yard next to the compost heap. Now, with 900 campers eating three veggie squares a day, and an eco-correct, adamantly Green philosophy firmly in place, composting at Camp Granola is a serious business. This was no ordinary compost heap. It was a compost *ranch.*

But there we were, nostrils teased by the pungent perfume of rotting vegetable peels, mops in hand waiting to tee off. Right about then I copped a quick peek at my watch: if I checked out now, I could be back in New York by cocktail time. Nice dinner (steak), a little baseball on TV, early to bed—and tomorrow go somewhere and play some bleeping golf.

Fortunately, I stayed. For the next hour and every morning and afternoon the rest of the weekend, Mike led us through mop drills that—I am convinced of this—helped my golf swing.

We stood with our feet together and our eyes closed and swung our mops as if they were drivers. (Swing too hard and you lose your balance.) We practiced releasing the club/mop at precisely the top of our backswing so that it would fly directly toward the target. (Grip it too tightly and the release won't be smooth, causing the mop/club to go off line.) We practiced the

Nine Positions of the Swing (hint: No. 1 is Address) until we were able to move without pause to whatever position Mike called out (hint: No. 9 is the top of the Follow-Through). We practiced the putter-stroke take-away for the chip shot. (When done properly, the mop drags along exactly on line.)

We all agreed that if it weren't for the fourteen-club limit, we would add a mop to our bag.

Back in the classroom, we probed and pondered dozens, scores, hundreds of aphorisms, epigrams, observations, and eminently wise sayings. From Buddha to Bertrand Russell to Ben Hogan. On cue cards, projected onto the screen, written on the blackboard, spoken by Mike. The sacred texts of the inner game of golf.

That much wisdom can be difficult to absorb, much less to apply. Therefore, as a public service, I shall now explain how golfers might interpret several key tenets of Zen Golf as presented at the Om Country Club. On the left is the Zen message; on the right its translation into golf.

Zen	*Golf*
Think like a man of action, and act like a man of thought. 　　　—Henri Bergson	Drive for show, putt for dough.
'Tis the mind that makes the body rich. 　　　—Shakespeare	And three-putt greens that make it poor.
If the shoe fits, there is no room for growth. 　　　—R. N. Coons	Time to buy new irons.
What we have to learn to do, we learn by doing. 　　　—Aristotle	I'm taking a mulligan.
The past is but the beginning of a beginning. 　　　—H. G. Wells	The double bogey on the first hole will come back to haunt you.

How is it that little children are so intelligent and men so stupid? It must be education that does it.
> —Alexandre Dumas

My golf teacher is to blame

The bird of paradise lands only upon the hand that does not grasp.
> —John Berry

Don't grip the club so damned tight!

It does not matter how slowly you go so long as you do not stop.
> —Confucius

You're swinging too fast.

Good players are good because they've come to wisdom through failure.
> —William Saroyan

I'm taking another mulligan.

This was the Omega Institute's first-ever workshop on Zen Golf. They had added it to the end-of-summer sports weekend, a staff member who helped put together the catalogue told me, because "we had heard that interest in golf seemed to be growing." Translation: somebody on the staff had tried to get a Saturday tee time.

So how did the workshop work out? What was the student reaction? One hint came at the end of the first day when a fortyish guy in a snappy maroon warm-up suit stood and said, "I'd like to share something with everyone."

Whenever I hear somebody offering to share something, I start looking for the door, unless he or she is clearly referring to a piece of cake. "Sharing" in our times is usually group therapese for "I'm going to give you my manipulative self-serving opinion whether you like it or not." This was no exception.

"I have been coming to the Omega Institute two or three times a summer for five years," he said, establishing his credentials in a superior tone that put us all on notice. "I have taken workshops in various fields because I have a wide range of interests." (We, by process of elimination, were ignorant bozos with the intellectual curiosity of tree stumps.)

"This workshop appealed to me because I was curious to see how Zen, which I know a little something about, might be applied to something like golf." (The way he said "little something" meant that he was only a few credits short of becoming a Zen master; the way he said "golf" suggested he didn't know a two iron from a toothpick and was proud of it.) "Frankly, I'm disappointed: there's too little discussion of Zen, too much emphasis on golf. I just want everyone to know that I'm going to transfer to another workshop."

(Thanks for sharing that. And he did have a point, I figured. The course probably should have been called Zen Mops.)

Otherwise, the reviews were mixed. The low handicappers seemed to like the workshop a lot, several of the 80s and 90s shooters snuck off at lunchtime the second and third days to hit balls at the driving range, the 100-and-up people were mostly perplexed because they had no golf frame of reference, and the newlywed yups are probably divorced by now. (She had a much better mop swing, and I don't think he could handle it.)

Generally speaking, my classmates and I would probably all agree in some measure with yet another penetrating observation by the distinguished deconstructionist philosopher, the aforementioned Dr. Berra: "I can't think and hit at the same time."

While I believe that I am a better golfer for having attended the Omega Institute's workshop on Zen Golf, I am at a loss to explain exactly how or why, in part because I still do not fully understand what Zen Golf is.

The first time I ever heard of Zen was back in college when a teacher posed the fabled Zen koan: "What is the sound of one hand clapping?" I didn't know then; I don't know now. Later on, I read and loved Robert Pirsig's *Zen and the Art of Motorcycle Maintenance,* although I suspect now that certain mind-expanding recreational substances—it was a long time ago, you understand—may have had something to do with my reaction.

Later still, I read *Golf in the Kingdom* by Michael Murphy, one of the century's true geniuses. It's an extraordinary book, yet I suspect that one of the reasons I think it is the *best book ever written about golf* is that there is so much in it that I still do not understand. Two more readings, and I'm still struggling, particularly with the essays in Part II. If you haven't read *Golf in the Kingdom* before, read it now. If you have, read it again. We'll get together for a two-week retreat and meditate on it.

But if Zen refers to the attainment of sudden enlightenment through total, focused concentration, then professional golfers *do* understand it. Or at least they *experience* it.

Mickey Wright said once, "When I play my best golf, I feel as if I'm in a fog, standing back watching the earth in orbit with a golf club in my hands." Mark Calcavecchia says that "when I'm in a zone, I don't think about the shot or the wind or the distance or the gallery or anything; I just pull a club and swing." And Paul Azinger insists that "staying in the present is the key to any golfer's game: once you start thinking about a shot you just messed up or what you have to do on the next nine to catch somebody, you're lost."

And nobody in the history of golf ever closed out the world more completely and focused on the present more intensely than the ultimate Zen master himself, Jack Nicklaus.

Hey-There! Hi-There!
Fore-There!

A round of golf . . . partakes of the journey, and the journey
is one of the central myths and signs of Western Man. It is built
into thoughts and dreams, into his genetic code. The Exodus,
the Ascension, the Odyssey, the Crusades, the pilgrimages of
Europe and the Voyage of Columbus, Magellan's Circumnavi-
gation of the Globe, the Discovery of Evolution and the March
of Time, getting ahead and the ladder of perfection, the exploration of space and the Inner Trip: from the beginning our
Western World has been on the move.

> —Shivas Irons in *Golf in the Kingdom* by Michael Murphy

Spend many winters anywhere in the Snow Belt and sooner or
later you decide, the hell with it, enough of this cold and snow
and slush, I have simply got to play a little golf, and I'll be
damned if I'm going to sit around waiting for some stupid robin
to say it's okay.

So what you do is you take out an emergency loan from the
cookie jar or the kids' college fund, whichever has the higher
balance, and book flights, rooms, and tee times. Then you get
your clubs out of the closet and polish the golf shoes that you
put away wet and muddy three months before. Finally, you run
down to the golf discount store to buy four dozen balls at a
savings of $36 (plus tax) from what you would have paid for
them at a resort pro shop. (Can you *believe* what they charge for
a sleeve of balls at those places?)

Feeling fiscally righteous, you also pick up that new perimeter-weighted tetrahedron-shaped putter with the built-in peri-scope that you've heard so much about, plus a ninety-degree wedge (your fifth) for hitting straight up, new head covers to replace the ones knitted for you by your first wife (time to move on), and three new Nick Faldo golf shirts in competing Day-Glo shades of yellow, purple, and magenta—you know, the ones with the zigzag pattern that looks like Richard Nixon's last polygraph test.

Now, fully armed and ready to take up the relentless pursuit of quasi-athletic mediocrity you suspended in frustration last October, where do you go?

Why, to Florida, of course.

Florida has orange juice, sunshine, Dolphins, gators, hurri-canes, *Miami Vice* reruns, drug lords, two time zones, Shamu the Whale, 1,800 miles of overbuilt coastline, 13 million residents, the fastest growth rate of any state in the union, Jimmy Buffett, stone crabs, a panhandle, America's oldest city, spring training, a $29 billion tourist industry, the nation's only Tupperware Museum, lunker bass, Anita Bryant, the best thoroughbred race-horses this side of Kentucky, a maximum elevation of 345 feet, a golden-age retirement community with your name on it, the country's largest congregation of fire ants, a new major-league baseball club, and the Everglades (at least for the time being). Oh, yes, and Walt Disney World.

But most of all, Florida has golf.

In 1513, Ponce de León sailed north from Puerto Rico and discovered Florida. Sounds like something any fifth-grade geog-raphy student could do just by looking at a map, but it wasn't until he got all the way up the coast near St. Augustine that the Spanish explorer actually found land. Old Ponce—he was fifty-three at the time, Jack Nicklaus's age—was looking for the Fountain of Youth, but the closest he got was a swatch of marsh-land off Highway A1A about forty-five minutes south of what is now the TPC Stadium Course at Sawgrass.

Nothing much happened in Florida for the next 300 years,

probably because nobody could figure out a way to get through the summers without air-conditioning. In 1819, America bought Florida from Spain for $5 million. Aside from the Louisiana Purchase, this was the best land deal in U.S. history, at least until 1979, when Deane Beman bought 450 acres of meadow, marsh, and woods in Ponte Vedra Beach for $1 and the promise to locate PGA Tour headquarters there.

The arrival of the railroads in the 1880s in Florida produced a big real estate boom, followed swiftly by an equally big collapse. Another boom came in the 1920s, complete with creative land swindles and yet another bust during the Great Depression. Not until after World War II did boom times come to stay in Florida, as retired people, Cuban émigrés, Walt Disney, shivering tourists from the north, land developers, and golfers combined to make Florida the California of the East Coast.

Next to the drug trade, golf contributes more to Florida's economy today than any other industry. Oranges? If they were so important, developers wouldn't have spent the last two decades cutting down orange groves to put in golf courses. Florida is number one in phosphates, theme parks, satellite launches, sponges, and retirement condos, and right up there among the leaders in electrical equipment, fast-food joints, and humidity. But golf is the real deal in Florida, and it's getting bigger every day, with new courses coming on line at the rate of twenty-five a year.

As of the beginning of 1993, there were 1,052 private, semi-private, resort, and municipal golf courses in Florida. That's 189 more than you'll find in California, runner-up in this all-important measure of a nation's cultural wealth, and 589 more than in Scotland, where it all began.

Assuming an average length of 6,200 yards from the regular tees, that means Florida has 3,611 miles of golf, give or take an executive course or two. Laid out as a single hole, Florida's golf courses would stretch from Key West to Vancouver and play as a par 36,902. Figuring four rounds a week plus a modest allowance for rain-outs, you would need about five years to play all of

Florida's golf courses, assuming a construction moratorium on new ones until you rolled in your last putt.

Also:

○Florida is the residence of preference for pro golfers when they're not out on the road chasing birdies. Only three members of the PGA Tour were born in Florida, but forty-seven now live there.

○Florida plays host to five tournaments on the PGA Tour, more than any other state.

○The PGA of America's annual Merchandise Show, which this year attracted 28,000 club pros, buyers, manufacturers, and golf techies to ooh and aah over the latest gimcrackery and gewgaws guaranteed to heal hooks and solve slices, is held in Orlando.

○The national headquarters of the PGA Tour, the LPGA, and the PGA of America are located in Florida.

○Golf contributes $1.9 billion annually to the Florida economy.

No wonder the Sunshine State is willing to do just about anything—drain Lake Okeechobee, route cart paths through the Everglades, whatever it takes—to keep guys like me coming on down.

There's just one tiny problem with a winter golf vacation in Florida: in my experience, it's always been a prescription for disaster.

It starts on the plane. All the way down you worry that (a) your clubs will be routed to Jackson Hole instead of Jacksonville, (b) it will rain every day, just as *USA Today* forecasts, (c) the Cape Beach Dunes Waves Palms Resort Hotel will have screwed up your reservation, forcing you to sleep in the parking lot in your subcompact rental car, (d) the plane will explode into a ball of fire while landing, leaving no survivors with handicaps greater than fourteen, or (e) all of the above.

Even when the answer is (f), none of the above, you're so excited by the prospect of actually playing golf the following day that when you finally get to your room you don't fall asleep until

1:15 A.M. Suddenly, at 3:37 A.M., you snap awake with the star-tling insight that, after not having held a club in your hands for nearly three months, your game might be a shade rusty. You panic. You try to recall every golf tip you ever read in every golf magazine ever published, but can't remember which end of the club to grip. You take practice swings with a coat hanger until you catch a glimpse of yourself in the mirror and realize what you look like. You finally drift off after draining several little bottles snatched at random from the minibar—at a cost, you later discover, of $32—and dream you are running down a long tunnel, racing desperately to get to the first tee on time, when you discover you forgot to put on your pants.

The first day, after five cups of coffee to scald the cobwebs out of your brain, you play thirty-six holes of exceedingly ugly golf in a fuzzy, hung-over, slo-mo daze, then race back to the prac-tice range to work on the sick boomerang slice you thought you'd fixed last summer. The second day you're so stiff you can barely stand up, but you play twenty-seven more and replace the slice with a pull hook. The third day you're straight as an arrow off the tee, but you chili dip or skull everything within forty yards and miss eleven putts under four feet. Hopeless, you figure, utterly hopeless—until, on the last nine holes of your fourth and final day, you start playing the best golf of your life and decide, Hey, I can *play* this game.

And then you get on a plane and go home.

Sound familiar? Only to another golfer, I guess. I know it pretty well sums up my life. At least it did until the winter I fulfilled my ultimate dream: I went to Florida in January—and I stayed there, for a month, visiting all the best golf resorts and playing all the best golf courses.

I wanted, for the first time in my life, to do a winter golf vacation the right way. This time was going to be different. This time was going to be absolutely perfect: one solid month of golf in the warm, sunny southeast corner of America, a calm leisurely round every day, each at a different terrific course, no rush, no pressure, no anxiety about having to squeeze in thirty-six holes before sundown, plenty of quality time at the practice range, nothing to do for thirty days but fine-tune my game.

Hey, somebody had to do it . . .

The organizing principle for my trip came from four guys from Liverpool—no, not the Beatles—whom I had met two years before at a bed-and-breakfast in Dornoch, a small town and famous outpost of golf in northern Scotland. They were on a week-long holiday in which they were systematically playing all the best golf courses in Scotland that are easily accessible from route A9, the highway that runs straight north from the Firth of Forth to Wick. They had played Pitlochry, Blair Atholl, Inverness, Nairn, and Tain, and now they were in Dornoch to play thirty-six holes at one of the grandest courses in the British Isles, Royal Dornoch.

My variation on that theme: take a tune from Jimmy Buffett's songbook and play all the best golf courses easily accessible on and just off "the avenue that's called A1A," the state highway that begins at Fernandina Beach on Amelia Island and runs south for 373 miles to Miami Beach. "Changes in latitude, changes in attitude" would transform my golf game, I was sure of it—provided I steered clear of Margaritaville *and* kept my eye on the ball.

The map says Florida, but your eyes tell you something else. Geographically, culturally, every which way, Amelia Island is closer kin to the Carolina Low Country of *The Prince of Tides*. About the only thing this long, narrow strip of salt marsh and coastal forest north of Jacksonville has in common with the state's two more famous islands, Palm Beach and Miami Beach, is the Atlantic Ocean.

Gnarled live oaks draped in Spanish moss and thick stands of loblolly pines form a cool, green cathedral. At the coastal forest's western edge, a sea of marsh grass ripples in the warm afternoon breeze. Hidden from view, except to an osprey gliding silently overhead, meandering streams cut looping, random doodles in the marshland. On the other side of the forest, beyond clumps of palmettos and dense thickets of shrub, a muffled roar builds in volume behind a ridge of sand and saw grass, until there, through an opening in the dunes, the ocean finally appears, a sight as exhilarating each new time as it was the first.

What's amazing is how much of that original beauty was left intact when developers transformed 1,250 acres into Amelia Island Plantation, one of the country's premier golf resorts and the first one you encounter on A1A. After all, it could have been another Hilton Head.

"Plantation" is a developers' code word, first applied up the way at Hilton Head, for the resorts/condo communities built on Low Country islands over the past three decades. It has a good sound to it, but no relation whatsoever to the original meaning, so don't go there expecting Tara with sand traps.

Amelia Links, the original twenty-seven-hole course by Pete Dye that opened for play in 1975, is a short, testy hike through marshland and thick forest. Narrow fairways, small greens, marsh just beyond the rough, and water everywhere put a premium on straight shots. None of the three nines tops 3,000 yards from the regular tees, but spray the ball and you'll be writing down big numbers all day.

There's more of everything at Long Point Club, a younger (1987) but bigger brother to the Dye course. More live oaks, more water, more marsh, more yards (about 700 more from the back tees). Long Point is also more beautiful than Amelia Links, primarily because the bordering marshland precludes any building alongside the course, particularly on the back nine.

There is also a dress code, reprinted here in its entirety: "Golf shirts must be worn at all times. Shorts must be 17″ minimum from top of waist to bottom of hem. No tank tops, T-shirts, blue jeans, bathing suits, mesh shirts, or cutoffs are allowed. Women are not allowed to wear halter tops or short-shorts. This dress code is mandatory on both the golf course and the driving range, and applies to all golfers. If you are in doubt of your attire, please check with the golf-shop staff. Thank you for your cooperation."

Let me get this straight. You want me to check with the golf-shop *staff* if I have questions about my attire? Check with people who wear purple-and-orange poly-blend shirts, green Sansa-belt slacks, and two-toned shoes? For advice on *clothes*? No, thanks.

Not that there has to be, but there's a lot more to Amelia Island that golf. Exploring a four-mile stretch of beach, fishing for bass in surrounding lagoons, bicycling on trails through thick forests, visiting the funky old port of Fernandina Beach just up the road, and riding horseback on the beach can all fill your days if you forget to bring your clubs. (Or if, as I nearly did, you throw them in the nearest lagoon after your first round.)

How did I shoot? Come on, now—give a guy a break. This was my first time out in three months. The weather was pretty chilly. I didn't get to spend enough time on the practice tee. This was the first time I'd ever played either course. I was concentrating on getting my tempo. I didn't keep score.

Heading south from Amelia, A1A takes you from heaven (the barrier islands north of Jacksonville) through hell (the spread-out, scruffy commercial fringe of Jacksonville) and out again (to the plush, manicured golf communities southeast of Jacksonville) in less than two hours. You can't see the ocean on the left or the golf courses on the right, but you know they're there because the sign says "Ponte Vedra Beach," and a good job it does because there is nothing else, absolutely nothing else, to indicate that the string of malls and fast-food joints and low-slung glass office buildings and gas stations constitutes a single entity of any kind, much less a town.

Welcome to Sawgrass.

Mention the word "Sawgrass," and just about anybody who's ever spent any serious time watching golf on TV flashes the image of a single golf hole. Yeah, *that* one. But, believe it or not, there are seventeen *other* golf holes at the TPC Stadium Course at Sawgrass, home of The Players Championship. Yet the only one to conjure up an instant mental snapshot, even if you've never seen it in person, is the most imitated par three of the last decade . . . the toughest easy hole in golf . . . the infamous Dyevil's Island.

Yes, fellow hackers, I'm talking about No. 17, "the one with the island green."

○No. 17 measures 132 yards from the championship tees, 121 from the blues, 97 from the whites, and 80 from the reds, but just about everybody who plays there hits from the back, just like the pros.

○A local rule posted at the tee limits each golfer to two tee shots. Unless the course is unusually backed up, this rule is routinely ignored.

○Each year, over *80,000* balls are fished out of the lake surrounding the green. If anyone from Sawgrass is reading, I'd like my two back, please.

○The toughest pin placement is front right.

○Robert Gamez scored an eleven there in the 1990 Players Championship.

○There have been two aces scored at the seventeenth since The Players Championship moved to the Stadium Course in 1982.

○The alligator that used to live in the lake has been relocated. Rumor has it that he was suffering from acute depression brought on by witnessing so much human ineptitude.

○The prevailing wind is from the northwest, which sweeps across the green and into your face at a forty-five-degree, left-to-right angle. *That's* why the toughest pin placement is front right.

○Forget the water and hit the damned ball—it's not *that* tough a hole!

Now, as to the rest of the course, it is either a great, imaginative design, one of Pete Dye's finest, or a "bleeping tricked-up pile of bleep," as one touring pro described it. It sort of depends on whom you talk to.

The fact is, most of the golfers on the PGA Tour hate the Stadium Course because it makes them look bad. They grouch about its nontraditional design, the dipsy-doo undulations of its greens, the severe contouring of its fairways—and they're right: Pinehurst No. 2, it ain't. But remember this: any time you hear a pro say of a course after a practice round that it's "tough but fair, an honest test of golf," it means he's just shot 66 and thinks he can top that when the gun sounds on Thursday. And if he uses the words "tricked-up" and "gimmicky" and "unfair" to describe the course, it means he just carded a 74 and has visions of spending Saturday morning watching cartoons.

More objective observers give it high marks. *Golf Digest*, for instance, ranks the Stadium Course number forty-four among "America's Top 100 Courses" and figures it's the third-best track in Florida after Seminole and Black Diamond, both of which are private.

But this does *not* make it a whole gang of fun to play, particularly for duffers like me. It's not brutally long (just 6,400 yards from the blue tees, another 400 from the tips), but the landing areas are too tight, the bunkers too punitive, and the greens too severe for a round there to seem like anything but hard work. The five finishing holes are especially punishing, with the seventeenth the least of your troubles. But tough as it most certainly is, the Stadium Course is one other thing as well: memorable.

Stay in the area long enough and you'll probably find yourself playing three rounds at "Old Sawgrass" (i.e., Sawgrass Country Club) for every time you put yourself through the torture chamber of "New Sawgrass" (i.e., TPC Stadium Course). Not that the former is a pushover: at just over 7,000 yards from the back tees, it's plenty of course and then some. But compared with the Stadium Course, Old Sawgrass is more direct, less punitive, more accessible, less tricked-up, more fun. A fairer test of golf. (Yes, I did shoot five strokes better at Old Sawgrass than at New Sawgrass. How did you guess?)

The customary base of operations for golfers testing the Stadium Course is Marriott's Sawgrass Resort, a 557-room standard-issue Marriott that looks like an IRS regional office with good landscaping. Stay there and you get to play the Stadium Course; the TPC Valley Course, a solid track that lives in the shadow of its glitzy big brother; and Sawgrass Country Club, a classy Ed Seay design that hosted the Tournament Players Championship (as the event used to be known) from 1977 to 1981.

But an even better place to bunk is The Lodge at Ponte Vedra Beach. The Lodge is small: just sixty-six rooms. It's lush: you spend $18 million to build sixty-six rooms, you get lush at no extra charge. It's on the beach: every room has an ocean view. It's new: open since 1989. It's beautiful inside: *novo* Mediterranean design, with lots of terra-cotta, pale wood, pastels, and open space. Best of all, The Lodge at Ponte Vedra Beach gives you the best golf deal in town because Lodge guests get to play at Marsh Landing Country Club, a beguiling Ed Seay layout that winds through a virtual nature preserve.

Get the picture? You can stay at a big, impersonal golf barracks a couple of miles from the ocean and play the Stadium Course, Old Sawgrass, and Valley Course. Or you can stay at a small, intimate, luxury hotel on the beach and play those three *plus* Marsh Landing, an otherwise private course whose front nine (says Dan Jenkins) is "simply the prettiest and most intriguing nine in the area."

Your call.

How did I shoot? The pros are right: the Stadium Course is just plain unfair. At Old Sawgrass, I hit a lot of good shots but caught some bad breaks. And at Marsh Landing, well, let me tell you that Marsh Landing is so danged pretty you don't care how you score.

An hour south of Jacksonville on A1A, the town of Palm Coast was created from whole cloth (i.e., oceanfront, scrub oak forest, marshland) by the ITT Corporation and is proud to be "one of the largest planned communities in America today."

Don't let that scare you off, though, because if you bunk at the Sheraton Palm Coast, you get to play at Hammock Dunes Links

Course, a 1989 Tom Fazio design that is shooting up the charts faster than a Michael Jackson single. Fazio says the Hammock Dunes site reminded him of what Seminole must have looked like when Donald Ross began routing that Florida treasure. Better hurry, as access is "for a limited time only" (i.e., until they sell enough of the pricey homesites around the private course so that they can manage without our greens fees).

How did I shoot? Whew, when the wind is blowing hard off the ocean, the way it was the day I was there, this is one tough mother of a course.

Moving on down the coast, I resist the temptation to drop by Vero Beach and see what Dodgertown feels like without the Dodgers. Forget baseball. Have to stay focused on golf. Next stop: PGA National at Palm Beach Gardens.

PGA National is to golf what Flint used to be to Buicks. Here you have assembly-line golf at its fine-tuned best, with an army of bag toters and club cleaners and rangers and pro-shop people working feverishly to keep the line moving. Five courses: the Champion (a Nicklaus redo of a George and Tom Fazio original) is big and tough, the General (by Arnold Palmer) is big and boring, the Haig and the Squire (also by the Fazios) are good, clean fun. The fifth course (the Estate, by Karl Litten) is somewhere off campus, so why bother?

PGA National, you will be pleased to know, has the largest croquet complex in the Western Hemisphere. Seriously. Either that, or they've cleverly used a lot of wickets to disguise a really big turf farm. If you ask me, a croquet pitch is a waste of a good putting green.

A few years back, PGA National was sued by the family of a golfer who died of a heart attack brought on, the suit alleged, by a nasty encounter with fire ants. In the lawsuit, the family contended that PGA National had been negligent in failing to exterminate fire ants on its courses and by not warning people of the safety hazard they represented. Not so, said PGA National's lawyers, who argued that fire ants are a scourge throughout the Southeast and that nobody anywhere had figured out how to get rid of them. (They're right. Recently an advanced scouting party of the little pests was spotted as far north as the outskirts of Knoxville, and scientists project that they will reach the Great Lakes by the turn of the century.)

Anyway, lawyers for PGA National suggested, the forty-eight-year-old golfer's heart attack may have had less to do with fire-ant bites than with the fact that the victim was thirty-five pounds overweight, had high blood pressure and elevated cholesterol, and smoked two packs of cigarettes a day.

Case dismissed.

But it did lead to one local rule: If your ball lands on an anthill, take a free drop.

How did I shoot? Heck, I was too busy looking out for fire ants to keep my eye on the ball.

They say the only three things that matter in real estate are location, location, and location. But if you can't have location, you can always fudge it. The Palm Beach Polo Club isn't in Palm Beach—it's in *West* Palm Beach, the town that grew up on the mainland across from Palm Beach to house the hired help. Much of West Palm is scruffy, run-down, poor. Willie Smith partied in *Palm* Beach, but he stood trial in *West* Palm Beach. The Breakers is in *Palm* Beach. Days Inn is in *West* Palm Beach. Wouldn't *you* fudge the name if *you* were the Polo Club?

The Palm Beach Polo Club is one place where you *do* want to put your cart before your horse. The guest villas are swell, the grounds are immaculate, the horses are beautiful, the tennis is first-caliber, the restaurants are good, the whole place gives new meaning to the term "casual elegance." And golf? With a tough new eighteen holes by P. B. and Pete Dye, a sneaky linkslike track by Ron Garl and Jerry Pate, and a testy nine-hole walkaround by Tom Fazio, the golf you'll find at this polo club is a darned sight better than the polo you'll find at your average golf club.

How did I shoot? I was doing great until I fell off my horse.

• • •

Just across Lake Worth in Palm Beach—the *real* Palm Beach—stands the dowager queen of Florida's grand old resort hotels, The Breakers. Once upon a time the center of the social universe (Eastern Seaboard Division), The Breakers has lost none of its snootiness, pretension, or snob appeal, even though it now depends on convention business rather than society balls to keep its doors open.

You can marvel at the pretentious grandeur of stylized excess, play croquet till your wickets stick, spot Burt Reynolds and Loni Anderson sipping $600-a-bottle Bordeaux, bump your credit-card limit on Worth Avenue, look down your nose at the conventioneers who've replaced the carriage trade, spend $2,200 a night for the Presidential Suite, take high tea, and pay an obligatory visit to Au Bar.

You can even play golf on the front yard, if all you're looking for is an excuse to get outdoors. They say the hotel course is a Donald Ross track. Maybe. But if it is, then the Master must have been on holiday at the time. (One grace note: you can walk.) Another eighteen about a quarter hour inland (the Breakers West Course, designed by William Byrd) is more interesting, but not by enough to make the Old Gray Lady of Palm Beach a *primo* stop for the serious golfer.

Fortunately, there's plenty of other stuff to keep you busy. Or you can take the money you'd spend there in a week and buy a new car.

How did I shoot? C'mon, everybody knows you can't expect to score well on a course that isn't challenging enough to keep your attention.

Everything is so swell about the Boca Raton Hotel and Club, one of the great old hallmarks of Florida luxury since 1926, that you kind of wish that "Boca Raton" in Spanish didn't mean "Rat's Mouth." If it bothers you too much, you can try what a nongolfing friend of mine does. She's married to a Brit, so she gives Boca Raton a limey twist, calling it "Ratsmouth," as in "Portsmouth."

The Boca deserves special preparation. If you visit, and you should, see if Hertz or Avis can come up with a yellow Stutz Bearcat for the occasion, because once you slide past the guard booth in front of the pink-stucco Mediterranean palace designed by society architect Addison Mizner, you enter another age. Once there, don't jump when Wilfrid Hyde-White appears at your side near the lobby registration desk to offer you a glass of champagne. And don't stand dumbstruck in the lobby (as I did), gaping at the elegant vaulted room, richly ornamented in dark wood and terra-cotta and well-faded tapestries and carved stone. People might take you for a tourist.

Just pretend that you're F. Scott Fitzgerald looking for a golf game.

Given the posh atmosphere and neo-Alhambran elegance of the place, you'd be willing to forgive and forget if golf at the Boca were on the ho-hum side. No need to worry: the original Boca course, a solid, traditional layout by William Flynn (1926) that Joe Lee retooled a couple of years ago, is a delight to play—tough enough to be interesting, but forgiving enough to let your spirits soar.

But even if the only golf within driving distance were a rubble-strewn muni with sand greens, you'd *still* have plenty of good reasons to stay at the Boca, not the least of which is the key lime pie at Nick's Fishmarket, one of Boca's two blue-ribbon restaurants.

What chili is to Texas, key lime pie is to Florida: a food group unto itself. Nobody makes a tastier one than Nick's, just across the Intracoastal from the main hotel at the Boca Beach Club. In fact, when the AAA and Mobil people last sat down to allocate their customary five diamonds and five stars to the Boca, I suspect it was right after polishing off several servings of Nick's rendition of the official state dessert.

Forget the stale graham-cracker crust and glutinous yellow mess that masquerade under the name key lime pie on most menus. At Nick's you get a light, flaky pastry shell about the size of a golf hole that's been filled with an ethereal lime mousse, topped with whipped cream and a single fresh raspberry, cast adrift in a shallow pool of raspberry sauce, and surrounded by a picket line of still more raspberries. (There you have it—the key to key lime pie is . . . raspberries!)

If Nick's key lime pie were a golf course, it would be Pine Valley.

How did I shoot? Better. Maybe it was the pie.

Trucking on down A1A, closing in on Miami but still in the high-rent district, you come to Turnberry Isle Resort and Country Club. What the Boca was to the 1920s and 1930s, Turnberry Isle is to the 1990s—stylish, hip, posh.

Political junkies will make a pilgrimage to Turnberry Isle to see the spot where Gary Hart and Donna Rice disembarked on *Monkey Business.*

Movie buffs and L.A. Lakers fans will want to go to Turnberry Isle because that's where Jack Nicholson acquired his recent addiction to golf. (A tip for those who never saw *The Shining:* if you spot Jack Nicholson coming toward you with a big grin on his face and a two iron in his hands, let him play through.)

Middle-aged tennis junkies will be pleased to learn that Jimmy Connors is a semiregular on Turnberry Isle courts when he's not beating the tail off kids half his age.

Shoot, you might even want to stay at Turnberry Isle just for the golf, which comes in the form of two Robert Trent Jones courses, one of them stronger than yesterday's coffee.

But the best reason for staying at Turnberry Isle is the room and board.

The new Magnolia wing at Turnberry Isle sets a new standard for Florida Modern design (hotel division). Fourteen-foot ceilings and huge ceiling-to-floor French doors opening onto small balconies overlooking the golf course impart an expansive, spacious feel that is positively exhilarating. The bathrooms, which are smaller than Bermuda but not by much, have all the right touches, from a separate shower to a jet-propelled Jacuzzi.

As good as the guest rooms at Turnberry Isle are, its dining room—The Veranda—is even better. Too many hotel restaurant chefs in Florida remain mired in the rut of "gourmet continental cuisine," whatever in Chef Boyardee's name that might be. Not Veranda head pro Robbin Haas, who runs his kitchen the way Seve Ballesteros plays golf—with dash, style, and imagination.

How's this for a hip version of surf 'n' turf: pan-seared venison loin with guava-tamarind barbecue sauce and garlic mashed potatoes, and sauteed Marathon Key mahimahi with red and golden tomato relish and saffron pearl potatoes. Or maybe you'd prefer pumpkin-seed-dusted pompano with lump crab meat and papaya salsa, and pan-seared and cumin-scented tenderloin of beef with horseradish mashed potatoes. Either way, start with tiered portobello mushrooms with grilled vegetables, goat cheese, and black-truffle vinaigrette.

Yum.

If the Turnberry Isle chef were as handy with golf clubs as he is with pots and pans, he'd be wearing a green jacket along with his toque.

How did I shoot? Maybe it was something I ate . . .

The Doral Ryder Open (formerly the Doral–Eastern Open Invitational and—before the era of corporate sponsors—the Doral Open Invitational) has been one of the pros' favorite stops on the PGA Tour since 1962. It always attracts a strong field, in part because it's the first of four straight Florida tournaments and the pros want to get reacquainted with Bermuda greens in a hurry. It's also popular because so many of the pros live in Florida, and they get to play close to home. Finally, the pros like the tournament because they love the track—the Blue Course (aka the Blue Monster) at the Doral Country Club and Resort.

Once the definitive Florida golf resort, the Doral had slipped noticeably in recent years. The Blue Course was still a Monster, but the other four tracks had gotten a little scruffy. Also, many of the rooms and public spaces were showing their age. The good news: many millions were spent on renovations over the past three years to bring the resort and its courses back up to par. (Or back down. Whatever.) Also, the Doral Saturnia Spa remains the region's top stop for sybaritic and healthful pursuits, and there is still an awful lot of great golf to be played just steps from your front door.

How did I shoot? I think I left my game on the masseuse's table at the spa.

The central, inescapable, defining fact of contemporary Florida is Walt Disney World.

All roads in the Sunshine State lead there. Even while tooling down A1A, you feel this irresistible tug toward the Magic Kingdom. There's no getting away from it. Wherever you are in the state, there's a billboard to remind you that you're just fill-in-the-blank miles from Mickey, Goofy, and all the gang.

So, you might as well give in gracefully. After you finish your round at the Blue Monster, find the Florida turnpike, set the cruise control to seventy, point the rental car northwest, and start reconstructing every round you've played since you first teed off at Amelia Island. That should take a while, assuming you count every stroke, and before you know it you'll be on the outskirts of Greater Disney World. (Don't worry about missing the turnoff: everything turns tacky and garish at Kissimmee.)

But don't make a beeline for the Magic Kingdom. You need to come to it gradually or all that jolliness will give you the bends. The best places to steel your nerves for a visit to the Magic Kingdom are a few minutes away at Bay Hill and right next door at Grand Cypress.

Florida is chock-full of posh, glitzy resorts outfitted with luxurious rooms aplenty, more fancy restaurants than France, enough activities to tire out a cruise ship, an oo-la-la spa where you can get scrubbed with stiff brushes and packed in mud, and a ho-hum golf course (maybe two) that will lower your handicap.

And then there is Bay Hill.

While it is a resort, technically speaking, the Bay Hill Club and Lodge is actually a great golf course with a motel grafted onto the pro shop.

Okay, that's not fair: the sixty-four guest rooms, twelve condominium units, and three guesthouses at Bay Hill are comfortable, tastefully appointed, and spacious. There is a swimming pool and a restaurant that serves decent grub. And you're just fourteen minutes from the Magic Kingdom. But my point is that you don't stay at Bay Hill for a great resort experience. You stay at Bay Hill because that's the only way you get to play Arnold Palmer's home course.

There are actually twenty-seven holes at Bay Hill, but the eighteen that concern you are the Challenger and Champion nines, which together form the course that hosts the Nestlé Invitational Tournament on the PGA Tour. Ed Seay is the designer of record, but the course has been tinkered with over the years by the club's owner and developer, Mr. Palmer.

If you watch much golf on TV, you already know the eighteenth hole, a 441-yard par four whose long, narrow green bends around a lake, with big traps to the left and behind to punish the timid. Most years it ranks as the PGA Tour's toughest finishing hole. If you haven't seen it, don't ask Greg Norman for details. Norman, who was on the verge of adding the Nestlé to his trophy case in 1990, was playing the seventeenth when tour rookie Robert Gamez holed a 176-yard seven iron on the eighteenth for an eagle to edge the White Shark by a stroke.

Even before you get to the eighteenth, you'll have done plenty of heavy lifting. Bay Hill is muscular, no-nonsense, no-tricks, in-your-face. The greens are faster and trickier than at most resort courses, but then Bay Hill is not really a resort course (except in the technical sense). It's Florida, so there's plenty of water and sand, but Bay Hill is not really a target course. First and foremost, Bay Hill is a big hitter's course—7,100 yards from the championship tees, 6,500 yards from the merely mortal tees, almost 6,200 yards from the old folks' tees.

So bring out your Big Bertha, wind up your wide-body, and

pop in your John Daly instructional tape. At Bay Hill, you'd better be ready to grip it and rip it.

If God is in the details, then the Grand Cypress Resort, located five minutes away from the Magic Kingdom, is a little slice of Golf Heaven. For instance:

○Walking is permitted. On the New Course at Grand Cypress, you can take a caddie, pull a handcart, or tote your own. Walking at most fancy-schmancy golf resorts will get you arrested for trespassing.

○Water *and* ice are dispensed on Grand Cypress courses—and you get large plastic cups instead of those stupid little paper cones that hold about one good sip.

○Each golf cart includes a packet of tees, a tool for repairing ball marks, and a towel for each golfer.

○You get to leave your shoes, change your clothes, take a shower, or just hang out in a clubhouse where Jack Nicklaus has a *permanent locker.*

Mere details, you say? Careful. You're dangerously close to blasphemy. After all, if God can be found in the details, chances are you can find a great golf resort in them, too.

Take the practice range. At too many blue-chip golf resorts, anyone not on a golf package has to pay three bucks or so for a small bag or bucket of range balls. Grand Cypress gives all golfers, packaged or not, unlimited range balls. At each station on the range, there's a pile of balls, and every so often an attendant in green knickers comes by to replenish the pile. This means you can play a round in the morning, have a little lunch, and hit balls until the sun goes down or your hands fall off, whichever comes first, without paying an extra cent for the privilege.

Don't you sometimes wonder how Florida resorts charging $60 to $100 and more in greens fees have the *nerve* to nick you another $3 for range balls? That's cheap-charlie bull-bleep at its worst. If they've got to have that extra few bucks, why not raise the greens fee $5 and *then* let you hit balls all day? And while they're at it, why not buy a few new range balls every five years or so? In California, most top-flight resorts (no pun intended) supply good-quality range balls gratis. But at most ritzy Florida joints the range balls are so lousy you'd get a better sense of trajectory by hitting rocks.

(The range balls at Grand Cypress are near mint-condition Spaldings, and if they didn't have that telltale stripe, my bag would be full of them right now.)

But I digress, and there are a lot of other things to consider about Grand Cypress, such as the housing options open to you.

If you feel like putting on the ritz, stay at the Hyatt Regency Grand Cypress. This is a whopping great 750-room hotel with special effects worthy of a Steven Spielberg movie, including the mother of all lobby atriums, a "Regency floor" where they tuck you in and tell you a bedtime story in between complimentary cocktails and complimentary breakfast, and a half-acre free-form swimming pool with a dozen waterfalls, three whirlpools, a swim-up bar, and a synchronized swimming team composed of fifty—count 'em—*fifty* live mermaids.

If you prefer to be far from the madding crowd, try the Villas at Grand Cypress, Mediterranean-style town houses clustered near the golf clubhouse about two miles from the hotel. Large and graciously appointed, the villa units range in size from one to four bedrooms and are no more than a nine iron away from a Caribbean-size swimming pool, should you crave an afternoon dip and not want to hop the turn-of-the-century trolley to the hotel. (No mermaids, though. They only work the hotel pool.) The villas come with full kitchens, but room service is only a heartbeat away for the terminally spoiled. At sunset, you can pull up a chair on your own personal patio, gaze out over a fairway or two, hum along with the crickets, and replay the day's round—minus the chili dips, snap hooks, and worm burners.

The golf at Grand Cypress is brought to you by Jack Nicklaus. It includes thirty-six holes of the Golden Bear at his very best (plus nine more holes at his only okay), one of the most re-spected golf schools in the business, a handsome clubhouse, and—as you may have heard—a particularly enlightened prac-tice-range policy.

The Old Course at Grand Cypress is not really all that old: the North and South nines made their debut in 1983, when Grand Cypress opened for business, and the East nine was added two years later. Conceptually, the North-South combo hails from the Heroic Period of the Golden Bear's architec-tural career, a time when Nicklaus moved heaven and a lot of earth to build the toughest, meanest, grandest course a devel-oper's money could buy.

Never mind that all he had to work with at Grand Cypress was several hundred featureless acres of an abandoned orange grove: "Flat land doesn't bother me," says the Golden Bear in the course guide. "I enjoy the challenge. We went down to the water table and created from there."

What he created was a spectacular collage of mounds, moguls, split-level fairways, huge elevated greens, and bunkers of every conceivable shape and size—grass bunkers, steep bunk-ers, shallow bunkers, pot bunkers, long bunkers, and *bunker* bunkers. Ten years ago, when it was new and raw, the Old Course (simply "Grand Cypress" then) had a tricked-up feel to it because it was unlike anything anyone had ever seen before, at least in Florida. Even so, it jumped onto *Golf Digest*'s top-100 list and stayed there until last year. (My prediction: it will be back.) Nowadays, with the mounds and moguls grown in, the Old Course looks perfectly natural, perhaps because some of its design themes have been echoed elsewhere.

(Note: The East nine of the Old Course, also by Nicklaus, is like a side dish you didn't order. Not necessarily bad, but not what you had in mind. On busy days, they'll try to put you on the East plus the North *or* the South. For $125, you have the right to just say No.)

The New Course at Grand Cypress (opened in 1990) pays

homage to the most ancient one of all, the Old Course at St. Andrews. Swilcan Burn protects the first hole, fourteen double greens open up the possibility of 150-foot putts, and Old Course landmarks such as the Principal's Nose and Hell Bunker punctuate the wide, undulating fairways at singularly inconvenient points. Mounds and swales around the green play visual tricks, while the absence of trees makes depth perception difficult— just as it is at the original. All that's missing from this new-old linkscape is the Royal and Ancient clubhouse.

There are, you will not be startled to learn, a few other attractions at Grand Cypress to placate any nongolfers in your party. Among them: a world-class equestrian center that gets the horsey set all in a lather, enough tennis courts to shame Wimbledon, a health spa for no pain–no gain fanatics, jogging and biking trails that are blissfully flat, and the obligatory croquet pit for people who don't mind looking really silly.

And, best of all, there's even a back entrance to the Magic Kingdom so you can slip in incognito.

The number one golf resort in America, measured solely by the quality and quantity of its golf courses, is—are you sitting down?—Walt Disney World.

That's right: Walt Disney World.

Not Pebble Beach. Not Pinehurst. Not Sawgrass. Not The Boulders, The Broadmoor, The Cloisters, The Homestead, or any of the other "The" resorts. Not Amelia Island, Innisbrook, or Doral in Florida. Not La Costa, La Quinta, or La Anything in La-La Land.

I'll say it again: Walt Disney World.

Take quality. The three "old" courses at Disney World—Magnolia (1971), Palm (1971), and Lake Buena Vista (1972), all designed by Joe Lee—are good enough to host a stop on the PGA Tour, and Palm and Magnolia are fixtures on *Golf Digest*'s "Top 75 Resort Courses in America" list. Not bad, but two new WDW courses that opened last year—Osprey Ridge (Tom Fazio) and Eagle Pines (Pete Dye)—are *even better* than their three older stablemates.

Pete Dye literally hollowed out Eagle Pines from the flat, wooded terrain, sculpting fairways that barely change in elevation but make up in subtle contouring what they lack in drop-dead drama. There's not a single building (other than a New Age clubhouse) to be seen from either Eagle Pines or Osprey Ridge, and there never will be. So when local egrets, ibises, and herons realize that construction is over and stake out claims in the newly dug lakes and ponds and untouched marshlands, playing Eagle Pines will be like spending the day in a nature preserve.

Where Dye burrowed, Tom Fazio built up. In creating his half of the new Disney double feature, he used spare dirt excavated at Eagle Pines to put the ridge in Osprey Ridge. The result will never be mistaken for a Carolina mountain course, but substantial elevation of key tee boxes provides unexpected vistas, while Fazio's signature mounding along fairways and around greens gives the course dramatic definition. As soon as enough people play it for word of mouth to spread, Osprey Ridge will earn top billing in the wonderful world of Disney golf.

Now take quantity. Other places have an individual course that is superior to any in WDW's lineup, but no other resort in the entire country has *five* courses this good. Put another way, the weakest link in the Disney chain—the Lake Buena Vista course—is better than the number two track at most other resorts.

Consider this: WDW bigwigs have a master plan for holding three professional tournaments in a single week. The Walt Disney World/Oldsmobile Classic, already a stop on the PGA Tour, at Palm, Magnolia, and Lake Buena Vista; a Senior PGA Tour event at Osprey Ridge; and an LPGA tournament at Eagle Pines. Don't bet that they can't pull it off. For an outfit that has just successfully invaded France, staging three golf tournaments in a single week is a piece of *gâteau*.

And yet . . . I have this, uh, problem with Walt Disney World attaining superpower status in the wide, wide world of golf resorts.

My problem is idiosyncratic and utterly irrational, not something I'm at all proud of. It's no doubt a result of closed-mindedness and a stunted imagination, and maybe someday I will overcome my prejudice. But the plain, honest-to-God truth is that Walt Disney World gives me the yips.

Part of it has to with size. Just knowing that WDW covers 28,000 acres, has 10,000 guest rooms, contains half a dozen separate theme parks, and can handle 17,000 conventioneers at a pop raises a scary question—suppose they all decide to play golf at the same time? It's enough to drive a fellow to the long putter.

Yet what really curdles my whey is Walt Disney World's aura, its gestalt, its essence. So clean. So neat. So wholesome. So well organized. So clean. So cheerful. So Stepford. *So damned clean.*

Do I sound like a maniac? I suppose so. And none of this bothers me in the least when I'm out on WDW's golf courses. But at the nineteenth hole, I get twitchy at the thought of spending the night in a place where the innkeeper is a sixty-five-year-old mouse with four fingers, of going down to breakfast and running into Goofy in the coffee shop, of losing it altogether and smashing in the next smiling face that says, "Hello, have a nice day."

Don't mind me, though: I'm just a cranky eighteen-handicapper with an acute case of rodentaphobia. Go ahead, especially if you have kids, and stay at Walt Disney World. You don't have to stay there to play there, but what the heck, you might as well. After all, you couldn't ask for a better baby-sitter than Goofy.

And you'll know it's time to go home when you find yourself singing a little ditty that goes something like this:

> Hey-there! Hi-there! Fore-there!
> Who's that standing on the tee?
> It's M - I - C - K - E - Y
> M - O - U - S - E . . .

The Old Course Owes
Me a Mulligan

The more I studied the Old Course, the more I loved it; and
the more I loved it, the more I studied it. So that I came to feel
that it was, for me, the most favorable meeting ground possible for an important contest. I felt that my knowledge of the
course enabled me to play it with patience and restraint, until
she might exact her toll from my adversary who might treat
her with less respect and understanding.

—Bobby Jones

Breakfast is the most important meal of the day, right? So at 7:00
A.M. on this morning before I play the most famous golf course
in the world for the first time in my life, day of days, I scrutinize
the breakfast menu in the dining room of Rusacks Hotel in St.
Andrews, Scotland, as if it were the Rosetta stone. In one hour
and forty-eight minutes I will tee off in a pro-am tournament
preceding the Dunhill Cup matches at the Old Course. I am
petrified.

Come, come, old sod. Must get a grip. It's only a wee bit of
gawf, innit now? Let's see here. What's to eat?

My eyes refocus, and my hands stop shaking long enough for
me actually to read the words printed on the menu. The "High-
land Grill" sounds promising. Bacon, sausage, haggis, eggs,
potatoes, grilled tomatoes, toast, coffee, and choice of juice
(orange, grapefruit, tomato, or prune). Hmmm. Maybe I'm
hungry after all. Yes, I think I'll . . .

Haggis?

Oh, sure. What could be more appropriate, prior to my first round ever at St. Andrews, than a little offal and oatmeal that's been boiled inside the lining of a sheep's stomach? Maybe I should order a double portion.

Instead, ordering toast and coffee, I make a mental note to add "haggis maker" to the growing list of occupations I pray never to have. ("Hi, honey, I'm home." "Have a good day?" "Just great. I stuffed thirty-seven sheep's stomachs with chopped-up lung, heart, and congealed blood. Only one of them broke." "That's fine, dear. Wash your hands for supper.")

The toast is served in the customary British manner, cold and limp, and I don't dare more than a couple of sips of coffee, lest too much caffeine short-circuit an overheated neurological system. Breakfast over, I overtip for good luck—are you watching, God?—and check my tee time (9:12 A.M.) for the thirteenth time since dawn. Next stop: the practice range.

The Links Committee of St. Andrews, the entity that manages the five golf courses owned by the municipality, has finally decided, after about a century and a half of studying the matter, to construct a proper practice facility. Not a bad idea, considering that they do play the odd British Open at the Old Course from time to time and most players like to get in a few warm-up hacks before teeing off. The Links Committee will probably get the new range sorted out, as the British say, well in time for the Royal and Ancient Golf Club's tricentennial celebration in 2054 of the founding of St. Andrews Society of Golfers. But in the meantime the practice range for the 1989 Dunhill Cup Pro-Am is a jerry-rigged slice of the Eden Course just to the west of the Old Course Hotel, where bags of balls are distributed to pro-am contestants from the back of a lorry. Pros get a bag of brand-new white Titleists; ams get orange balls. Makes sense: they need some way to tell us apart.

On the practice tee, my hands are shaking so hard that I need adhesive tape to form an overlapping grip. While my narrow escape from a plate of haggis may have something to do with this case of hyper yips, a more likely cause is the enormity of what I am about to do. For the first time in my golfing life, I am going to be playing in a honest-to-God tournament, in a field that includes the likes of Greg Norman and Curtis Strange and Tom Kite and Mark Calcavecchia, at the oldest and most famous course in the world, *and I'm not going to be allowed a single mulligan.*

Now, I respect the Rules of Golf, and for the most part I abide by them. I can live without rolling the ball in the fairway (unless it lands in a particularly deep divot). I haven't used a foot mashie in the rough in years. I don't break off tree limbs or uproot shrubs to give myself a clear shot. If a lie is unplayable, I take my penalty stroke like a trooper. I'd die before I'd ground a club in a bunker.

But no mulligans? That hardly seems fair.

It's not that I'm necessarily going to *need* a mulligan, you understand; it's that I need the *idea* of a mulligan. For millions of hackers all over the globe, the mulligan—the idea of a second chance, now and then, whether you deserve it or not—is what makes the game of golf tolerable. When you first start out, the mulligan keeps you from giving up the game in utter despair; without it, most of us would have quit after six months. The better you get at this most exquisite form of self-torture, the more you want to get a fix on just how good you are, so the less you rely on the mulligan. And at some point, I suppose, you forgo the mulligan altogether. But my game hasn't reached that point yet, and I don't suspect it will in this lifetime, so *I need to know my mulligan is there even if I don't take it.*

In the meantime, I'm hitting the ball better than I've ever hit in my life. Monster three woods, 230 yards and straight, with only a whisper of a fade at the very end. Majestic five irons, dropping softly on a patch of green the size of a tablecloth 170 yards away. Crisply nipped half wedges, proud seven irons high and true, even a few wind-cheating three irons rifled low and hard to an imaginary green 190 yards away.

"Oh, God," I began to intone the old golfer's prayer, one we've all prayed after a good session on the practice tee. *"Please don't let me hit all my good shots here."*

The starter's kiosk at the Old Course is located about seventy-five paces from the first tee on the right of the first fairway. I check in there forty-five minutes before tee time and am told politely to come back at twenty till. I walk around, putt on the small putting green nearby, walk some more. Check watch: forty-one minutes and ticking. More walking, more putting, although it's doggone hard to putt when you have no feeling whatsoever in your hands. The ball floats half an inch above the green, guided by electronic beams from outer space.

Suddenly, I feel dizzy, light-headed, a pain in my chest. Heart attack? No, I've just forgotten how to exhale. Check watch: twenty-nine minutes. (What does Greenwich Mean Time mean?) Check pockets: two brand-new Pinnacles in right pocket, golf glove in right hip pocket, six white golf tees in right pocket. If I were truly cool, I'd have a flask of old brandy in my golf bag. Of course, if I did, I'd be dead drunk by now. Check watch: twenty-four minutes to go. Omigod! Where's the loo? Through there, across the street, just beyond. Can I make it in time?

"Mr. Waggoner, you will have Ronnie today," says the calm voice behind the window at the starter's kiosk. "Ronnie is a Class 2 caddie and a good fellow."

"Class 2" means that his normal bag fee is eight pounds (a Class 1 caddie gets ten). Does "good fellow" mean that there are some bad ones who might have been assigned to me instead? Meanspirited Dickensian rogues who would mimic my swing to raucous laughter in low pubs for weeks to come? Diabolical avengers who would sneak into my hotel room and slit my throat in the name of defending the honor of the Grand Old Game?

As I ponder the possibilities, Ronnie presents himself with an outthrust hand and a neutral good morning. Ronnie is compactly built, about 5'8" tall. Gray tweed golfer's cap, gray wind-breaker, white shirt, tan pants. He could be in his late twenties or early forties; it's impossible to tell. The florid face and redness around the eyes suggest an excessive fondness for good Scottish ale, a common affliction among St. Andrews caddies. No matter: he's my new best friend.

I start apologizing for my game as we shake hands. This is my first time here, I'm not a very good golfer, this is my first pro-am, I'm not a very good golfer, Scotland is beautiful, I'm not a very good golfer . . . the usual. What else can I do? If I don't forge some kind of bond between us now, Ronnie's likely to stop speaking to me altogether. I know, I know—it's pathetic. But so is my golf swing.

"On the tee, from the United States, Mr. Glen Waggoner."

Oh, God.

I look around. Nobody else steps forward, so I guess the starter must mean me.

Oh, God!

"One of the least alarming tee-shots in existence," wrote Bernard Darwin in *The Golf Courses of the British Isles* of the first shot on the Old Course. "In front of us stretches a vast flat plain, and unless we slice the ball outrageously onto the sea beach, no harm can befall us."

"Piece of cake," Curtis Strange had said in the bar of the Old Course Hotel the night before. "All you have to remember is to keep it to the left on the way out and keep it to the left on the way back."

Ronnie whispers the same advice seconds before the starter calls out my name: "Hit it anywhere to the left. Just don't hit it right."

Okay, okay. I get the picture. The first and eighteenth holes at the Old Course share this huge expanse of fairway with no rough and no hazards, and there is more forgiveness on the left than in all the great world religions put together. But I still have one question: How do you hit it left or anywhere else when you can't draw back the club?

The tabloid headlines flash before my eyes: "YANK GOLFER TURNS TO STONE IN ST. ANDREWS." Even though she's an ocean away, I hear my wife saying, "I told him so." But something, probably fear that the starter would announce my name again, breaks the spell: I step up to the ball and actually swing my club.

Have you ever flushed a quail from cover in a meadow, watched it dart low and fast away from you at an angle, then stop in midair and swerve sharply to the ground after catching a tight pattern of shot from your 12-gauge? Well, I haven't, but it must look something like the half-smothered pull hook I send 185 skittering yards down the left side of the most famous fairway in the world.

Ugly? You betcha. But it's out there, the sun's still shining, and I have my health. What more can a mortal ask of his first shot at the first hole on his first visit to the Home of Golf?

"Take a full seven," says Ronnie, as we assay my second shot. "How far?" I ask, still drained from sheer relief at having gotten off the tee. "A full seven," Ronnie repeats, establishing firmly that his job is to give me a club and mine is to swing it. He cannot know that my full sevens can go anywhere from 135 to 165 yards and from east to west on the compass. No matter. This full seven travels about sixty-five yards, trailed for about forty-five of them by a divot the size of Ronnie's cap. "That's all right," he comforts me, "at least you didn't go into the burn."

What burn, I ask myself, looking around for smoke. And then I see Swilcan Burn for the first time. It's only the most famous little stream in golf, but my mind is a tabula rasa. I'm lucky to remember how to walk, much less that streams in this part of the world are called burns, and that this particular burn wraps around the first green. What was it, exactly, that made me take up golf in the first place?

But then something wonderful happens. I'm a full wedge from the flag, and I nail it perfectly. No skull. No chili dip. No burn. Neither fat nor lean. A perfect shot. Perfect by my standards, at least: on the green, just twenty feet from the pin. My putt slides six inches past on the right. Tap in. Routine bogey.

Bogey? While Ronnie commiserates and tries to pump me up for the second hole, I'm just about jumping out of my skin with joy. He's disappointed that I made a bogey; I'm ecstatic for having finished the hole. At this pace, I'll shoot 90 on the Old Course! Take me now, Precious Lord; I'm ready for my snow-white wings!

Too bad He didn't. If He had, at least I'd have crossed over to the other side buoyed by the belief that I was playing bogey golf at St. Andrews. Alas, it was not meant to be. Something unspeakably foul happened on the way to my 90, although to this day I'm still not sure what.

If there's one thing golfers are good at, it's being able to recount every waggle, every club selection, every swing on every hole of every round played, oh, for the last decade or so. The worst question a civilian trying to make polite conversation can ever ask a golfer is "How was your round?" Invariably, and in mind-numbing detail, the civilian finds out.

But not this time, not from me, not about my first round ever at the Old Course. The rest of what should have been the most memorable day of my golfing life is as elusive as September fog. Like disconnected fragments of a complicated dream, the round floats just out of reach, a slice here, a chili dip there, without ever quite coming together. It shimmers in front of my eyes, then fades into a haze, through which I spy a character who appears to be auditioning for a part in *Night of the Living Dead.* He stumbles out to the end of the shepherd's crook[1] and back

---

[1]The people who say the Old Course is shaped like a shepherd's crook can also look up into the night sky and spot bears, archers, belts, and dippers of assorted sizes. Your call.

toward the Auld Grey Toon,[2] stopping frequently to strike a little white ball. How do I know that I am the somnambulant golfer in this out-of-focus picture? Only because I have the scorecard to prove it, plus a few random scratches on my memory chip that simply will not go away.

There is, for instance, a drive on the second hole that slices far, far right onto a foreign fairway beyond the line of heather and gorse bushes separating the Old Course and the Jubilee Course. When we get to the point of the ball's departure from Old Course airspace, Ronnie makes a beeline for a break in the shrubbery, obviously with the intention of tracking down my drive. I restrain him. There is no way that I'm going to cross to the far side of an adjacent fairway belonging to another course for the sole purpose of humiliating myself even further. Ronnie is appalled. Scottish caddies abhor the idea of abandoning balls. Then there is the little matter of the Rules of Golf, which require that I return to the tee and hit another ball. No way I'm doing that, either. Ronnie is shocked. Citing the Rules of *Hacker* Golf, I drop a ball, give myself a one-stroke penalty, and hit a perfectly respectable four iron in the direction that Ronnie grudgingly indicates.

I know what you're thinking. In clear sight of the Royal and Ancient Clubhouse, on the most sacred turf in golf, this guy knowingly violates the Rules of Golf. What am I supposed to do? Go back to the tee and tell the foursome there to hold up while I forfeit stroke *and* distance? Cross over onto the Jubilee Course, delay play there, and run the risk of hitting my next shot onto the beach? (The fact that it's the beach seen under the credits in *Chariots of Fire* provides neither solace nor inspiration at the moment.) Disqualify myself before finishing the second hole on my first visit ever to the Old Course?

None of the above. What I proceed to do instead is provide a

[2]The by-laws of the Royal and Ancient require that everyone who writes about the Old Course refer (at least once) to St. Andrews as the "Auld Grey Toon."

lively demonstration of the flaws in my short game, pencil in a seven on my scorecard, and put an asterisk beside it as a reminder that the Rules of Golf were temporarily, but necessarily, suspended.

The next dozen holes I play in a daze. Ronnie gives me a line, I launch a shot to the left or right of it, then we go find my ball and repeat the process. He tells me the names of the most famous bunkers as we pass them, warns me about unseen hazards lurking ahead, and pumps me up after flubs. ("No matter. We can still save bogey.") Occasionally, he gives me a gentle needle: "This green," he says as I stand over a nine iron on the 514-yard Hole o'Cross (Out), "is the biggest green on the course. If you don't hit it, I'm walking off."

I don't, but he doesn't.

Sometimes golf isn't pretty. The other two arms in the foursome are better golfers than I am, but they're playing lousy—and not taking it well at all. Our pro is Gery Watine, the number-three man of the French entry in the Dunhill Cup, and his game reminds you that France is a nation of lovers and cooks. There's not a lot of gab in our group: Watine's English is on a par with my golf; the other two arms are too angry about their play to talk; and I'm catatonic. We get along famously.

Like all first-timers at the Old Course, I am unable to judge distance, primarily because there is so little change in elevation. Not that the Old Course is flat: on the contrary, it dips and bulges and rolls so incessantly that I practically get seasick looking out from the tee, trying to figure out which swell is obscuring the next green. Wad up a legal-size piece of paper, then smooth it out with your hands, and—presto!—you have a relief map of the Old Course.

Normally a decent putter, I'm having big trouble on the greens, despite Ronnie's accurate reads. I always seem to be putting down the side of a cliff and watching helplessly as the ball slides six feet past the hole. Even though I get a stroke a hole with my "eighteen" handicap,[3] too many three-putt greens prevent me from helping our floundering team. Indeed, the greens are a mystery to me in more ways than one.

Seven of the putting surfaces on the Old Course are double greens, each serving two holes. Only the first, ninth, seventeenth, and eighteenth holes have single greens. Even golfers who've never seen the Old Course know that much about it, right? Sure, but they haven't played the front nine in a trance: not until the eleventh hole, when I notice that the green I've just missed has two flags, does it dawn on me that others before have been similarly outfitted.

The High Hole (In) at the Old Course is one of the great par threes in the world—and possibly the toughest. At 172 yards it's not overly long, but if the wind is blowing into your face off the Eden estuary, the eleventh plays like 271. A double green serves holes eleven and seven. Shallow and slightly elevated, the hard, fast putting surface slopes sharply down from back to front. Behind, a sharp incline leads down to the rough and sand bordering the Eden estuary. In front, two malevolent bunkers stand guard, to the left the ten-foot-deep Hill and to the right the even more unforgiving Strath, the Scylla and Charybdis of golf.

"Trouble once begun at this hole," warned Bernard Darwin back in 1910, "may never come to an end till the card is torn into a thousand fragments." A bit melodramatic? Not at all, as none other than the immortal Bobby Jones would make clear a decade later at the 1921 British Open. After a 46 going out in high winds and heavy rain during the third round, Jones took five strokes on the eleventh but was still one putt shy of a triple, whereupon he decided to hell with it, tore his card into a thousand fragments, and stormed off the course.

[3]My real handicap at the time was between twenty and twenty-six, depending on the time of year and phase of moon, but eighteen was the maximum permitted in the Dunhill Cup Pro-Am, so I lied. Hey, don't look at me that way. Most people lie the *other* way.

Whatever you do, Darwin cautioned, steer clear of Strath, because from its depths a golfer is a long, long way from home: "With a stout niblick shot the ball may be easily dislodged from Strath, but it will all too probably bound over the green into the sandy horrors of the Eden. From there it may again be extracted, but as it has to pitch on a down slope, it will almost certainly trickle gently down the green till it is safely at rest once more in the bosom of Strath."

Amazingly enough, I manage to avoid Strath with my tee shot even though—are you ready for a shocker?—*at the time I had not yet read Darwin's warning!* Weird, isn't it, how we sometimes surprise ourselves by rising to the occasion? Whatever the reason, whether from an instinctive feel for the game or just plain blind luck, I come off a four iron and sail a half boomerang into a little hollow off the double green, a good twenty yards to the right of Strath and smack-dab in front of the seventh flagstick.

That's where I get a tip from Greg Norman.

Walking rapidly toward my ball, I'm praying that I can get to it and play the damned thing before the group coming into seven arrives. Suddenly, over my left shoulder, a voice rings out a hearty "G'day!" Crocodile Dundee isn't entered in the Dunhill Cup, so it can only be one other person: the White Shark.

Sure enough, Norman is in the group that's playing into seven, and our paths cross where the two fairways intersect. We're not exactly mates, you understand; in fact, he doesn't know me from Grantland Rice. But I have talked to him in several press tents and the occasional bar, and we are heading for the same place, so we match strides toward the green.

"What in bloody hell are you doing over *here?*"

Good question, one posed by Norman with the broadest of grins on his face, as we walk up to my ball, safely away from Strath but much closer to the seventh flag than the eleventh. Rather than demonstrate the swing that got me here, I smile wanly and turn to Ronnie for a suitable tool and guidance, but Ronnie is looking unbudgingly out to sea, so embarrassed he is to be where we are.

"Look," says Norman, perhaps sensing that I could do with a mite of help, "whatever you do, don't quit on the shot. You've got to carry it to the flag or it'll roll back into the bunker."

He is, I discover, absolutely right: when I quit on the little half sand wedge, it plops short of the flag and rolls right back into the bottom of the dreaded Strath. Thanks, Shark.

From that point, Darwinian theory takes hold: out of Strath but over the green, onto the green but back down into Strath, onto the green again but above the hole, a six-foot downhill putt that slides five feet past, and a confidently stroked, laser-locked uphiller that dead-centers into the bottom of the cup. Bobby Jones, eat my dust!

Perhaps because I play the eleventh hole better than Bobby Jones did on his first visit to St. Andrews, or possibly because with the quadruple bogey any dream of a good score is now long gone, I suddenly start playing better. Decent drives, fair approaches, solidly stroked putts. No greens in regulation and no pars, but no doubles or triples, either. I stay out of Coffins and Lion's Mouth, avoid the Beardies, and don't get trapped in Hell. I do drive into the Principal's Nose[4] on sixteen, but I come out sideways at Ronnie's insistence ("If you don't, you'll end up in his glasses, I promise you") and hit a good approach to save bogey.

Yet despite this stretch of lights-out golf, I don't feel exactly brimming with confidence as I stand on the tee and contemplate my drive on the seventeenth, the Road Hole. I don't feel exhilarated by the prospect of playing the best-known golf hole in the world. I feel nauseous.

And for good reason. Just fourteen yards short of regulation par-five distance, the Road Hole is even more treacherous than it is long. The blind tee shot over a facsimile of the railway shed that once sat in front and to the right of the tee. The punitive

---

[4]The Principal's Nose is a pot bunker in the middle of the sixteenth fairway, with two other pot bunkers—the principal's glasses—immediately beyond.

rough on the left. The out-of-bounds on the right. The cavern-ous Road Bunker eating into the green on the left. The gravel-topped road immediately beyond the green. The long, narrow, elevated green that treats approach shots the way . . . Are you feeling sick yet?

It was at the Road Hole that Tom Watson belted a three iron from 195 yards that hit the green, bounded over the road, came to rest near the stone wall, and cost Tom the 1984 British Open Championship. It was here that Tommy Nakajima hit the green in regulation in the 1978 Open, whereupon he then putted into the Road Bunker (a clear and present danger if the hole is cut near it), took four whacks getting out to finish on his way to a nine, and endowed the Road Bunker with a permanent nick-name, "The Sands of Nakajima." It was here in 1990 that Nick Faldo confirmed Bernard Darwin's assessment of the Road Hole ("Many like it, most respect it, and all fear it") by laying up four times on the way to his second Open title.

And, more to the point, it is here that I pull my drive into the left rough, scuff a seven iron about fifty yards deeper into the gunch, hack out with a wedge, punch-and-run a deft little five iron onto the green, and two-putt for a six—a double bogey that means I must par the eighteenth in order to break 100.

Of all the great finishing holes in golf, the Home Hole at the Old Course in St. Andrews is surely the easiest.

Picture the heroic eighteenth at Pebble Beach, curving left around the crashing waves of the ocean down below, challeng-ing the golfer who needs a birdie to find the courage to start a driver over the water and bend it back onto the left side of the fairway. Picture the final hole at Augusta National, which re-quires the golfer to hit a perfectly controlled fade uphill be-tween towering pines and then a middle iron to a two-tiered, lightning-fast green guarded front and right by bunkers. Now picture a fairway as wide as a football field, a well-manicured grassy expanse without so much as a blade of rough, and a large, inviting green with nary a bunker and with the flagstick stuck right in the middle.

Welcome to the Home Hole at St. Andrews.

For a hacker like me, there's only one thing wrong with this picture: the gallery. Behind the white picket fence that runs the length of the hole on the right, behind this historic boundary between the Old Course and the old town that symbolize the game of golf, people are standing four-deep. They are standing in the narrow street that runs past Old Tom Morris's golf shop and along the back of Rusacks Hotel, where Bobby Jones always stayed when he came to St. Andrews, and then past Granny Clark's Wynd, a public footpath that leads across the eighteenth and first fairways to the *Chariots of Fire* beach beyond. (Pedestrians, not golfers, always have the right-of-way.)

They are standing there, these golf fans by the hundreds, waiting for me to hit my tee shot.

Not all of them, I suppose, have come out on this fine, sunny September day just to see *me* play the Home Hole. Norman, Strange, Kite, Calcavecchia, Sandy Lyle, and Christy O'Connor, Jr., are in foursomes spread out behind me, so a few members of the gallery may have turned out to see them finish. If I could have one wish granted at this moment, it would be that everybody in sight would go off somewhere and have tea, or whatever it is that Scots do when they're not playing or watching golf, and let me hit my drive in peace. But no, here I stand on the tee, needing a par the way a martini needs an olive, and I have to try and get it in front of an audience.

"Aim for the clock," Ronnie says, echoing advice given by St. Andrews caddies to golfers on the eighteenth tee since 1854, when the Royal and Ancient erected its stately clubhouse on a slight rise behind the first tee of the Old Course. The timepiece in question is set in the second-story façade of a sturdy, four-square edifice that is as familiar a landmark to golfers as Stonehenge was to the Druids. Everyone, pro and am alike, aims for the clock. A drive struck along that line takes full advantage of the wide, open spaces to the left, steers well clear of Rusacks Hotel on the right, and leaves the golfer with the safest approach to the green.

"Piece of cake," Strange had said of the Old Course. "Keep it to the left on the way out and keep it to the left on the way back."

I hit it right.

My ball starts off well left, on a beeline for the R&A clock, but then, as if remembering who hit it, veers off in a grand, sweeping arc to the right, on a beeline for the bay window of Rusacks's tearoom. "Bloody God!" Ronnie exclaims, but he needn't have worried: I didn't hit it *that* hard. Sure enough, my tee shot rolls to rest about 210 yards directly in front of the tee, well short of Granny Clark's Wynd and a good fifteen yards shy of the out-of-bounds fence on the right.

Piece of cake.

As we clackety-clack across the 850-year-old stone bridge over Swilcan Burn, I am calm and confident. And with good reason: my ball's in the fairway, I have an unobstructed 140 yards to a big green with no bunkers or other ugliness to contend with, and all I have to do is get close enough to two-putt in order to break 100 in my first round ever at St. Andrews. *Piece of cake!*

As I walk up to my ball, I do a quick mental inventory of all the pertinent instructional tips I can recall from *Golf* and *Golf Digest.* Should I ever drown, I'm sure that a lifetime's golf tips will flash before my eyes as I go under for the third time. Never mind that all those tips, laid side by side, would cancel each other out faster than a "Tastes Great!"/"Less Filling!" debate. These are the crutches we golfers live by; they are the ones we'll die by.

Most golfers have a favorite club, one they feel more comfortable with than any other, so I'm delighted when Ronnie hands me my eight iron. I love hitting my eight iron. For some reason, I tend to hit a seven iron too hard. For some other reason, I tend to baby a nine iron. Like Baby Bear's chair, porridge, and bed, an eight iron for me is just right. (There's no rational explanation for it, of course, but neither is there a rational explanation for golf.)

Just before addressing my ball, I force myself to think of Ed Norton and Ralph Kramden. Remember the episode of *The Honeymooners* when Norton tried to teach Ralph golf, beginning with "How to Address the Ball"?—"Hello, ball!" I never play a round of golf without thinking about that scene, and I never think about it without laughing. Should I think about it now on my backswing, when by making par I can break 100 on the Old Course at St. Andrews, I'll either whiff or hit the ball sideways. So I bring Norton and Ralph back for another rerun, smile, and step up to address my ball for the most important golf shot of my life.

"Hello, ball!"

A golfer always know instantly that he's hit a ball solidly when he doesn't actually feel the contact. There's no jarring, no sense of an actual blow, just a smooth, rhythmic movement accompanied by a magical sound. *"Cleck!"* That's the sound of a squarely stroked eight iron, which is exactly what I proceed to hit. The ball takes off fast and rises quickly, arching high on a dead-straight line. It's a perfect shot except for one little thing: it's heading too far right.

At first, I think it's going to be okay. It's not slicing, fading, or cutting; it's as straight as any arrow ever shot by Robin Hood. But Ronnie sees at once where it's heading and starts talking to it: "Come back! Come back!" Gently, at first, then sternly. For a moment, it seems to have a chance, but the fence line is too close. As the ball reaches the apex of its climb, I know it's gone. I start to worry about killing somebody.

"Fore right! Fore right!"

(Ronnie and I shout in unison.)

"Clop!"

(Ball strikes pavement pin-high, bounces two stories above crowd.)

"Back in!"

(Ronnie pleads vainly for someone to swat it over the fence.)

"Clop!"

(A second, shorter bounce, farther up the road.)

And then it is gone, a souvenir for some redheaded schoolboy who has cut class to get Greg Norman's autograph. Gone, too, is my chance to break 100 at the Old Course.

A well-hit shot, perfect distance, but pushed just a tiny fraction too far off line to the right. From over on the left side of the fairway, where my drive should have been, the same shot would have ended up safely on the right side of the green, leaving me two putts for par and a final score of 99.

Keep it left, Strange had said. Keep it left. I had lost it right.

"You know what you have to do now, don't you?"

"Umph." Glassy-eyed and numb from what I've just witnessed, it's about all I can manage in response to Ronnie's question.

"You have to drop another ball and do it again," he says, knowing that I know it.

Right. Again. Of course.

After all, some people may have been daydreaming and missed my humiliation. Got to give those folks a mulligan, even if I don't get one. Maybe this time I can pop a ball through the plate-glass window of Old Tom Morris's golf shop. Maybe I can conk some little old lady's corgi and get embroiled in a nasty lawsuit. Maybe I'll stand there and hit eight irons into the street until I run out of balls. (No, there are only two dozen brand-new Pinnacles in my bag, but Ronnie can always go fetch some more if necessary.) Maybe . . .

Maybe I should just stop worrying, reload, and fire.

Cleck!

Another smooth, easy swing. Another solid meeting of club face and ball. Everything feels exactly the same, a mirror image of the first shot. Only this time, my ball stays exactly straight, exactly on line.

Perhaps this time my shoulders turned a millimeter more or my hands a nanosecond sooner, or my feet were lined up a fraction of an inch more to the left, or my left hip cleared a bit quicker, or my ears wiggled during my waggle.

Who knows?

Who ever knows about golf?

All I know is that my second ball hits pin-high again, but this time on the green, fourteen feet right of the flag, where it stops dead and waits to be putted twice for a double-bogey six and a final score of 101.

Jack Nicklaus once said that there is no greater feeling in the world than winning an Open championship at St. Andrews. You walk up that eighteenth fairway toward the Royal and Ancient Clubhouse, toward the huge green wedged in against the fence on the right, toward a grandstand and streets packed with the most knowledgeable golf fans in the world, and as you cross Granny Clark's Wynd, the marshals step aside and the gallery rushes in behind you, while up ahead the cheers build into a roar.

Guess I'll have to take Jack's word for it because I seriously doubt I'll ever know that feeling firsthand.

But I do know it felt pretty doggone good to hear the polite applause for my second eight iron as I walked up the fairway of the Home Hole at the Old Course. The polite clapping didn't cause the windows in Rusacks to rattle; there was no echo of the roar that saluted Nick Faldo on his victory march in 1990. But even if the people applauding were doing so out of sheer relief that they were no longer under fire, I would take it any day.

I didn't shoot bogey golf on my first time on the Old Course. I didn't even break 100. But I'll be back.

And next time, I'm taking my mulligan.

The Cockermouth Open and the Worthington Classic

That was always the plan. Tennis at 25, skiing at 35, and golf at 50. I waited so late to take up golf because I wanted to feel the swing and the arc and feel the calmness inside. One minute it's fear and loathing, but hit a couple of good shots and you're on top of the world. I've gone crazy over this game.

—Jack Nicholson,
in *Golf* magazine

"That's a lot of bull," said Ziggy, the first to reach the second tee.

Zig might well have been referring to the number of strokes reported by Peter for the first hole, there being some lingering difference of opinion on the issue of "intent to hit" in what Peter insisted was merely a fully realized dress rehearsal for his actual stroke.

Or he might have been responding to Charlie's demand that my asterisk par (i.e., a par four achieved off my second drive) on the first hole not be counted on the multitier bet that Charlie had constructed for the day.[1]

[1]The bet included a "simple" Nassau at match play with presses allowed on all even-numbered holes; greensies, sandies, and barkies; team and individual stroke play; most greens in regulation; a longest-putt contest; and a modified Stableford System match with three points for birdie, two for par, one for

When the rest of us arrived at the tee, though, we followed Ziggy's gaze and realized that in fact he was speaking the literal truth.

Since returning to golf after my long hiatus, I had faced a lot of tough tee shots: the ninth and tenth holes at Pebble Beach, the island green at TPC-Sawgrass, the eighteenth at Bay Hill and at Doral's Blue Monster, and the Road Hole at the Old Course in St. Andrews. But not until I played in the Cockermouth Open had I ever encountered a tee shot that required a 150-yard carry over a 2,000-pound moving hazard with four hooves, one tail, two immense horns, smoke pumping out of its nostrils, and the biggest set of balls this side of a bowling alley.

That *was* a lot of bull.

Students of the Romantic poets will recognize Cockermouth, a village at the northern end of England's Lake District, as the birthplace of William Wordsworth. Until the first Cockermouth Open a few years ago, however, it was not known for its championship golf.

Unfortunately, the correct pronunciation of Cockermouth is "*CAH*-kur-muhth," the last two syllables delivered with lips tightly pursed in one's best Jeeves imitation. Saying it the way it is spelled is more fun, of course, but we're dealing here with England, where Leicester is Lester, Gloucester is Glahster, and the hood of a car is a bonnet.

We had been lured to Cockermouth by Kathleen, a close friend who had decided a couple of years earlier that she wanted to celebrate her fortieth birthday with her husband, Dominick, in one of her favorite places in the world, the Lake District in

---

bogey, and minus-two for triples and above. (It was here that Charlie questioned my asterisk par, even though mulligans had not been explicitly addressed in the original bet.) Fortunately, we had an objective referee present in Nancy, Zig's life companion, who had come along along in her official capacity as scorekeeper, photographer, golf Annie, and gallery of one. She told Charlie to shut up and hit.

England, with as many friends as she could entice into accompanying them.

When she first broached the subject, everybody said sure, what a great idea, because nobody thought it would ever happen.

It didn't figure to be easy, persuading a dozen active, busy adults to drop everything and fly across the Atlantic Ocean at great personal expense to watch someone else open presents. It would require significant inducements—something beyond the promise of warm beer, bad weather, long hikes in the soggy English countryside, a photo opportunity next to a statue of Wordsworth in the town of his birth, unlimited quantities of English food, and the chance to be killed while driving on the wrong side of the road.

For four of us, the only thing that might possibly guarantee our presence was golf, without which Kathleen would have to settle for cabled best wishes and overly expensive gifts. And the outlook for golf was dicey at best: the northern edge of the Lake District is roughly equidistant from Royal Troon and Turnberry, neither close enough for an easy one-day golf outing and return.

The promotional campaign for Operation Lake District (code name: OLD) began in earnest eleven months before D day with a newsletter from Kathleen explaining how much there was to do in Greater Cockermouth and how much fun it was all going to be. Golf was mentioned in passing, but no details were furnished.

Every six weeks or so for the next eight months, prospective celebrants received newsletters with OLD status updates:

○We were told what to pack: mostly rain gear, waterproof boots, extra socks, and traveler's checks.

○We were advised of cheap flights via airlines with safety records so spotty that our life-insurance policies probably wouldn't be valid.

○We were given detailed directions on how to find Watergate Farm, the nine-room farmhouse Kathleen and Dominick had rented: the final twelve miles required half a typed page, single-spaced, to plot a route through a maze of winding roads, lanes, tracks, and footpaths, all of them filled with sheep.

○We were promised a trip to Cockermouth's principal cultural attraction, the fabulous Pencil Museum. (It's a little-known fact, but the pencil had more to do with beating Germany in World War II than the Spitfire.)

But still no concrete golf arrangements, and I began to work on my excuses for not being able to go.

And then, early in the spring, an OLD newsletter arrived with a copy of a letter from R. D. Pollard, the Hon. Secretary of the Cockermouth Golf Club. Visitors would be most welcome, the Hon. Secretary confirmed: "The course comprises 18 holes and yardage-wise is rather shorter than many conventional courses, but the views from many points on the course are unsurpassed. I feel sure that if you do decide to play you will thoroughly enjoy the experience and you will receive a very warm welcome."

Golf-wise, I was there.

The plane wasn't hijacked, Pete didn't exceed ninety-five mph on the drive from Manchester to Cockermouth, it took only an hour and a half to find Watergate Farm, the trip to the Pencil Museum turned out to be optional, it didn't rain for four straight days, we didn't have to climb a fell,[2] no one died on the four-hour forced march previously billed as an "easy hike," and the gala birthday dinner at the Trout Hotel in Cockermouth was surprisingly edible. All in all, OLD turned out to be the greatest birthday party of all time.

And the golf? Oh my, the golf was sublime.

What made it truly special was that it reminded me so much of my favorite golf course back home, which had come to symbolize the fundamental appeal of the game. And that, in turn,

[2]"Fell" is the Lake District's word for "hill." Don't ask *me* why: *they* invented the language.

made me think of a conversation a few years earlier with the secretary of state.

The secretary of state was a busy man.

Secretaries of state are always busy men, but George Shultz held the office while Ronald Reagan was president, so he was especially busy. Not only did Secretary Shultz have to manage the nation's foreign affairs, he also had to explain them to the former president of the Screen Actors Guild. ("Okay, let's try it again. *Italy* is the one shaped like a boot; *Ireland* is where the little people live.")

"Fifteen minutes," the State Department official said politely but firmly. "The secretary has an extremely tight calendar today, and he can only give you fifteen minutes."

Check. The photographer and I had already been told this at least fifteen times, so we had pretty much dismissed any idea of spending all day chatting about world affairs. For our magazine assignment, the photographer's job was to snap a reasonable likeness of Mr. Shultz. Mine was to plumb the depths of the man's character, find out what made him tick, learn his private plan for securing peace in the Middle East, discover his prescription for reversing America's cultural and political decline, and get him to admit his dimwitted boss was to blame for everything. In seven and a half minutes.

We waited on the seventh floor of the State Department Building in a reception room normally reserved for major dignitaries from minor countries. And waited. The secretary was fifteen minutes late. Twenty. (Who knows? Maybe he was off somewhere being lied to by Oliver North.)

Finally he arrived, accompanied by an outwardly calm and collected administrative aide, a court stenographer, and a Secret Service agent who obviously suspected I was Yasir Arafat in disguise. The photographer took Mr. Shultz out on the balcony where he had set up the shot to take advantage of the natural light, the administrative aide began checking her watch, the court stenographer set up his transcribing machine *and* a tape recorder, the G-man kept an eye on me for false moves, and I tried to make small talk. It was a one-sided conversation.

The photo shoot completed, Mr. Shultz returned from the balcony and took a seat on the sofa across from me. The court stenographer clicked on his tape recorder and positioned himself behind his transcribing machine. I flipped open my notepad, turned on *my* cassette recorder, and wondered what sort of recording took place at, say, nuclear-disarmament talks.

For the next seven and a half minutes, I fired probing, tough questions worthy of Bob Woodward, but the secretary of state sidestepped each of them with the deftness and grace of Fred Astaire. He might as well have been giving a civics lesson to a first grader. About the most controversial thing I could get him to admit was that America is a great country. I was getting nowhere. But I had a secret weapon.

Precisely fifteen minutes after Mr. Shultz had entered the room, the administrative aide stepped forward, smiled sweetly, and reminded us that the secretary had to leave for his next appointment. Mr. Shultz smiled, shrugged, and stood up. So did I. We shook hands. It was over. Almost.

"Thank you, Mr. Secretary," I said as he turned toward the door. "By the way, I understand you belong to the Worthington Golf Club. The seventh hole there is something else, isn't it?"

He took another step, then stopped and turned back toward me. The automatic-pilot switch in his brain flipped from on to off, and he looked at me as if I had just materialized in the room. He asked: "Do you know the Worthington course?"

"Yes," I said, trying not to smile like a salmon fisherman who had finally set a hook after a morning of near misses. "A friend of mine lives just behind it. We play there a lot."

The secretary, a very busy man who had an extremely tight calendar that day, suddenly decided he had a few minutes to spare. The Arabs and the Israelis could go arm-wrestle or something: the secretary wanted to talk a little golf.

And so we did. George and I stood there in the reception room as if we had just bumped into each other in the men's locker room at the clubhouse. We talked about the seventh hole at the Worthington Golf Club, the condition the course was in, how tricky the approach shot to the second hole was, when he had played there last, when he planned to play there next, and how, yes, it was a bit odd to play with several Secret Service men in dark suits walking in the rough ahead of him, checking behind bushes and trees.

The photographer packed up and left. The court reporter turned off his tape recorder and stenographic machine.[3] The administrative aide checked her watch and turned ashen. The Secret Service agent kept his eyes peeled for terrorists who might be lurking under the couch. And Shultzie and I kept talking golf.

The golf course that caught the secretary of state's attention and caused him to expend five nonscheduled minutes from a busy day is located in Worthington, Massachusetts, a town of about 1,200 people in the Berkshire Hills in the western part of the state.

Too far from Boston and New York to be a prime weekend retreat for Beautiful People, Worthington was a farming community for most of its history since its founding in the mid-seventeenth century. What is now second-growth forest used to be cleared land: walk in the woods today and everywhere you see the remains of stone fences that once enclosed pastures and fields. Much of Worthington's land area is still farmland, but a majority of its current residents commute to work in nearby Pittsfield and Northampton. There are also summers-only people from Springfield and Albany, as well as a handful of artisans, artists, academics, and writers. The Marquis de Lafayette slept there in 1825.

[3]At the State Department, you apparently have to be sitting down for anything you say to be official and on the record.

Most of the nearby Berkshire hill towns have a similar composition. (Lafayette probably slept in many of them, too: when touring in 1824–1825 the former colonies he helped liberate, the penurious Lafayette permitted himself to be fed and sheltered just about everywhere.) The next town over, Cummington, is where George Shultz has his place. But only Worthington has a golf course.

"In 1904," writes the official town historian, "several young men who had played golf in other places laid out a six-hole course off Old North Road. Later, the present Golf Club property was acquired and a nine-hole course was laid out. This club is the hub of summer social life in Worthington today and has been largely credited with the growth and development of the town, ranking high with the town water system installed in 1910."

The first president of the Worthington Golf Club was Elisha Brewster, an ancestor of Kingman Brewster, who was president of Yale University and later ambassador to Britain. But the Worthington Golf Club was never a club of privilege; it's always been a club of just plain folks. Annual membership dues are $400, which includes all greens fees and the right to play in club tournaments, but it's not necessary to be a member of the club to play there.

George Shultz, an avid golfer who belongs to several clubs around the country, including Cypress Point and Augusta National, is a member in good standing of the Worthington Golf Club. So are two of my regular playing partners, Okie and Darrell. All just plain folks.

The Worthington course is a nine-hole track laid out on the side of a hill.[4] It's short—just 5,629 yards (twice around) from the back tees. Par is 70. There is one water hazard, a drainage

---

[4]Actually, with the recent addition of a new par three that replaces the sixth hole when one plays the "back" nine, there are now ten holes at Worthington. The membership is divided over whether this attempt to add a little spice to the course represented a wise use of funds. It will likely be the subject of debate well into the next century.

ditch in front of the seventh green. Several of the greens are elevated, and all but one are defended by bunkers, none of which are particularly severe. All the fairways are wide, but the rough is extremely rough and the woods are worse, so it pays to avoid slicing off sidehill lies. The course rating is 66.8; the slope rating is 115.

Doesn't sound like much, does it?

But while it may not register high on the Richter scale of golf courses, Worthington has a special quality that places it, in my opinion, very close to the heart and soul of golf—a special quality shared by the site of the Cockermouth Open.

The morning of the first (and final) round of the Cockermouth Open was warm, sunny, and clear—and I was worried. It was vacation time in England, and on such a beautiful Friday the course might well be crowded, and we did not have confirmed tee times.

Everything else about OLD was meticulously planned, from the punishing jog around an immense lake to the pub lunch at the halfway point, from the restorative selection of single-malt whiskies at the farmhouse to the tea scheduled at a pleasant country hotel for four o'clock, when the winner of the golf tournament would receive his trophy. But without confirmed tee times, I feared, we might have an interminable wait. And if the course was really crowded, we might have to cut the round short to make it back for the stupid tea. As far as I could tell, the whole raison d'être of the trip—aside from Kathleen's birthday, of course—was in serious jeopardy.

The Cockermouth Golf Club is located on a hill—sorry, a fell—just off a country road a few miles north of downtown Cockermouth. When we arrived, there were a couple of cars in the parking lot, but there was no one in the clubhouse, not a soul. My first reaction was panic: maybe by some idiotic local custom the course was closed on Fridays to everyone but fell climbers.

But then, next to a closed office door with the words "The Hon. Secretary" stenciled on it, we spotted a side table with a small metal box on it, and propped behind the box was a sign with a neatly printed message: "Greens Fee £6. Thank You. C.G.C."

We checked the box: in it were a few bills and coins—My God! The place was run on the honor system! (Wait until the guys up at Van Cortlandt Park in the Bronx heard about *that*.)

Ziggy was so pleased by the notion that he emptied at least six pounds of coins from his pockets into the box. An institutional investor for a large brokerage firm, Ziggy was accustomed to buying and selling millions of dollars' worth of stocks and bonds every day, but he was utterly baffled by the British monetary system. In the country for six days, he had been paying for everything with paper currency because he was unable to decipher the coins of varying shapes and virtually illegible inscriptions that he received in change.

"I'm leaving this country in four days," he explained, as he topped off the box with another handful of coins, "and it's too late to try to figure this stuff out now. This way, I can get out of here without tearing holes in all my pockets."

There was a stack of scorecards and pencils on the table, but no course map. Fortunately, as we rounded the corner of the clubhouse looking for the first tee, we ran into a golfer coming off the eighteenth green. He gave us a quick orientation and pointed us in the right direction.

"Oh, and one more thing," he said as we parted ways. "Apologies on behalf of the club, but according to an agreement with local shepherds, the fairways don't get mowed until June fifteenth."

What? It was the end of May, and they hadn't mowed the fairways all spring? That's just great: we're going to be playing in rough that's knee-deep. What kind of goat track is this? Not a goat track at all, we discovered when we stepped up to the first tee, but a *sheep* track. There, up ahead, spread out over the first fairway, was a herd of about fifty big, fat, woolly sheep.

"So what are we supposed to do," said Pete, "ask them to let us play through?"

Ziggy teed up his ball, took a couple of practice swings, but hesitated: "What if they don't get out of the way? I don't want to hit one."

"Just hit away," said Charlie. "I'll yell 'Fore!' "

(At the time, it seemed like a perfectly sensible idea.)

As it turned out, the sheep were just out of range, and when we got up to our balls, they moved out of the way. Except for the odd "b-a-a-a" from a lamb, the sheep went quietly about their business, which apparently was to keep the fairways shorn, at least until June 15.

The first hole played 345 yards straight up a hill. The sheep had done a good job on the fairway, and our balls sat up well on the turf. (Who needs a mower if you can get sheep to work for nothing?) The tournament was on, we had all gotten off the tee well, and everybody was concentrating on his shots. It wasn't until we reached the green at the top of the hill and stopped to look around us that anyone recalled the Hon. Secretary's words: "the views from many points on the course are unsurpassed."

Who could have guessed that he was given to understatement? The sky was cloudless and pale blue, the air crisp, and we could see miles in every direction. The first green was clearly one of the points on the course the Hon. Secretary had in mind.

We were on the top of the world, looking out over an endless series of lush, rounded green cones stretching to the horizon. Not just one shade of green, but many, dark greens and pale greens, their gradations determined by the angle of the late morning sun. We could see roads and farmhouses nearby, a lake glimmering up from a valley to the south, and the edge of Cockermouth down below. But in the middle distance and beyond, we saw only the tops of other green perches like our own, rolling out to the edge of the sky.

The fells of the Lake District were unlike any hills or mountains I had ever seen. They had relatively few trees or outcroppings of naked rock, the absence of which made even the steepest of them seem softer, more accessible. From what we could see, most served as grazing ground for large herds of sheep, like the ones tending to our fairways. A couple of the fells we could see showed a rugged face, scarred by a mountain stream that emptied into a lake in the valley below, but from a distance most seemed smooth, benign, even gentle.

No wonder Wordsworth starting writing poems at such an early age.

"Look, you guys, it's really pretty up here and all," Charlie said, "but what are we going to do about that goddamned bull?"

Here's the picture. We were standing on the tee. Directly in front of us about fifteen yards away was a sturdy wire fence. Leading over the fence was a stile, on the other side of which was a large corral (or whatever it was they called it in that part of the world) about 150 yards wide and twice as long. On the other side of the corral was the second fairway. Inside the course were a dozen or so cows, ranging from heifers to matrons. Also inside the corral was the bull.

You see our problem.

Maybe it was the old Ryder Cup spirit talking, or maybe it was because Nancy was there for us to impress with our machismo, but we didn't give a thought to canceling the Cockermouth Invitational on the spot, heading for the nearest pub, and getting to know our British cousins a little better. We came all this way to play, not to be cowed by some damned bull.

So we talked it over. We figured that if we hit our drives over the fence on the other side of the pen, then walked confidently but quietly across the corral without making eye contact with the bull and making *certain* not to startle him with any abrupt movements, then everything would be okay. He had to be a tame bull, as bulls go, didn't he? Not even Brits would stick some crazy mad killer bull in the middle of one of their fairways, would they? On the other hand, it was springtime, and we sure didn't want him to get the idea that we were trying to horn in on one of his heifers.

We also created several Local Rules on the spot:

Local Rule No. 1. A player would be permitted unlimited mulligans as necessary until he hit a tee shot that cleared the corral. Under no circumstances could balls hit into the corral be retrieved: they would belong forevermore to the bull.

Local Rule No. 2. After all tee shots cleared the corral, all players (and Nancy) would cross over the stile individually, but wait at the fence line until everyone was over. The group would then cross together and in close order to the other side, except that if the bull should show signs of charging, all bets would be off and it would be every man (and Nancy) for him(her)self.

Local Rule No. 3. If an errant tee shot should either hit the bull or hit close enough to the bull to visibly annoy him, then the tournament would be canceled forthwith and the player who struck the errant tee shot would be required to buy all drinks at the pub until closing time for all the other players (and Nancy).

Miraculously, all our tee shots carried beyond the fence on the other side. We all negotiated the first stile without incident. We held rank almost all the way across the corral. (With thirty yards to go, certain of the players—not Nancy—broke from the pack and ran. They know who they were.) We crossed over the stile on the other side. And we all made par on what was mutually agreed to be the number one handicap hole on the course.

The bull? Other than swishing a few flies with his tail, he never made a move. Maybe he was conserving his energy for more important things.[5] Or maybe he'd seen our swings and decided we had enough problems already.

We spent the rest of the round scampering around on the fell,

[5] A young bull and an old bull are standing together on the top of a hill. Down in the valley below them is a herd of cows. "Hey," said the young bull, "let's run down the hill and screw one of those cows." "No," said the old bull, "let's walk down the hill and screw all of them."

making friends with the sheep, hitting the usual mix of good and horrible shots. We played over stone fences that dated from the Enclosure Movement in the eighteenth century. We made sure to avoid the single strand of electrified wire strung around each green to keep the sheep out. We teed off from the edge of cliffs with sheer drops of 200 feet.

Like its analogue in Worthington, the Cockermouth course is about a hundred years old. And also like Worthington, it's quirky. Just shy of 5,900 yards long, the little country course in the Lake District has small greens, only a couple of fairway bunkers, no water hazards, and a lot of grassy swales and mounds. It's a little raggedy around the edges, but the greens are in good shape and surprisingly fast.

The Open? Ziggy won individual honors, Pete and Charlie won the team event, and I shelled out a small fortune in indecipherable British coins.

The Cockermouth Open was the single most exhilarating, most liberating day I have ever spent on a golf course. Better than Pebble Beach. Better than the Masters. Better than the Old Course at St. Andrews.

I think I know why. It has to with the beauty of the setting and the simplicity of the place. You look around you, you play, you have fun. You hit the ball, go find it, hit it again. No distractions, no rituals, no dress code, no noisy carts, no golf bags the size of steamer trunks, no halfway house, no condos on the course, no pro shop.

The sheep and the bull were more than oddities: they helped make the day playful, helped keep the game a game. And though the course was short, the fairways wide, the hazards minimal (with one *big* exception), you still had to make the shots. If you didn't, the game would bite you on the ankle, the way it always does, to remind you who's boss.

Worthington has a similar appeal. Simple. No frills. Just a golf course. A few gas carts are available, but most people carry their bags or use pull carts. Unless there is a tournament going on, the typical waiting time to tee off is however long it takes you to get your clubs out of the trunk, put your shoes on, and walk across the road to the first tee. A round takes a foursome three and a half hours. By yourself, less than three.

Like Cockermouth, the course at Worthington consists of a few silly holes, a few good ones, and one really fine golf hole, the seventh—the one I used to sucker-punch George Shultz.

It looks like a piece of cake: a straight-ahead par five, only 528 yards long. But a big tree intruding on the left of the landing area about 200 yards out forces you to fudge to the right. But the fairway slopes down and to the right, and if you push your drive too far off center, the ball runs down into the woods and your second shot is a punch-out back to the fairway.

But even for the big hitter who can fly the tree or bend his drive around it, the seventh is still a three-shot hole because there's no way anyone is going to hold the severely sloping green with a fairway wood.

On the other hand, a golfer willing to accept what the hole gives can sometimes outfox it. Pete Packard, the retired Worthington postmaster and George Shultz's longtime best friend in the area, used to hit three five irons on the seventh. That's the sort of thing a course like Worthington makes you do—or lets you do, if you have the wisdom to give in to the game, rather than try to make it give in to you.

Over a period of five years and about seventy-five rounds of golf at Worthington, I've parred the seventh exactly once, and that was with a twenty-foot no-brainer after mishitting my approach to the green and scuttling on in four. The one time I did hit the green in regulation, I three-putted. (Why do you think golf spelled backward is flog?)

I would rather birdie the seventh at Worthington than the eighteenth at Pebble Beach. Or even the Home Hole at the Old Course.

For me, then, Worthington is an almost perfect course. All it needs is a herd of sheep. I can live without the bull.

19TH HOLE

Acknowledgments

Acknowledgments

Why is it that people whose generosity, support, and encouragement make a book possible are always let off the hook during assignment of responsibility for the author's errors, omissions, flawed thinking, and lapses of taste? Somehow it doesn't seem right, but that's the way it's always been, and that's the way it is here.

Thanks go first and foremost to my editor and sometime golf partner, Peter Gethers. His extraordinary patience and forbearance as I hacked around the course were exceeded only by his creativity, his wit, and his ability to scramble.

Next up on the tee is my agent, Dominick Abel, whose only character flaw is that he thinks golf is a silly game. That notwithstanding, he provided wise counsel and steady guidance while enduring more golf stories than you've had hot meals.

If Nick Faldo ever decides to write about golf instead of play it, he should fire David Leadbetter and get in touch with T. R. Reinman, my own personal swing guru. Nobody knows the game better, loves it more, or writes about it with greater understanding and insight.

Without the creative and conceptual guidance of two members of my regular foursome, Lee Eisenberg and Daniel Okrent, I would still be out in the woods looking for my ball. Max and Morris, I owe you. Our other playing partner, Michael Pollet, deserves thanks for constantly reminding us all by his approach to the game that golf is supposed to be fun.

Good friend and driving-range companion Kathleen Moloney gave me so much help in so many ways that I am keeping my promise not to reveal the color of her golf bag.

Anyone looking for a game would do well to hook up with the likes of John Alderman, Jim Apfelbaum, Jim Climer, Ian Devenish, Charlie Hayward, Mike Mulhearn, Len Riggio, Darrell Shedd, and Kenny Scott (wherever he is).

If copy editor Jeff Smith could read greens as well as he reads manuscripts, he'd win the Masters every year.

At regular PGA Tour events, the golfers play in threesomes, each of which is called a pairing. Why pairing? Why not trioing? I don't know, but I do know the following pairings of golf-beat reporters went out of their way to make a rank greenhorn feel comfortable in the press tent: Jaime Diaz, Steve Hershey, Ivan Maisel; Bob Green, Gary Van Sickle, Gordon White, Jr.; Bob Baptist, Larry Dorman, Tom McCollister.

Thanks also to three pros from the PGA Tour's media relations operation: Marty Caffey, Tom Place, and Sid Wilson.

And more of the same to Kathy Watson, Marie Burnett, and Bev Norwood, who helped open doors both on and off the Tour.

When it comes to golf, Sharon McIntosh is a great volleyball player. Yet, even during those rainy days when I was inclined to deep-six my clubs again, she remained steadfast in her belief that I could shoot par. Or at least finish the round. She provided moral and material support, read the manuscript with a discerning eye, and laughed when she surely wanted to scream.

How do I thank someone who has meant so much to me? Well, for starters, by *not* taking her with me on my next trip to Pinehurst.

A native Texan, GLEN WAGGONER spent his formative years hacking around on a scruffy municipal golf course in Dallas. He didn't learn until much later that, at about the same time but on the other side of town, Lee Trevino was doing the same thing. More or less. He—the author, not Trevino—was graduated from Southern Methodist University, acquired a couple of advanced degrees in European history from Columbia University, and decided against pursuing a career in golf. After serving a seventeen-year stretch in the groves of academe, first as an overworked junior faculty member at the University of Michigan and later as an unappreciated midlevel bureaucrat at Columbia, the author became a senior writer at *Esquire* magazine. There he wrote about manners, food and drink, travel, fashion, baseball, health and fitness, football, movie stars . . . and golf. Now a contributing editor of *Men's Journal,* Waggoner is the author of three other books: *The Traveling Golfer, Baseball by the Rules* (with Kathleen Moloney and Hugh Howard), and *Esquire Etiquette* (with Kathleen Moloney). He is also editor of *Rotisserie League Baseball,* currently in its seventh edition, and one of the game's founding fathers. He lives in New York City with his wife, Sharon McIntosh. His handicap hovers between 18 and 20, depending on how often he can get away from Manhattan on a golf assignment.